Center for Basque Studies
Basque Diaspora and Migration Studies Series, No. 7

THE BASQUE DIASPORA WEBSCAPE

Identity, Nation, and Homeland, 1990s–2010s

Pedro J. Oiarzabal

Center for Basque Studies - University of Nevada, Reno
Basque Diaspora and Migration Studies Series, 7

This book was published with generous financial support from the Basque Government / Eusko Jaurlaritza.

Center for Basque Studies
Basque Diaspora and Migration Studies Series, No. 7
Series Editor: Joseba Zulaika

Center for Basque Studies
University of Nevada, Reno
Reno, Nevada
http: //basque.unr.edu

Cover art: Jone Arzoz

Library of Congress Cataloging-in-Publication Data

Oiarzabal, Pedro J.
The Basque diaspora webscape : identity, nation, and homeland, 1990s-2010s / Pedro J. Oiarzabal.
pages cm. -- (Diaspora and migration studies ; no. 7)
Includes bibliographical references and index.
Summary: "Study of Internet and web usage among members, associations, and organizations of the Basque diaspora and diaspora-related institutions"-- Provided by publisher.
ISBN 978-1-935709-41-1 (pbk. : alk. paper) 1. País Vasco (Spain)--Social conditions. 2. Basques--Social conditions. 3. Basques--Ethnic identity. 4. Communities of practice. 5. Information technology--Social conditions. 6. Information society. I. Title.

HN590.P275O36 2013
306.0946'6--dc23

2013027042

In memory of Sergio Oiarzabal (1973-2010)

"No finaliza el viaje. No. Yo nazco en la palabra.
Ella es el carmín rojo de los deseos."

Table of

Contents

Preface

This book engages questions central to the study of diasporas and digital technologies, by analyzing the Basque case in depth. It is about how one diaspora group—the Basques—are using the Internet to preserve its identity and culture. It also examines the way Basques in the diaspora are using the Internet to create online communities and a kind of digital nationalism that links all Basques, whether living in the contemporary homeland or scattered around the world, into a single self-identifying people. My research focuses particularly on the websites created and maintained by Basque social and benevolent organizations in sixteen countries in North and South America, Australia, and Western Europe, prior to the popularization of the so-called Social or Collaborative Web or Web 2.0. That is to say, I examine the ways these websites represent the organizations of which they are a part, and the ways they depict Basque culture, homeland, nationhood, identity, and political aspirations. I also examine the support provided by the Basque government, both quantitative and qualitative, for these websites and the diaspora organizations they represent from the early 1980s to the first decade of the twenty-first century.

The current work presents a clear "still" photograph of a particular time in the history of the web's development and its usage by a diaspora group and how complex social practices offline move online. It explores the evolving Basque institutional presence on the web, taking into account its ephemerality as an intrinsic characteristic of the web. This historical dimension enriches the final product as information and communication technologies research frequently focuses on very recent and short term trends and developments.

There are limitations to this kind of investigation that must be acknowledged. First, although I take into account the fact that the websites are the official online "homes" of their organizations, the websites cannot be considered to reflect the views or interests of every member of each organization that I have studied. The Internet is not a tool used by all diaspora Basques. Many of the older generation are not computer literate, and many Basques of all ages lack the time or incentive to concern themselves with their organization's website. However, even though an organization's webmaster may work alone, his or her work is rarely done without the guidance and scrutiny of other members as well as that of the officers and board of directors. So, we may conclude that a website would represent, in general at least, the views and values of the organization's members and institutional leadership.

Second, one might argue that Basque culture and history reflected by these websites is not always consistent with the current realities of life in the Basque Country, or Euskal Herria, as it is known in Basque. The qualitative and comparative analysis of the content of over ninety diaspora institutional websites yielded some conclusive results regarding such a disjuncture between homeland and diaspora. Most diaspora Basques are many years—and sometimes many generations—removed from Euskal Herria. For many, knowledge of the Basque homeland is at best second-hand, the product of familial memories or occasional written or telephone contact with relatives in the homeland. Until recent advances in travel and long-distance communication, direct contact with the Basque Country seldom occurred after emigration. Few emigrants were ever able to return to their homeland, even for a brief visit, and contact with family and friends left behind was largely limited to letters and sporadic telephone conversations. Consequently, for most older living emigrants and exiles and for the descendants of émigrés of the past, the homeland was encapsulated in memory, forever unchanging, and these memories were passed down through the generations, preserved like a fly in amber, untouched by the realities of daily life in Euskal Herria.

But this limitation, if it can be considered one, is nonetheless important to this study. One of my interests in undertaking this research has been to examine the diaspora's contested perceptions and heterogeneous discourses of Basqueness in both "online" and "offline" dimensions. There are many books that discuss contemporary life in the Basque Country, and others that examine the lives of Basques in various parts of the diaspora. One of this book's intentions is to consider how Basques in the diaspora define themselves as Basque, which symbols or traditions they use to illustrate the fundamental nature of the Basque people, how they perceive the distant homeland, and how they try to articulate their own place in an increasingly technological and interconnected Basque world.

I discuss the methodology of my research later in the book. I would like to add here that this book could be considered a case study of how a single diasporic group is using rapidly evolving and changing media technologies to define itself, preserve its culture and traditions, and connect with other members of the diaspora and with its homeland. The same methodology could be used to examine the way other migrant and diasporic groups are utilizing the Internet and the web to preserve their community and culture. Indeed, such studies could lead to fruitful discussions about the impact of the emerging media on "globalized" populations.

Pedro J. Oiarzabal
Bilbao, June 16, 2013

Acknowl

edgments

This book would not have been possible without the enthusiastic support of the Center for Basque Studies at the University of Nevada, Reno and its editorial team. I feel especially indebted to Jose Luis Agote, Kate Camino, Daniel Montero, Cameron Watson, and Joseba Zulaika for their professional assistance and Kimberly Daggett and Joannes Zulaika for their editorial assistance. I would like to specially acknowledge Andoni Alsono, Margaret Dalrymple, Charlotte Dihoff, Carl Mitcham, Sara Velez-Mallea, and Linda White for their valuable contributions to previous drafts of this manuscript. Many thanks to the board of directors and webmasters of Basque diaspora institutions worldwide, and to their respective memberships; the personnel at the Basque Studies Library of the University of Nevada, Reno; and those who took part in this effort by participating in surveys and interviews.

Fore

word

Virtual Euskal Herria: Measuring a Special Population's Web Ties

The Basques, this ancient people originally living on the Western shores of Europe, before hunger, civil war, industrialization, and the hopes for a better future drove many of them to the New World, are one of the smallest peoples with one of the largest diasporas. According to some accounts, more than three quarters of all Basques live outside of their original homeland.

Pedro J. Oiarzabal has taken on the monumental task of documenting the voices of communities of Basques who have emigrated from their homeland, Euskal Herria–the Basque Country, and their descendants, as these voices manifest on websites. His book is to be seen as part of a larger effort by him and his colleagues, with works spanning from his books: *La Identidad Vasca en el Mundo* (Oiarzabal and Oiarzabal, 2005), *Gardeners of Identity: Basques in the San Francisco Bay Area* (Oiarzabal, 2009), *Diasporas in the New Media Age* (Alonso and Oiarzabal, 2010), and *Sailing in New York* (Oiarzabal, San Sebastián and Aguirre, forthcoming), to our recent special issue of the *Journal of Ethnic and Migration Studies* on "Migration and the Internet: Social Networking and Diasporas" (Oiarzabal and Reips, 2012).

The present book moves the focus to the virtual world; it builds and provides essential groundwork for any further studies of the modern Basque diaspora in light of the new era of social media. When, where, and how the diasporic Basques organized their online presence for the first time on the Internet will be the basis for any study that compares the Basque diaspora to other diasporas. It will also inspire researchers to provide similar accounts of other diasporic communities—accounts of diasporas in exploration and transition from pre-Internet times to social media. Future generations will look at this era of the current generation with curiosity like we look at the generation that first experienced book printing. How did their lives and their communities change with the new medium?

Between chapter 1, "Imagining the Basques," and the concluding chapter, "Beyond Cyber-Imagination," Oiarzabal leads us through a colorful landscape of websites and internationally transformed diasporic reflections of community identities—a *webscape*, as he calls it. This webscape almost exclusively consists of sites from the Americas, suggesting that European diasporas more easily connect with and directly engage in the homeland, because of geographic proximity. Almost cursorily, Oiarzabal leads us to important places of discussion (for example of the term "diaspora"), through the blossoming history of imagined online communities (chapter 4), to shores of online self-representations, colorful forests of pictures from diaspora websites (e.g., variations of depictions of the Gernika tree), and along streams of identity discourses. Chapter 3, "The Mirror of Euskal Herria," is an excellent summary of the Basque diasporas' history with pre-Internet media. It leads nicely to a later analysis on the effects of new Internet technologies. Oiarzabal's empirical analyses reveal high intra-diaspora connectivity, suggesting diasporas are learning from each other—as diasporas. We can expect this interconnectedness to grow in the social media revolution, just as the interconnectedness of diasporas with the homeland. In his captivating style that is both rich in anecdotal evidence and empirical rigor, Oiarzabal analyzes in chapter 5, "Imagining the Basque Country," how diasporic Basques and homeland representatives tend to imagine Euskal Herria. Images are ordered along a dimension past-future and the analysis reveals that only very slowly a primordial sense of Basque identity is left behind in favor of a globalized, mobile, digital identity. There are few traces of the latter, if any at all. From my perspective, it would be interesting to explore if this finding from the Basque diaspora webscape could be replicated elsewhere, for example in the process of "Basquification" of those who move to the Basque Country, both foreigners and those returning from the diaspora. With chapter 6, "Online Politics," the author reveals more interesting facts about the detachment of political views between many diasporas and the homeland. Some of the resulting dynamics (also visible in a wonderfully researched and narrated episode of Basque children who flew to the United Kingdom in 1937) are certainly due to the general situation of diasporas in their host countries, while others come from mystification and lack of detailed experience with everyday life in the homeland. For example, many Basque diasporas portray themselves not in a heroic way but rather as victims. Diaspora groups also exhibit a great level of criticism of the Basque government.

Oiarzabal's groundwork includes a very carefully researched collection of data from the full or near full population of Basque diaspora websites, and an analysis of this trove of data. The author provides an inspiring outline for future research in the concluding chapter of the book, in which he highlights the importance of "longitudinal studies, [and] a comparative examination between the Basque diaspora online and other digital diasporas." Of course, this analysis will have to be further complemented by research of those who do not make active use of these online and digital diasporas. As Oiarzabal notes, "Only 0.4% of Basques abroad are members of diaspora institutions." Future research will try reaching those outside the institutional context. The social media revolution will make this task much easier than it was in the past (Reips 2008, 2013).

Not surprisingly, given self-selection, historical development, and funding opportunities for the Basque diaspora institutions, the author finds that "the Basque diaspora has internalized the nationalist interpretation of Basque ethnicity." Interestingly, and in stark contrast to a nationalist interpretation, the author also finds, for example, that "Although the Basque language is highly regarded by diaspora institutions as one of the most powerful Basque identity markers, its actual use on websites is residual, limited to a few sentences, words, and introductory epigraphs." A wonderfully funny episode is the issue of *subdivision ad infinitum* in identity management. At the core of current unrest and of nationalism and separatism debates, the question of the appropriate level of social identity asks from the point of view of a Basque individual whether he or she is part of a unit at a certain level *exclusively*—without acceptance of the next higher level (Spain/France) as a valid concurrent unit of identification. (Even higher levels, like Europe or the United Nations seem not to be in question.) Simultaneously, that same view is not granted to others who identify similarly with a lower level unit. Oiarzabal writes: "Only 4% of total websites refer to the Basque Country as the political-territorial administration of the Basque Autonomous Community (BAC) of Spain, while the two Navarrese websites refer exclusively to Navarre . . . The BAC official coat of arms refer to three Basque provinces—Araba, Bizkaia and Gipuzkoa—the fourth space is blank, but its red color symbolizes the Navarrese coat of arms and the wish to incorporate Navarre into the BAC. Significantly, the BAC parliament has 100 seats, but only seventy-five are used. The remaining twenty-five await the Navarrese members . . . Some emigrants from Navarre and their descents belong to Basque diaspora clubs, while others participate in Navarrese institutions abroad that identify with a Navarrese identity over a Basque identity. . . The diaspora politics promoted by the different political administrations of Navarre has stressed a clear-cut sense of Navarrese identity in opposition to a Basque identity as a reflection of their anti-Basque nationalist orientation back home, and, for instance, Basque language is clearly absent on their websites. The Navarrese websites identify exclusively with the Navarrese coat of arms and the Navarrese government."

Similar views are shared in Catalonia, in their relationship with Spain and the Valencians. However, it remains to be seen in comparative future research whether this is reflected in their diaspora webscape.

Virtual Euskal Herria—the Basque Country as a land on the Internet. It raises connotations to the idea of an ideal state, of a utopian country, of an imagined past, of mythical stories in light of bare facts, and of escapism (webscape escapism) from the realities of life. This is precisely what drove most diasporic Basques or their ancestors away from the homeland to seek a new beginning. So by definition, Virtual Euskal Herria is a better place and thus may contain helpful advice for the homeland and those who remain there. It also contains projections of identity, and of course it contains more practical information for the dispersed local communities. The newly elected president of the Basque Autonomous Community, the *Lehendakari* Iñigo Urkullu Renteria, wrote a letter to the Basque diaspora, saying that his government's first priority will be "to internationalize the Basque Country" (Urkullu Renteria, 2013). He and his government may find very helpful ideas in Oiarzabal's book if they read and listen to the voices from afar.

Congratulations on a very exciting book, I hope it will find many readers to share in the pleasure of discovering the web of Virtual Euskal Herria!

—Ulf-Dietrich Reips

University of Deusto; IKERBASQUE Research Professor, Basque Foundation for Science

Getxo, Basque Country, March 2013

References

Alonso, Andoni and Pedro J. Oiarzabal. (2010). *Diasporas in the New Media Age: Identity, Politics and Community.* Reno: University of Nevada Press.

Oiarzabal, Agustín M. and Pedro J. Oiarzabal. (2005). *La Identidad Vasca en el Mundo: Narrativas sobre Identidad más allá de Fronteras.* Bilbao: Erroteta.

Oiarzabal, Pedro J. (2009). *Gardeners of Identity: Basques in the San Francisco Bay Area.* Basque Diaspora and Migration Studies Series. Vol. 4. Reno: Center for Basque Studies, University of Nevada, Reno. Second Edition.

Oiarzabal, Pedro J., Koldo San Sebastián, and Anna M. Aguirre. *Sailing in New York: The Social Origins of the Basque Club of New York, 1905–1955.* Forthcoming.

Oiarzabal, Pedro J. and Ulf-Dietrich Reips. (Eds.). (2012). Migration and the Internet: Social networking and diasporas [special issue]. *Journal of Ethnic and Migration Studies* 38, no. 9: 1333–1490.

Reips, Ulf-Dietrich. (2008). "How Internet-mediated research changes science," in A. Barak (ed.) *Psychological Aspects of Cyberspace: Theory, Research, Applications.* Cambridge: Cambridge University Press.

Reips, Ulf-Dietrich. (2013). La investigación científica con la ayuda de la Internet. Special issue "20 años de internet público | 20 years old public Internet". *Infoamérica-ICR: Iberoamerican Communication Review.* Invited manuscript, forthcoming.

Urkullu Renteria, Iñigo. (2013, February 1). *Letter to the Basque community abroad.* Retrieved March 6, 2013, from http://www.blogseitb.us/basque_boise/wp-content/uploads/2013/02/lehendakariaren_gutuna_en1.jpg.

Imaging

(01)

the Basques

> Every social community reproduced by functioning of institutions is imaginary, that is, it is based on the projection of individual existence into the weft of a collective narrative, on the recognition of a common name and on traditions lived as the trace of an immemorial past (even when they have been created and inculcated in the recent past). But this comes down to accepting that, in certain conditions, only imaginary communities are real.
>
> — Etienne Balibar 1991, 346

You ask me, "Where is Euskal Herria, the Basque Country?" Euskal Herria is everywhere. It is in the Australian sugar plantations of North Queensland, in the high desert of the western United States, in the pampas of Argentina, in the industrial and technological hubs of Europe and Asia, and in cyberspace, the last frontier expanded by our imaginations. Like a constellation of stars, the different Basque platforms on the World Wide Web (web) are connected by imaginary lines or links, drawing a picture that speaks of a new landscape that I call *webscape*. More than ever, Basque culture is uprooted, diasporic, and deterritorialized. It expands, bringing light to an expanding space. That is, the Basques—diaspora and homeland alike—are constructing an identity atlas: a sum of geographies, times, generations, and individual identities, by-products of lived experiences and inherited traditions.

Cyberspace as a constructed and shared electronic social and cultural space is the new backyard of the Basques, their new plaza.[1] This webscape of the new Basque village is created through mailing lists, forums, websites, weblogs, and social network sites, among other online platforms. Similar to Bernardo Atxaga's description of Obaba, the imaginary setting of his novel *Obabakoak*, as "the country of my past, a mixture of the real and the emotional," the Basque diaspora online is also an emotional but real landscape (*The Guardian,* October 20, 2001). In a sense, the Basque Country is the Obaba of diaspora Basques—a country of memories, where idealization, through nostalgia and melancholy, becomes central in defining Basque identity in the diaspora. For many diaspora Basques, there are places we cannot physically return to, so instead we visit them through our memories.

Based on this country of memories, the Basque diaspora has established an ephemeral and ever-changing online space and has begun building a network nation, a network ideology. The Basque diaspora is utilizing the web as a twenty-four-hour easy-to-use and inexpensive communication platform in order to create an image of who the Basque people are, and to project what they do and how they do it. It is a self-image—not an image created and/or imposed by others—that is distributed to the entire world. Diaspora Basques can claim ownership of their online space and their projected image while searching for social, cultural, and political recognition in both physical and virtual spaces.

Over twenty years ago, before the popularization of the Internet, electronic mail (e-mail), and the web, nobody could have predicted that those technologies would become daily domestic electronics that influence the ways that we entertain, interact, study, work, and even conduct research. The web is defined by its global reach or global audience, its ubiquity, and its lack of synchronicity. Accessibility to the web is fast and widespread. The web text can be found anywhere and can be simultaneously read by different people at different places and times. Computer "navigation" enables continuous and stable communication, independent of where users live, which was unthinkable just three or four decades ago (see Carlson and Goldman 1991; Haythornthwaite 2001; Wellman and Haythornthwaite, eds. 2003; and the Center for Digital Future 2004). Having said that, we need to take into account the issue of the so-called digital divide in relation to the penetration, accessibility, and use of the aforementioned technologies by developing countries and segments of the population such as the elderly and women. In this sense, the impact of the Internet is uneven and asymmetric (see Ragnedda and Muschert 2013).

Diaspora groups' use of distance and time-shrinking telecommunication technologies, such as e-mail and the web, have attracted the attention of scholars (e.g., Adams and Ghose 2003; Alonso and Oiarzabal, eds. 2010; Jon W. Anderson 1997; Brinkerhoff 2004, 2006; Dentice-Clark 2001, 2004; Ignacio 2002; Lal 1999; Oiarzabal and Reips, eds. 2012a; Parham 2004; Rai 1995; Shichor 2003; Stubbs 1999; and

---

1 For further definitions on cyberspace see: Diamandaki (2003, online); Hakken (1999); Kolko, Nakamura, and Rodman (2000); Mitra and Schwartz (2001, online); Poster (1998); and Sökefeld (2002).

Wong 2003) from a variety of disciplines, such as anthropology, political science, philosophy, psychology, sociology, mass media, and computer-based communication. The widespread use of computer-based technologies, such as the Internet and the web, constitute a new dimension in the study of emigrant and diaspora identities within the context of current processes of globalization. At the same time, the web has also become a new platform for students and scholars of migration and Internet studies from which they carry out interdisciplinary research.

The aforementioned authors have focused on how emigrant communities utilize online technologies to communicate, interact, maintain identity, and enhance political mobilization, while assessing these technologies' impact and implications on diasporic emigrants' daily lives. In short, the study of virtual ethnicity, digital diaspora, and online communities has become a substantial body of theoretical consideration and empirical research.

Several authors (e.g., Alonso 1998; Alonso and Arzoz 1999b; Arzoz 2002; Echeverría 1992; Fernández 1998; and Krutwig 1984) have addressed the repercussions of the technological advancement of the Basque Country from the theoretical point of view of the philosophy of technology, cybernetics, and computer science. However, beyond a few partial and peripheral pioneer studies on the presence of the Basque diaspora on the Internet (e.g., Alonso and Arzoz 1999a, 2003; Douglass 1999, 2000; and Uberuaga 2000), there is no known major scientific academic study on this matter.

Those studies that focus on the potential impact of the Internet on the networking of Basque diaspora communities as well as on the potential for identity maintenance are mainly theoretical. They portray the Internet as an antidote for the assumed disjuncture or dislocation resulting from spatial and temporal distance between the Basque diaspora and its homeland. For example, William A. Douglass stated, "The Internet is essential to maintain Basque identity outside the Basque Country. If the Internet didn't exist I would be more pessimistic about the future of the [Basque] diaspora" (Euskonews & Media 1999, online).

Consequently, I shall examine the ways that the Basque institutional diaspora self-represents, imagines, and portrays Basque identity, nationhood, and homeland by following the multiple narratives and discourses, called "networks of texts" by Mitra and Cohen (1999), of cultural and political self-identification and reimagination as they are constructed on current organizations' official websites. As we will see, Basque diaspora websites are platforms for communication, social interaction, and representation. This study is the first worldwide comparative research on the presence of the Basque institutional diaspora on the web, as well as the first systematic investigation of its structural dimension through the use of the Internet. It is also the first book-length academic inquiry of its kind into the political and cultural implications of new media technologies in relation to the Basque diaspora.

Within the temporal framework of the present work, as of December 2005, the Basque diaspora had engendered 189 associations—federations of clubs, *euskal etxeak* (community-based social clubs), and cultural, educational, political, and business organizations—throughout twenty-two countries: Andorra, Argentina, Australia, Brazil, Canada, Chile, Colombia, El Salvador, France, Germany, Italy, Mexico, Paraguay, Peru, Puerto Rico, Spain, Switzerland, the Dominican Republic, the United Kingdom, the United States, Uruguay, and Venezuela. Back then, Basque associations, registered with the Basque government, from Colombia, Brazil, El Salvador, Paraguay, Puerto Rico, and the Dominican Republic, had no presence on the web. My database combines my research findings with the Basque government's registry or database of Basque institutions abroad, which was used to draw the sample of my population. Other sources, such as Eusko Ikaskuntza's (the Society of Basque Studies) project on the Basque diaspora called EuskoSare (The Basque Net), estimate that the number of Basque diaspora associations is over 200. However, I opted for using the public database provided by the Basque government because other sources do not present as much consistency and accuracy on the number of existing diaspora associations as the Basque government's does. The Basque webscape encompasses all diaspora associations regardless of their registration with the Basque government. (Significantly, no political diaspora association is registered with the Basque government.) The result of my database of the Basque diaspora webscape is a website, http://euskaldiaspora.com, that has become a useful tool for accessing diaspora sites as well as an experiment in hypertextuality.

More than half of diaspora associations (ninety-eight) were online in sixteen countries with a Basque institutional presence as of November 2005. The first Basque website was created in the diaspora by Blas Uberuaga in 1994 (www.buber.net). (Uberuaga is also the webmaster of the New Mexico Basque club's site www.buber.net/NMEE.) The first Basque institutional diaspora website was created in 1996 by the political association Asociación Venezolana de Amigos de Euskal Herria (Venezuelan Association of Friends of the Basque Country; Caracas, Venezuela, http://earth.prohosting.com/avaeh/). The Basque government established its first websites in October 1996. Prior to this, the Basque presence on the Internet was related to two mailing lists: Basque-L (December 1993) and soc.culture.basque (July 1996) (for the historicity of the Basque diaspora online, see Oiarzabal 2011).

By June 2007, the Basque institutional diaspora increased by nine new associations and two new countries—China and Cuba. At that time, 123 diaspora associations (over 62 percent) had a presence on the Internet in nineteen countries (nearly 80 percent of the total). The new associations from Brazil, China—the first Basque diaspora association in Asia—and Colombia finally joined the Basque diaspora webscape.[2] However, as of June 2007, the Basque associations from Cuba, El Sal-

2 According to the Spanish National Institute of Statistics (INE 2002-2012) 30 Basques went to China—the new global industrial powerhouse—in 2002. The figure increased to 100 in 2008. Coincidentally, in 2004, 17 people founded the Basque Club of Shanghai. The founding president of the club was Juan Ignacio Mutiloa, the then president of SPRI, the Basque government's entreprenership development agency, in China, and since 2012 the Basque government's vice-minister of industry and energy.

vador, Paraguay, Puerto Rico, and the Dominican Republic still had no presence on the web (see appendix: tables A.1, A.2, and A.3; and tables A.4 and A.5 for a full list of websites). As of this writing, the organizations from Cuba, Puerto Rico, and the Dominican Republic remain digitally excluded.

These associations, self-defined as Basque, materialized with strong group self-awareness, sustained over a considerable period of time. The majority of these associations are by-products of the massive nineteenth- and twentieth-century Basque emigration waves. It is roughly estimated that nearly two hundred thousand Basques, from both sides of the Pyrenees, immigrated *legally* into the New World from the 1830s to the early 1900s.[3] During the eighteenth and nineteenth centuries, the Basque land was plagued not only by extreme socioeconomic mishaps, but also by overwhelming political instability in the form of revolutions and wars, which pushed many Basques to emigrate in order to improve their quality of life or simply to save their lives. In general terms, the traditional family-primogeniture system of inheritance forced non-heirs to emigrate in search of a better future. The dismantlement of the same kind of rural legal structure in the northern part of the Basque region after the French Revolution obliged non-heirs to leave the household in order to avoid breaking up the inheritance. Also, the finite agricultural economy based on small socioeconomic family units of production was a powerful factor in Basque emigration. In other words, the *baserri* or farmstead was based on a traditional economy of subsistence that was not able to provide for all members of a household. In addition, rural overpopulation and drastic crop failure provoked serious episodes of hunger (e.g., 1846–1847 and 1904–1906).

Simultaneously, a tumultuous chain of political and military events, including the French Revolution (1789); the Napoleonic military campaigns on the Basque territories of Spain (1808–1809); followed by civil wars (1833–1839 and 1872–1876) between liberals and traditionalists (called Carlists because their candidate to the Spanish throne was Carlos/Charles of Bourbon) shook the Basque territories.[4] The liberal victory put an end to the *fueros* or traditional law system of the Basque provinces in Spain, and therefore traditional privileges such as exclusion from mandatory military service were abolished.

The twentieth century was no kinder to the Basques than the previous eras were. The Spanish Civil War (1936–1939) and the two World Wars (1914–1919 and 1939–1945) forced thousands of Basques into exile. This exile was the last massive wave of Basque emigration in the twentieth century.[5] Since the 1960s, Basque emigration has nearly ceased.

---

3 The lack of a database on those who returned to Europe or migrated to secondary destinations makes those estimates extremely unreliable.

4 Carlism was the movement created to defend the ideals of the Carlists.

5 On the reasons for migration and its history see for example: Bilbao (1992); Douglass and Bilbao (1975); Douglass (1989, 1999); Escobedo, Zaballa and Álvarez (1996a, 1996b); Iriani (2000); and Pescador (2004).

At the present, the historical Basque territories are divided into three main political administrative areas—the Basque Autonomous Community (BAC), or Euskadi; the Foral Community of Navarre (Nafarroa in Basque; Navarra in Spanish) in the Spanish state; and three Basque provinces, or Iparralde,[6] in the Department of Low Pyrenees within the Aquitaine region in the French state—with a total combined population of nearly three million people. The Basque territories have historically enjoyed significant local and provincial decision-making authority and a broad degree of cultural unity based on language and common traditions. Since the restoration of democracy in Spain, the BAC and Navarre had developed substantial institutional powers, while the Basque provinces in France lack of any political autonomy (see chapter 3 for further explanation).[7]

On the other hand, the size of the population of the Basque diaspora is nearly impossible to determine, as it depends on the operational definition of being Basque as well as on a complete statistical database. Nevertheless, the Basque government estimates that the diaspora population consists of 4.5 million people (Gobierno Vasco 1996, 47). Lately, the government argues that the number of diaspora Basques or "the children of the Basque Country in the twenty-first century" is six million (*Deia,* July 10, 2008). However, this figure is extremely difficult to corroborate. Given that the diaspora is about 1.5 times as large as the population in the home country with an institutional presence in over twenty countries, the issue of communication and contact—and information and communication technologies' role in it—is of enormous importance.

Defining Diaspora

> The multiplicity of different definitions of diaspora notwithstanding, all [is] based upon a decisive condition of space: the spatial separation of the diaspora community from "its" homeland. Diaspora is about not being there.
>
> — Martin Sökefeld 2002, 111

I conceive past and present Basque emigrant and exile communities as diasporas (see Douglass and Bilbao 1975; and Molina and Oiarzabal 2009). Diasporas are composed of scattered, deterritorialized emigrants and exilees, who shared a collective identity in their homeland, and who have been forced by socioeconomic or political conditions or have chosen to leave their land of origin to settle in other countries. There, emigrants and exilees and their descendants collectively develop and maintain cultural, religious, and political expressions of their identity, and consequently they form a collective identity distinct from that of their host societies' dominant culture. Within this collective identity, they have instituted specific social

---

6 Iparralde, or the Northern Basque Country, is that part of the Basque Country to the north of the international frontier between Spain and France.

7 For a further reading on the history of the Basque Country as well as its institutionalization and culture, see: Ahedo (2008); Douglass and Zulaika (2007); Irujo and Ibarra (2011); and Lecours (2007).

identities, institutions, and networks. Contemporary Basque diaspora associations constitute transnational networks that maintain explicit and implicit personal and institutional ties of a cultural, social, economic, political, and business nature with the homeland and other countries of Basque presence.[8]

The links developed between Europe and America provided information and means of travel for potential emigrants. Information networks and exchange of knowledge between homeland and host societies accomplished over centuries have traditionally helped Basques to settle in particular areas. Subsequent Basque migrations benefited from the important positive social status of the Basques as a collectivity and the existence of an institutional network that supported the newly arrived immigrants to help ease them into the new ways of the host societies.

It is interesting to note that during the Second World Congress on Basque Communities (Vitoria-Gasteiz 1999), a small but significant number of representatives of Basque communities from Argentina refused the term diaspora as used by the BAC government officials, "As it has connotations of nations with no territory of their own" (Gobierno Vasco 2000b, 59). Significantly, Josu Legarreta, the then Basque government's director for relations with Basque communities (1995–2009), stated, "I'd rather prefer to use [the term] Basques in the world" (Euskonews & Media 2000). However, in 1956, Pedro de Basaldua, the Basque government-in-exile's delegate to Argentina (1951-1982), defined the Basques abroad as a historical diaspora (Gobierno Vasco 1981, 439).

The institutions and networks, formed by the collective identity of the diaspora, favor transnational or cross-border interactions and ties with the homeland and co-diasporans or diasporic members, as well as the formation, development, and maintenance of their identities. Diasporas constitute a world-spanning web of attachments and allegiances, which combine and share an identity from a particular place and culture belonging to a particular time and generation. That is to say, diaspora is an evolving historical social concept subject to time and space, which represents a shifting historical reality.

Diasporic people such as the Basques map an identity atlas that occupies multiple geographical locations. This atlas also constructs different discourses, speaks different languages and dialects, represents different degrees of assimilation into their host societies, and maintains different degrees of connections among themselves and with the homeland. The Basque diaspora is a community not of place, but of identity.

According to Roland Robertson (1990, 1992), within the process of "glocalization," particularity is becoming a global value, while global flows become locally appropriated, integrated, and altered. Diasporas are at once local and global (Brah

---

8 For a further analytical exploration of the concept of diaspora, see Safran (1991, 1999), Tölölyan (1996), Cohen (1997a, 1997b), Glick Schiller (1999), Sheffer (1999), Schnapper (1999), and Butler (2001). See also Alonso and Oiarzabal (2010).

1996). Diasporas as global institutionalized and interest networks are rooted in local communities, and they function as meeting points between the local and the global, and between the particular and the universal. For example, the Basque diaspora constitutes a web of local connections and attachments rooted in their local cultural communities as well as a web of interactions among other co-diaspora communities and the homeland.

In this sense, diaspora communities constitute a unit of analysis of identity formation and maintenance that helps us to understand the interconnectedness of social identity realities across transnational spaces. Nina Glick Schiller et al. introduced the concept of transnationalism as a new analytical framework for understanding migration past and present and defined it as a process "by which immigrants build social fields that link together their country of origin and their country of settlement" and consequently "take actions, make decisions and feel concerns, and develop identities within social networks that connect them to two or more societies simultaneously" (1992a, 1–2; see also Glick Schiller et al. 1992b, 1995; and Glick Schiller 1999).

Following Victor Turner's conception of liminality as a state of being "betwixt and between" as "neither here nor there" (1969, 95), I would argue that the diaspora concept also refers to a condition of "in-betweenness" or a third space between the homeland and the hostland, which is characterized by its lack of unity, purity, or fixity. For instance, the Basque diaspora is not only a physically dispersed community formed by segments or nodes within a transnational space, but also a psychological or emotional interconnected community among co-diaspora communities and the country of origin. Diasporic identity is a psychological or emotional state somewhere, between a sense of being and a sense of belonging, in which memory and remembering are key elements in the reproduction of a homeland by means of imagination, as a collective image created in and for the present. This sense of belonging is the result of what I describe as nostalgia from emptiness, which brings about the need for a sense of fulfillment or self-completion. Identity endures because of an individual and collective nostalgia, as part of a strategy on maintaining identity (Oiarzabal and Oiarzabal 2005). "Being there" or "the return to the birthplace or the homeland" are in Lacanian terms the emigrants and exiles' "*object petite a*"—the lost object, and therefore desired—and which existence is due to the simple fact that has been lost or is absent (see Dashtipour 2009).

Drawing on the theories of cultural mourning and object loss,[9] Ricardo Ainslie argues that

> When an immigrant leaves loved ones at home, he or she also leaves the cultural enclosures that have organized and sustained experience. The immigrant simultaneously must come to terms with the loss of family and friends on the one hand, and cultural forms (food, music, art, for example) that have given the immigrant's native world a distinct and highly personal character on the other hand. It is not only the

9 See Volkan 1981.

> people who are mourned but the culture itself, which is inseparable from the loved ones whom it holds. (1998, 287; quoted in Plaza 2010, 155)

According to Ainslie, immigrants and their descendants, consequently, build a new space where they re-create the lost activities as a way to address their feelings of loss.

Diasporans such as the Basques, particularly the emigrant generation, find themselves between a "here"—attached to a hostland by the presence of their descendants born in the new country, and which is future-oriented—and a "there"—attached to the homeland by the presence of their ancestors and their memories, and which is past-oriented. This situation forces or empowers them to create their own temporal or permanent space that they can call "home," which is present-oriented. This diasporic space re-creates a psychological bond between their ancestors and their descendants. It is a space or "bridge" between the homeland and the hostland, a space that shares both worlds—their parents and their children's "homes"—and where they might go back and forth between cultures, but they are never entirely in either. In this sense, Edite Noivo highlights how "diasporic spaces may actually represent entirely new emotional geographies—places that emigrants enter and exit in a constant, permanent crossing of cultural and psychological borders. Those grounds are also less physical than imaginary homelands although those concrete spaces may unconsciously represent sanctuaries of identity" (2002, 272).

This situation produces specific dual or multiple identities and consciousnesses (see, for example, DuBois c.1903/1961; and Vertovec 1997). As an example of this, a Basque emigrant in the United States says, "We have two countries. We love the one which we remember with emotion and this one in where we live . . . All our lives we have been sponges, absorbing the beauty and the culture of both shores of the Atlantic" (Nere Garate Arostegui, quoted in Ascunce and San Miguel 2004, 419; see also Oiarzabal and Oiarzabal 2005).

Similarly, the Basque diaspora online is also structured alongside different digital platforms, such as electronic newsgroups, forums, listserves or mailing lists, and websites or nodes connected throughout cyberspace. Consequently, the Basque webscape encompasses those websites authored or commissioned by Basques in the homeland as well as in the diaspora. My interest lies within the framework of the web landscape established by the Basque diaspora institutional websites, which create a common networked set of online discourses across geographical, political, and linguistic barriers, discourses that I shall analyze in chapters 4 and 5.

In this sense, it is not difficult to think of the Basque diaspora online in terms similar to those used to discuss the offline diaspora. The Basque diaspora online as a psychological community also transcends geographic, temporal, generational, and ideological frontiers. In short, the Basque diaspora is a global community under a generic name that can be created and re-created by acts of imagination—either self-imagined and/or imagined by others.

Communication Technologies and Technological Diasporas

> All distances in time and space are shrinking . . . Man puts the longest distances behind him in the shortest time . . . What is created as a consequence of this technological innovation is a world in which everything is equally near and equally far: the distance prevails.
>
> — Martin Heidegger, 1971, 165–67

Time- and Space-Shrinking Technologies

The impact of technological progress implies a re-comprehension of our modern perceptions and preconceptions of time and space as well as the ways we think, behave, and live. Rick Parrish (2002 260, 280) refers to the telegraph and telephone as the first post-geographical technologies, which began to alter the ways that community interaction had been happening until then, that is, a face-to-face interaction rooted in physical proximity. Technological advancement in transportation—such as the airplane—and in communications—from the first instant communication technologies, such as telegraph, telephone, and fax, to satellite-based networks and computer-based networks, such as the Internet—promote worldwide interactive participation in real-time, dissolving old temporal and spatial constraints (see Harvey 1989; Brunn 1996).

The intensification of communication processes implies an increase in number and intensity of social contacts in time and space, as well as a decrease of the distance between the transmitter and the receptor on a global scale, resulting in a more networked society. To some extent, these technologies modify our understanding of place as a self-evident reference for cultural distinctiveness and belonging, while creating a globally interconnected and shared space. It shifts the focus from geography of territories to geography of identities. Anthony Giddens argues that, "We are dealing with the intensification of world-wide social relations which link distant localities in such a way that local happenings are shaped by events occurring many miles away and vice versa" (1990, 64).

The nature of any diaspora is intrinsically defined by physical or geographical dispersion as well as psychological separateness from the homeland, which creates, to some degree, longing and nostalgia. Global technologies of information, telecommunication, and transportation have accelerated contemporary diaspora formation and maintenance as well as linkage between co-diaspora communities and the homeland. Those "distance shrinking" technologies have reduced not only the physical distance, but the emotional distance between diaspora communities and the homeland by facilitating closer social relations.[10] They help to overcome

10 See also Harvey's (1989) "Time-Space Compression" and Giddens' (1990) "Time-Space Distanciaition" concepts.

or at least ameliorate a "tyranny of distance" (Blainey 1966; Cairncross 1997) as a result of such temporal and spatial dislocations.[11]

Diasporas have profusely used and are still using old and new forms of "distance shrinking" communication technologies, from mail, telegraph, ships, trains, cars, radio, telephone, television, fax, and airplane, to the Internet and particularly the web since the 1990s (see Karim 2003).[12] For example, Mark Poster defines the Internet as a "space-time relativized medium of global exchange of simultaneity without physical co-presence" (1998, 194). The Internet, as a global communication system networking computers and people, has significantly provided the ability for groups such as diasporas to connect with, maintain, create, and re-create social ties and networks to both their homelands and co-diaspora communities (see Morley and Robins 1995). In this regard, Poster describes the Internet as a "many-to-many medium" (1998, 194).

I argue that diaspora individuals and associations are more likely to continue to establish, retain, reconnect, or rediscover ties to the homeland by utilizing the Internet due to its low cost, effectiveness, and speed. Additionally, the Internet offers the ability for diasporas to exchange factual information regardless of geographical distance and time zones as they have twenty-four-hour access to vast resources.

In a sense, the Internet might facilitate the formation of a diaspora because it might help to regain and/or increase its consciousness of belonging to the same human group as such. It might empower a specific diasporic identity in cyberspace as a fundamental source of social meaning (Castells 1996, 2001; see also Dahan and Sheffer 2001). That is, the Internet offers the possibility of sustaining and re-creating a global imagined community by reaching a borderless audience. Through the web, the power to represent and imagine Basque identity might become more widely distributed and available to a wider audience. Minorities, such as the Basques, are projected into the global arena by using the Internet, which underpins their identity on a planetary scale (Diamandaki 2003, online; Sökefeld 2002; Poster 1998). As we will see in the following chapters, some of the potentialities of the Internet and the web described here will be borne out in the Basque case.

The Basque Technological Diaspora

The Basque diaspora has not been immune from the use of space- and time-shrinking technologies. Historically, diaspora Basques have made significant efforts to retain a connection not only with the homeland but also with co-diasporans, and they have used a variety of networking resources to overcome the barriers of distance. In diaspora communities where migration had ceased, the need to recon-

11 See also Aksoy and Robins (2002); Kolko et al. (2000); Rheingold (1993); and Shain (2002).

12 Tim Berners-Lee invented the web in 1990, and by 1991, it was established as a publicly available service on the Internet. By then, Berners-Lee had also written a web browser called the *World Wide Web* (later on renamed Nexus) and the *Hypertext Transfer Protocol* (HTTP). Mosaic (later on Netscape Navigator), invented by Marc Andreessen and Eric Bina in 1993, would become the first commercially available web browser.

nect became imperative. In this regard, the Basque club Euzko Etxea of Necochea, Argentina, established in 2004 an annual cultural "sojourners" program called Hator Hona (Come Here) that enabled young homeland Basques to live in Necochea for a month in order to teach local Basques diverse aspects of Basque culture, such as language, dance, music, cuisine, or sports.

Also, diaspora Basques published several periodicals for Basque diaspora communities in America. Some of them were also circulated among subscribers in Europe and information flowed back and forth.[13] According to Adolfo Ruíz de Gauna (1991), 108 Basque periodicals were published outside the Basque Country from the nineteenth century to the late 1970s: forty-three in the United States, sixty-five in South America, Central America, and Cuba, and one in the Philippines. In the nineteenth century, there were nine periodicals exclusively related to Basque emigrant communities and their institutions. Two were found in Madrid and Paris, two in the United States, three in Argentina, one in Uruguay, and one in Cuba. In addition, a Parisian association created by Basque, Béarnaise, and Gascon emigrants published the periodical *L'union Pyrénéenne* from 1899 to 1913.

In Buenos Aires, one of the most important diaspora publications called *La Vasconia—Revista Euskaro-Americana* (1893–1901), and later known as *La Baskonia* (1901–1943), was distributed in American areas populated by Basques as well as in Europe. Significantly, the first-ever, short-lived, weekly diaspora newspapers in the Basque language were printed in Los Angeles, California.[14] Those were *Escualdun Gazeta* (1885) and *Californiako Eskual Herria* (1893–1898), which was renamed in 1897 as *Eskual Herria* under the motto of "Yainkoa eta Sor-Lekuoa"—"God and the Homeland" or "Native Country." They were also distributed in San Francisco, San Diego, Mexico City, La Havana, and Río de la Plata (today's Argentina and Uruguay). In Buenos Aires, the newspaper *Euskal Herria—Journal Basque-Français du Rio de la Plata* (1898) was also published in Basque and in French. In addition to these Basque diasporic and transnational periodicals, we find the weekly *Revista Sociedad Vascongada de Montevideo*, called *Laurac Bat* (1877–1882, in the Spanish language), and *Vascones*, (1898) both from Montevideo; *Revista de la Sociedad Vasco-Española de Buenos Aires,* called also *Laurac Bat* (1878–1893, 1911, 1921–1922, 1930–1931, 1960–1970, in Spanish), and *Haritza* (1896) both from Buenos Aires; and the weekly *Laurac Bat* (June 1886–August 1886, in the Spanish language) from Havana, Cuba, dedicated to the Basque-Navarreses' beneficence societies.

In the twentieth century, ninety-nine periodicals were published in the Basque diaspora, constituting a true golden era of diaspora publications. For example, *La Euskaria* (1906), both from Buenos Aires, *Euskal Erria* (1912–1960), from Mon-

---

13 See also Soraluze (1986), and Álvarez Gila and Tápiz Fernández (1996).

14 The first newspaper published in the Basque language in the Basque Country was the weekly *Uscal Herrico Gazeta,* according to Javier Díaz Noci (2001, 315–16; 320–21). This paper was published by Joseph Augustin Chaho in Baiona in 1848. It only lasted for two issues. Another periodical was *Aurrera* published in 1883 in Madrid in the Basque language. The first scientific journal in Basque, *Euskara* (1886–1896), was published by non-Basques in Berlin, Germany.

tevideo, and the *Voice of the Basques* (1974–1977) from the United States were published by and for diaspora Basques. *Voice of the Basques* closed down due to insufficient subscriptions. Twentieth-century periodicals, mostly of a political nature, were related to the Spanish Civil War, the defeat of the Republican side, and the establishment of the Basque government-in-exile and political parties-in-exile, particularly the Basque nationalist parties. For example, there were early Basque nationalist periodicals published in the Americas, such as *Irrintzi* (1902–1923) from Maipú (Chile), *Euzkotarra* (1907)—first published in Mexico and later on in New Orleans (United States) under the name of *Askatasuna* until 1909—*Euzkotarra* (1913) from Buenos Aires (Argentina), *Aitor* (1915) from Rosario de Santa Fé (Argentina), and *Aurrera* (1917) from Santiago de Chile (Chile).

Since the nineteenth century, the Basque diaspora has used diverse means of communications, such as the aforementioned periodicals, which have contributed to the initial construction of a common Basque transnational, transatlantic, and diasporic identity and consciousness. They have helped to shape and articulate diaspora Basques' own particular sense and understanding of Basqueness and culture, openly influenced by the interaction with homeland ideologies and by the cohabitation with other groups in their host societies. It resulted in multiple interpretations of a generic sense of being Basque.

Basque diaspora media contributed to certain cohesion of identity and cultural maintenance, while resisting assimilation. It increased the awareness of interconnectedness among Basques, who shared common experiences of migration and identity across borders, in distant parts of the Americas, and on both sides of the Atlantic. Those experiences entailed physical and psychological uprootedness—migration understood as trauma, crisis, and loss—and physical and psychological adaptation and resettlement—migration as gain (see Grinberg and Grinberg 1989).

For the last decade, the Basque diaspora has added the Internet and the web to other more traditional forms of communication such as diaspora-based newspapers, newsletters, or radio programs, which are, to some extent, reproducing the same role of the old periodicals.

The proliferation of radio stations deserves a mention here. As of July 2007, there were ten Basque diaspora radio programs hosted by local radio stations from Argentina and France, and of which five are offered through the web: *La Voz del Centro Vasco-Euskal Etxeko Ahotsa* (The Voice of the Basque Center, Centro Vasco del Chaco, Argentina; www.radiochaco.com.ar), *Presencia Vasca* (Basque Presence, since 1990, Asociación Vasca Urrundik, Entre Ríos, Argentina; www.lasogaweb.com.ar/fmuniversidad/fmonline.htm), *Palabra de Vasco-Euskaldunon Hitza* (Basque Word, Centro Vasco Euzko Etxea de la Plata, Argentina; www.lr11.com.ar), *Zenbakaitz!* (Uncountable! Hiru Erreka Euskal Etxea, Argentina; www.radio105.com.ar), *Palabra de Vasco* (Basque Word, Centro Vasco Zazpirak Bat, Rosario, Argentina), *La Hora de los Vascos* (The Hour of the Basques, Centro Vasco de Chivilcoy, Argentina), *Eskualdunen Biltzarra* (Bordeaux, France), and *Txalaparta Irratia* (Paris,

France), which was established in 1980 and is hosted by Radio Pays (www.radiopays.org). In addition, the Federation of Basque-Argentinean Entities (FEVA is its Spanish acronym) produces a weekly one-hour radio program that broadcasts to fifty cities with Basque centers. FEVA produces forty-five minutes of the program, and the local Basque centers produce the remaining fifteen. As of July 2007, FEVA consisted of ninety-five club members (seventy-six are registered with the Basque government) (Ayesa and Orbaiceta 2008). There have also been historical radio programs, such as the Basque Program (1937–1997) from Buffalo, Wyoming, and Radio Euzkadi, the clandestine radio station of the Basque government-in-exile, which broadcasted from Iparralde from 1946 to 1954 and then from Caracas, Venezuela, from 1965 to 1977.

The proliferation of specific websites dedicated to Basque diaspora communities reflects contemporary Basque identity from a transnational and polycentric perspective. The contemporary process of Basque diaspora networking and communication via the Internet and the web has been facilitated by the establishment of the Basque government in 1979 as a way to reconnect with the homeland as well as with co-diaspora communities.

Connecting Basques and the Basque Government

Public Law 8/1994, May 27, passed by the BAC Parliament, is the current legal framework of institutional relationship between the BAC and the diaspora, which was established in order to "preserve and reinforce links between Basque Communities and Centers on the one hand, and the Basque Country on the other hand," and to "facilitate the establishment of channels of communication between Basque residents outside the Basque Autonomous Community, and the public authorities of the latter" (Gobierno Vasco 1994).

Law 8/1994 was partially the result of a petition by diaspora institutional leaders and delegates of the Basque American Congress in Euskadi (1982) to institutionalize the relations between the Basques abroad and the then–newly established Basque government, successor to the historical Basque government-in-exile. In addition, the diaspora delegates demanded a means of communication, which was taken into consideration by Law 8/94. The delegates argued that due to the lack of efficient means of communication, there was a need to establish "a system which will contribute to the maintenance of Basque identity" and that should include news, radio programs, Basque learning methods, and an intra-diaspora magazine called *Euskal Etxeak* (*Basque Studies Program Newsletter* 1982).

The Basque government has edited and published *Euskal Etxeak* since May 1989, and it distributes 36,500 copies—87 percent are in Spanish and 13 percent in English—to 115 countries. Since 2001, there has been a weekly electronic version of the *Euskal Etxeak* magazine, called *Euskal Etxeak Virtual*. As of March 2002, *Euskal Etxeak Virtual* was being distributed to ten thousand e-mail addresses throughout the world (*Euskal Etxeak* 2002). As of 2007, the number of subscribers to *Euskal*

Etxeak Virtual was approximately nine thousand (Ugalde Zubiri 2008). As of 2007, the BAC Public Radio and Television (EiTB in its Basque acronym) had five radio stations and four television channels—two of which are satellite televisions. ETB Sat (established in 1996) focuses on the European audience, while Canal Vasco (Basque Channel, established in 2000) focuses on the Americas (see chapter 3 for further information). EiTB also offers two satellite radio stations. Since 2000, the radio stations and the ETB Sat channel are available free of charge online through EiTB's website, www.eitb.com. Since March 2006, EiTB has also provided Canal Vasco in high definition via the Internet.

Within the context of the contemporary relationships with the Basque government, this is one of the earliest diaspora arguments establishing that communication between the homeland and the diaspora is necessary for maintaining identity. This argument, by the way, would become a constant goal for the Basque diaspora throughout the years. The connections between homeland and diaspora, between emigrants and those who stayed behind have been interrupted temporarily or permanently and have deteriorated with the passage of time, and those connections must be reestablished. That is, there is an urgent need to retain and even increase the ties, in a synchronic manner, with the Basque Country. In this sense, technologies of information and communication play a significant role.

By 1992, the Internet became generally available to the public. According to the Center for Digital Future (2004), back then about two million computers were connected to the Internet. Returning to the 1990s and the celebration of the first American Congress of Basque Centers (Buenos Aires, November 1997), there were already sixty-one Basque diaspora institutions registered with the Basque government, but there was only one diaspora association online: the political site Asociación Venezolana de Amigos de Euskal Herria (AVAEH; Caracas, Venezuela, http://earth.prohosting.com/avaeh/). However, diaspora delegates were already aware of the Internet and its potential for diaspora communication, thereby recommending the use of the Internet for Basque-language teaching as well as "the direct access to the Internet to members of the Basque Centers" (Fundación Juan de Garay's site, www.juandegaray.org).

Language learning via the Internet has been ongoing. Since 2004, the Basque government has implemented the Internet-based program for learning Basque called *Boga*, which replaced the 2001 *Hezinet* program. Since 2003, the government has also offered the Basque-teaching program called *Euskara Munduan* (Basque in the World), which was established following the successful program *Argentinan Euskaraz* (Basque in Argentina), set up in 1990. By January 2008, seventy-five Basque clubs in America, Australia, and Europe were participating in *Euskara Munduan*. One hundred teachers had been trained, and there were 1,500 students in America and 1,000 in Europe. In addition, the government has financed Basque lectureships in twenty-four universities throughout twelve countries, with a total attendance of 700 students as of January 2008. Law 3/2007 approved the creation of the Etxepare Basque Institute, similar to the Catalan Ramon Llull Institute or the

British Council, in order to project internationally the Basque language and culture (Gobierno Vasco 2008). Furthermore, in October 2008 the Education Department of the Basque government began also to promote a new online method to learn Basque called *Ikasten* (To Learn; www.ikasten.net) to complement other initiatives such as *Boga*.

By the time of the Second World Congress of Basque Communities (Vitoria-Gasteiz, October 1999), the Basque government had provided computer equipment and Internet connection to all 108 registered diaspora associations in existence at that time, "enabling reliable and rapid communications with the Basque government and with each other through the use of electronic mail," as well as enabling them to access the web. The estimated cost was €240.000 (approximately $330,000) (Gobierno Vasco 2000, 44). As of October 1998, there were only seven diaspora websites from Argentina, the United States, and Venezuela. Over 79 percent of total diaspora websites were in fact created after 2000.

In 2000, the Basque government's youth diaspora program *Gaztemundu* (Young World), established in 1996, focused on new technologies and identity maintenance. Thirty-eight participants from Argentina, Canada, Chile, Mexico, Peru, the United States, Uruguay, and Venezuela suggested the creation of a global virtual community called "vascos.com" as a "space to communicate or transmit information of general interest related to the Basque world . . . Euskadi, the Basque centers,

and their activity [as well as] to promote Basque identity as a support for cultural, professional and commercial exchanges, using the advantages of the Internet [and] to show a real and positive image of the Basque world . . . which has been so blemished lately by the terrorist outrages" (*Euskal Etxeak* 2000, 13–15). The 2009 edition of Gaztemundu exclusively focused on the use of Euskaletxeak.net portal.

Finally, the Four-Year Plan for Institutional Action (2004–2007) elaborated by the diaspora delegates at the Third World Congress (Vitoria-Gasteiz July 2003) proposed, in an unprecedented manner, the application of new technologies "to boost the creation of a comprehensive cooperation and communication network to extend and optimize the links between Euskal Herria and the [d]iaspora through Internet and other means and tools," while focusing on the creation of websites and portals and a network of webmasters (Gobierno Vasco 2004, 255, 257–58). In November 2008, the Basque government created a specific website, www.euskaletxeak.net, in collaboration with the different diaspora federations, with the goal of becoming a virtual meeting point for Basques abroad by highlighting its inclusive and participatory elements. The site expected to host forums and communities where users would generate most of their content. However, this goal has never entirely been accomplished. For the last three decades, the Basque government has played an increasing role in networking the Basque diaspora as an attempt to enhance transnational channels of communication. Some of the underlying reasons for such involvement will be discussed in chapter 3 as part of the examination of the government's ethnonational discourses on the diaspora. All the steps taken, particularly by the Basque government and diaspora associations, toward the creation of new telecommunications infrastructure have the potential to increase exponentially and in an unmatched fashion not only the flow and exchange of information and ideas, but the number and frequency of connections between the different diaspora communities and the homeland. That is, regardless of where diaspora populations are located in the physical world, the Internet enables them to "get together" in cyberspace. As of June 2007, 123 Basque diaspora associations (or over 62 percent of the existing associations throughout nineteen countries) had a presence on the web, compared to just a few years prior when the number of sites could be counted on one hand. This trend demonstrates a powerful potential for Basque diaspora expression online.

Imagined Online Communities

> In the fifteenth century, news was a social event: when someone walked into town, everyone gathered to find out what was happening up the road . . . Printing put villagers in touch with broader groups they had not identified with before. People who didn't speak the same language or live anywhere near each other began to join together, to go to war over ideas promoted by the millions of copies of Martin Luther's work. The Protestant Reformation brought together what Benedict Anderson called "imagined communities," and which I would be tempted to call "virtual communities."
>
> — Howard Rheingold 1999, 18

Richard C. Carlson and Bruce Goldman raised similar opinions as those expreseed by Rheingold by arguing that "the small personal computer is the Protestant Revolution of technology" (1991, 4).[15] The arguments within the academic and non-academic worlds about whether online aggregations resulting from individual online interactions are indeed communities are polarizing. On the one hand, authors such as Amitri Etzioni and Oren Etzioni (1997, 1999), William A. Galston (2000), Joel Snyder (1996), and Shawn P. Wilbur (1997) argue that online aggregations cannot be considered "real" communities because they lack the characteristics that communities must have in order to be defined as such: identification with the same specific physical place and time, common ties, and indirect verbal or non-verbal, face-to-face social interactions, described as intimate, holistic, and all-encompassing (Bateman and Lyon 2002, 375, 378). On the other hand, authors such as Michael Benedikt (1991), Mark Dery (1996), Andrew Feenberg and Maria Bakardjieva, (2004), Steve Fox (2004), Howard Rheingold (1993), Nessim Watson (1997), Barry Wellman and Milena Gulia (1999), and Wellman (2001) strongly argue that online communities are communities as authentic or real as the ones in the physical world, and they are treated as such by their members.

---

15 The concepts of online, virtual, and cyber are used by many authors as interchangeable. I prefer to use the terms *cyber* or *online*.

I argue that the term *community* is not essential in describing these aggregations. The significance lies in the participant's own perception of being part of a community where communication and interaction is felt to be meaningful. Consequently for those participants, the Internet is a community-forming device where they meet and interact, thereby constituting social networks and online or cybercommunities—placeless, deterritorialized, and without face-to-face interaction. Such online communities can take the form of multi-user dungeons (MUDs) or multi-object oriented (MOOs), weblogs or blogs (online diaries), newsgroups, web forums or bulletin boards (BBs), Internet relay chat (IRC), or instant messaging sessions (IMS) or software-driven communications programs that provide a real-time chat facility. MUDs and MOOs are text-based virtual games, where multiple users can interact with each other and the environment. The original BBs were the precursor to websites and online forums. According to Avtar Brea, they were created as "an ideal model of participation, attempting to replace the traditional unidirectional and vertical scheme of emitter-receptor with that of a disseminated rhizome of users." However, they "failed as multi-media browsers appeared and the communicative potential of the medium far exceeded the limitations of a mere notice board" (2003, 4–6 online; see also Bromberg 1996; Fox and Roberts 1999; Oiarzabal 2010; Miller and Slater 2001; and Watson 1997).

In a sense, online individuals may never meet face-to-face, but they might form what Howard V. Perlmutter describes as "communities of [common] interest" or affinity, limited by neither space nor time, which combine the interests of individuals and the interests of the collective (quoted in Cohen 1997a, 173–174; see Perlmutter 1991). Already in the mid-1960s, Joseph C. R. Licklider and Robert Taylor, both of whom worked in the Advanced Research Projects Agency of the Pentagon (headquarters of the United States Department of Defense at Arlington, Virginia) and were pioneers in promoting development of the Internet, had defined online interactive communities as communities "not of common location, but of common interest" (1968).

Furthermore, the literature reviewed establishes a relation between the role of imagination in the construction of the modern nation-state by its members, which is theorized by Benedict Anderson as an "imagined community," and the impact of "print capitalism," as well as the impact of "microelectronic transnationalism" (Spivak 1989, 276), "electronic capitalism" (Appadurai 1996, 7), or "digital capitalism" (Shani 2002), and the production and reproduction of other types of imagined communities, such as online or cybercommunities. Anderson emphatically argues that within the context of nineteenth-century nation-state building, "All communities larger than primordial villages of face-to-face contact (and perhaps even these) are imagined" by their individual members (1991, 6).[16]

---

16 For a critical account on Anderson's concept of "imagined communities" see, for example, Chasteen and Castro-Klarén 2004.

Similarly, online communities—although non-territorial—are undoubtedly imagined communities in the sense of Anderson's "imagined community" concept. Online communities are also imagined by "often faceless, transient, or anonymous" individual members who, despite their geographical location, may feel that they are a part of their communities (Foster 1997, 25). That is to say, the web helps individuals consolidate a common image of a community, which is re-created by acts of imagination.

Online and offline communities as social constructs are dependent on the imagination of their members, and consequently we should consider the need to transcend the duality of "real" community versus online community.[17] I argue that online and non-online "worlds" are not completely detached or disconnected from each other as if they were parallel universes. Steve Fox (2004) and Mary E. Virnoche and Gary T. Marx (1997) argue that we should envision online and physical communities not as distinct communities but as part of a wider, single, imagined community that incorporates both physical and online interactions, a community whose members might share spaces both online and offline.

For example, the impact of the growing dependence on computers in our daily lives is closing the gap between both "worlds" as individuals progressively interact with their online and physical communities. Authors such as Katie J. Ward (1999), Ananda Mitra and Raelynn Schwartz (2001, online), and Etzioni and Etzioni (1999) argue that the interaction between the online and the physical realms creates a new hybrid, synthetic, or cybernetic space based on a combination of face-to-face and computer-mediated communities.[18]

Computer-mediated communication does not exist independently from face-to-face patterns of communication. The hybrid space is both physical and online simultaneously, as there is a symbiotic, reflexive, and inextricably woven relationship between online experiences and physical experiences. Cyberspace helps to maintain the networks of social ties existing within the wider physical community. According to Ward, a cybercommunity "requires the physical to provide it with meaning" (1999, 95) (see chapter 4 to learn about the application of the cybernetic concept in relation to the Basque diaspora).[19]

In this regard, diasporas have become the paradigmatic communities of virtuality and imagination. Geographical and temporal distance forces diasporans such as Basques to think of themselves as imagined communities that share a common origin, identity, and culture. "Real life" communities such as diasporas function as imagined communities and extend themselves into cyberspace and becoming cybercommunities. I consider diasporas like the Basque one to be cyber-expansions of themselves. In this case, the Basque diaspora community is an online imagined

17 See, for example, Diamandaki (2003, online); Hakken (1999); Fox (2004); Mallapragada (2000); Mills (2002); and Sökefeld (2002).

18 See Curry (2004, online); Kolko, Nakamura and Rodman (2000); and Sökefeld (2002).

19 See Boase, Horrigan, Wellman, and Rainie (2006); and Wellman and Gulia (1999, 179).

community that is part of a wider, heterogeneous, imagined Basque community that encompasses both the online and non-online communities.[20]

I refer to an episode that illustrates the argument that both online and offline spaces are dimensions of one same reality. Like the Basque Country, Catalonia is not a state recognized by the United Nations, and therefore it does not receive the two-letter designation code that states receive in order to be identified on the Internet, such as *.it* for Italy or *.ch* for Switzerland. (However, there are exceptions, such as the domain name for Palestine, *.ps*). On behalf of sixty-eight thousand individuals and associations—including those from the Catalan diaspora—the Catalan non-governmental association PuntCAT (www.puntcat.org) successfully lobbied to obtain the specific Internet domain name *.cat* for the Catalan linguistic and cultural community as a way to express Catalan identity on the web (e.g., Friends of Catalonia, Miami; www.friendsofcatalonia-miami.cat). The domain name *.cat* was obtained in September 2005, and it was the first ever domain of its kind (see Gerrand 2006, online).[21]

This provoked a heated protest headed by the Spanish political establishment. The Spanish government and the Spanish right-wing Popular Party (PP, in its Spanish acronym) manifested their opposition to any future demand for the domain name *.ct*—equivalent to *.es,* for *España* (Spain), or *.fr,* for *France*—as this would mean "the political independence of Catalonia on the Internet" (*Deia,* October 5, 2005). The Spanish Association of Internet Users (www.internautas.org) argued that the domain name *.cat* meant a radical virtual detachment from the Spanish Internet community identified by the domain name *.es* (*El País,* September 15, 2005). PuntCat has already begun working on the demand for the domain name *.ct.*

Similarly, as of April 2006, the non-governmental associations PuntoGAL (www.puntogal.org), PointBZH (http://bzh.geobreizh.com/www/bzh/default-eng.asp), and DotSCO (www.dotsco.org) were born in order to lobby for the top level domain names *.gal, .bzh,* and *.sco* for the respective Galician, Breton, and Scottish online communities (Vieiros, April 6, 2006). Voices from the Basque Country also began to demand a domain name for the Basque cultural and linguistic community on the Internet. The Basque homeland newspaper *Gara* (September 17, 2005) argued that the Catalan example was "the way to be followed" by Basque cultural associations in both the homeland and in the diaspora in order to obtain a specific domain for the Basque Country. Consequently, on April 2, 2008, eleven homeland linguistic, cultural, educational, and media organizations, including the Basque Public Radio

---

20 See, for example, Cohen (1996, 516); Diamandaki (2003, online); Kolko, Nakamura, and Rodman (2000, 9); Laguerre (2004, online); Schmidt (2002, 8–9); and Sökefeld (2002).

21 In a domain name, such as *euskaldiaspora.com*, *.com* is the so-called top-level domain (TLD), while *euskaldiaspora* is defined as second-level domain. There are two types of TLD: those that, theoretically, reflect the purpose of an organization (generic top-level domain), such as *.com* (commercial), *.edu* (educational), or *.org* (organization), and those that refer to a country (country code top-level domain), such as *.fr* for France, or *.ar* for Argentina. The Internet Corporation for Assigned Names and Numbers (ICANN; www.icann.org/) provides the "country codes" to states recognized by the United Nations and also manages the Domain Name Systems. In June 2008, ICANN approved the initiative to create domains by using any word or letter.

and Television, EiTB, the University of the Basque Country, and *Euskaltzaindia*, the Royal Academy of the Basque Language, constituted the association PuntuEUS (www.puntues.org) in order to obtain the domain name *.eus* for the online community of the Basque language and culture. Surprisingly, no diaspora organization is found among the founding institutions of PuntuEUS. The association PuntuEUS was officially presented to the public at the end of January 2009. It states, "The Basque language, Euskara, faces a new challenge: creating its own name on the Internet . . . something unnamed simply does not exist. [It] wants to achieve: the creation of a symbol that allows us its international recognition in the virtual space on the Internet: the .EUS domain [name]." In June 2013, ICANN finally accepted the *.eus* domain. During the public presentation of the domain, the current President of the BAC, Lehendakari Iñigo Urkullu, defined the new Internet territory facilitated by '.eus' as the "eighth territory of the Basque language," i.e., the point entry of the global world (*Deia*, June 22, 2013).

Notes on Data Sources and Methods

Data Sources

This book is of necessity a "work in progress" due to the volatility, ephemeral, and changing nature of the web, as it is constantly updated. This also applies to the Basque institutional diaspora presence on the web. During the research for and preparation of this manuscript, some Basque diaspora websites were newly established, some were renewed, others were under construction, a few were old, others had not been updated for years, and a small number disappeared and never emerged again.

For example, the Euzko Etxea de Necochea's site (Argentina, http://euzkoetxea.com.ar) was established in the fall of 2005, soon after my initial research. Then, during the fall of 2006, the North American Basque Organizations' (NABO) site was renewed as it merged with its Basque language's sister site (www.euskara.us) under a new domain (www.nabasque.org). As of March 2007, twenty associations had renewed the URLs (uniform resource locators) or web addresses of their sites (see appendix: table A.4 for further details). As for sites under construction, the Centro Vasco Laurak Bat of Buenos Aires's site (www.laurakbat.com.ar) was under construction between 2004 and 2008. Similarly, as of June 2007, the site belonging to the Basque choir of Buenos Aires, Coral Alkartasuna (www.coralalkartasuna.com.ar), was also under construction. Other sites had already been around since 1997, such as the political site Asociación Diáspora Vasca–Euskal Diaspora Nazioarteko Elkartea (Argentina, http://euskalherria.cjb.net), the educational organization from Buenos Aires Fundación Vasco Argentina Juan de Garay (Argentina, www.juandegaray.org.ar), and the Basque club from Seattle (United States, www.seattleeuskal.org). By contrast, the Basque Dancing Society at New Castle University Upon Tyne's site (United Kingdom, www.societies.ncl.ac.uk/basque.dancing), and the Centro Vasco Zingirako Euskaldunak (Argentina, www.chascomus.com.ar/centrovasco/), despite renewing its web address in 2007, had not been updated since 2001 as of this writing.

And finally, between October 2005 and May 2007, nine websites disappeared. Three were from Argentina: Centro Vasco Villegasko Euskaldunak (General Villegas, www.vascos.villegas.net.ar), Centro Vasco Denak Bat (Mendoza, www.denakbat.com.ar), and the advocate site Josu Lariz (www.josu-askatu.org); one from Mexico—also the advocate site 6 de México (www.6demexico.org); one from Spain—Euskal Etxea de Sevilla (Sevilla, http://groups.msm.com/EuskalEtxeaSE/home.htm); one from the United Kingdom—the Institute of Basque Studies (London, http://ibs.lgu.ac.k); one from Uruguay—Centro Vasco Euskal Erria (Montevideo, http://euskalerria.org.uy); and two from the United States—Gauden Bat (Chino, www.gaudenbat.com) and NABO's Basque-language platform Euskara.us (www.euskara.us).

The Basque diaspora presence on the Internet and particularly on the web is undoubtedly still unfolding. Although it would not be wise to prognosticate about any future trends of the Basque diaspora presence on the web, evidence shows an increasing tendency for articulating an online presence. For example, from the beginning of 2004 to the end of 2005, thirteen new diaspora institutional websites were created, and from October 2005 to June 2007, another thirty-four appeared (twenty-three sites and eleven blogs/photologs, mostly built by Basque-Argentinean dance groups)—the majority of which are Basque clubs, or *euskal etxeak,* and mainly from Argentina.

In addition, the Association des Basques de Montpellier et Languedoc (France, http://eskualdunak.midiblogs.com/) and the Centro Vasco de Caracas (Venezuela, www.euskoetxeacaracas.blogspot.com) replaced their respective sites with blogs. Furthermore, as of June 2007, a new phenomenon appeared. That is to say, four diaspora sites also built complementary digital platforms such as blogs, social network sites, and online groups as a way to connect people who share similar affinities. The first identified Basque diaspora association to establish a profile on a social network site (MySpace) was the Reno Basque club Zazpiak Bat (Nevada, United States) in 2007. My research identifies the Colorado Basque club (United States, www.coloradoeuskaletxea.com/) as the first club to establish a presence on the Basque digital diaspora's blogosphere. It goes back to April 2004. (However, those blogs were not identified until 2007. Consequently, they were added to the 2007 database.) It created two additional online platforms—the Members Blog (http://coloradoeuskaletxea.blogspot.com/) and the Topagunea Blog (http://topagunea.blogspot.com/), the second of which was established to facilitate the exchange of ideas on a Basque teaching program between the Colorado *euskal etxea* and the San Fermín Ikastola (Basque-language school) in Navarre (Nafarroa). Both blogs have been inactive since 2005 and 2004 respectively. The Basque club of Barcelona's official website was also supported by a blog (http://blog.euskaletxeak.org).

In November 1999, the London Basque Society (www.zintzilik.org/london/) created an online group for the members of its club (http://groups.yahoo.com/group/

euskaledge/). As of June 2007, it had eighty-six members. By March 2009, it had two fewer members. There have been no new messages posted since December 2008. In addition, between June 2000 and November 2001, the political group Asociación Diáspora Vasca from Argentina (www.diasporavasca.org) created five online groups or virtual *txokos* (Basque fraternities) in order to complement the activities of the websites. Those *txokos* are located at http://ar.groups.yahoo.com/group/vascosdiaspora/ (271 members in June 2007; in Spanish); http://groups.yahoo.com/group/diasporavasca-euskera/ (seventy members in June 2007; in Basque), http://groups.yahoo.com/group/diasporavasca-english/ (115 members in June 2007; in English), http://groups.yahoo.com/group/diasporavasca-francais/ (forty-five members in June 2007; in French), and http://groups.yahoo.com/group/diasporavasca-portugues/ (twenty-seven members in June 2007; in Portuguese). The groups were not to be found as of March 2009[22] (for further analysis on the social network sites of the Basque diaspora, see Oiarzabal, 2010, and 2012a).

Research Methods

I have conducted quantitative, qualitative, and comparative research on the online and offline dimensions of the Basque institutional diaspora in order to better understand its discourses on Basque identity, culture, and nation. The web is characterized by the multimedia of the text, consisting of a combination of written word, graphics, and audio-visual forms. However, the web is not just a compilation of texts and images, isolated from the offline world. Therefore, I have analyzed the context from which the sites take their meanings by carrying out comparative fieldwork on Basque diaspora communities and by interviewing Basque diaspora institutional leaders from diverse Basque communities around the globe. The analysis of institutional diaspora websites offers fruitful insight into their offline world institutions while providing further arguments related to the exploration of identity formation and reproduction in the online world. I argue that the significance of global technologies such as the Internet relies on why and how they are used to explore offline life.

22 As of March 2009, there were another eight diaspora associations that also created their respective online groups/mailing lists. All of them are hosted at Yahoo! Groups. Only the "Goizeko Izarra," the "CV Chacabuco," and the "Vascos de Castelli" groups are active since their creation. In Argentina, the Centro Vasco Lagun Onak de Pergamino set up the "Goizeko Izarra" group in August 2004 (thirty-three members; http://ar.groups.yahoo.com/group/goizekoizarra/); the Centro Vasco established the "CV Chacabuco" group in September 2004 (thirteen members; http://ar.groups.yahoo.com/group/CVChacabuco/); the Centro Vasco "Euskal Etxea" de Comodoro Rivadavia set up the "Haize Dantzariak" group in November 2004 (one member; http://ar.groups.yahoo.com/group/Haize_Dantzariak/); the Centro Vasco Denak bat de Lomas de Zamora, Province of Buenos Aires also set up in November 2004 the "Denak Dat" group (three members, http.//ar.groups.yahoo.com/group/denakbat); the Centro Vasco Castelli "Oneratu" established the "Vascos de Castelli" group in May 2006 (six members; http://ar.groups.yahoo.com/group/vascos_de_castelli/); and the Centro Vasco Ibai Txori de Concepción del Uruguay, Entre Ríos, created the "Ibai Txori" group in September 2008 (two members; http://ar.groups.yahoo.com/group/ibaitxori/). In Venezuela, the Centro Vasco de Caracas established a group in February 2002 (nine members); (http://espanol.groups.yahoo.com/group/centrovascodecaracas/); and in Spain, the Centro Vasco "Gure Toko" from Valladolid created a group in February 2006 (two members; http://es.groups.yahoo.com/group/gure_txoko/).

I combined different methods in order to collect and analyze the data, while utilizing the Internet not only as an object of study, but also as a complementary research tool. The methods used were fieldwork, interviews, content analysis, hyperlink network analysis, and surveys.

Between 2002 and 2009, I traveled throughout twelve Basque communities in both the United States and Argentina and I interviewed fifty-seven individuals from over twenty countries in order to gain insight into diaspora institutions and communities, including webmasters, diaspora institutional representatives, community members, and academics specialized in diaspora and migration studies. For example, I attended and participated in the Third and Fourth World Congress of Basque Communities (July 2003, Vitoria-Gasteiz, and July 2007, Bilbao, BAC), the First Basque-Argentinean Youth Congress (Necochea, Argentina, November 2005), several NABO and FEVA meetings and conventions, and multiple community gatherings.

I have applied a discursive and rhetorical analysis to ninety Basque diaspora sites from sixteen countries as of July–August 2005, which I have complemented by studying new websites that had been created since then up to June 2007 (see chapters 4 and 5). The time frame as a "snapshot of cyberspace" (Mitra and Cohen 1999) for the analysis and selection of contents was July and August 2005. At the time, it was not possible to conduct any content analysis on five of the websites because two were under construction—the Buenos Aires–based *euskal etxea Laurak Bat* (Argentina, www.laurakbat.com.ar/) and the Centro Vasco Danak Bat de Bolívar (Argentina, http://centrovasco.tripod.com/Informacion.htm)—and three sites reported "http 404-File Not Found," meaning, most likely, that they had been removed (temporarily or permanently) or that their domain names were changed. These three sites were the Centro Vasco Argentino Zingirako Euskaldunak (Chascomús, www.chascomus.com.ar/ArteyCultura/Baile/CentroVasco/index.html), the Centro Vasco Euskal Erria (Montevideo, Uruguay, www.euskalerria.org.uy), and the Arizonako Euskal Etxea (Arizona, http://members.cox.net/pescoz/arizonako/). As of July-August 2005, 63 percent of the websites were up-to-date (37.3 percent were up-to-date as of July 2005). Eighteen percent of the sites were updated before 2005. Nevertheless, for 17 percent of the sites, the date of the last update was unknown. It can be argued that the issue of updating the sites is a symptom of the sites' health and their respective associations' health; however, the lack of current content on some sites did not deter me from including them in the study. Like books written long ago but still currently available, the contents of the sites were still worthy of analysis.

Back in 2005, seven new Basque diaspora sites, of which five were *euskal etxeak*, were identified and/or published by the time I was conducting content analysis, and therefore were included in the analysis. These sites were the Colectividad Vasca de Concordia (Argentina, www.concordia.com.ar/Vascos/); the Sociedad Vasca de Villa Mercedes (Argentina, www.vascosvillamercedes.sergroup.com.ar/); the Euzko Etxea-Centro Vasco de Santiago de Chile (Chile, www.euzkoetxeachile.

cl/); the Basque club of North Queensland (Australia, http://basqueclubnq.com/index.html); and the Euskal Etxea de Sevilla Pitxurritu (Seville, Spain, http://groups.msn.com/EuskalEtxeaSE/home.htm).

At the same time, Euskara.us, an online educational platform, was created by NABO and sponsored by HABE (the Basque Language Department of the Basque government in Spain) in order to promote the Basque language in the United States. In addition, a Basque-business association, Asociación de Empresarios de Origen Vasco (EmpreBask, Association of Business Owners of Basque Origin) was created in Santiago de Chile (Chile, www.empresariosvascos.cl and www.emprebask.com), becoming the first of its kind in the entire Basque-diaspora cyberspace to utilize the opportunities that the Internet and particularly the web can offer, such as connectivity, networking, or speedy communication. EmpreBask Colombia and EmpreBask México (www.emprebask.com.mx) were also set up in 2007 as a way to strength the commercial exchange between their countries of residence and Euskadi. Similarly, other diasporas had already jumped into the online world, establishing business associations based on their common identity and heritage, such as the Asociación Catalana-Ecuatoriana de Negocios (Catalan-Ecuadorian Association of Business, www.acenecuador.org), the Federación de Entidades Empresariales de Ascendencia Catalana (Federation of Business Entities of Catalan Ancestry, Chile, www.fedaca.cl), and the Agrupación de Empresarios de Ascendencia Catalana (Association of Business Owners of Catalan Ancestry, Chile, http://aeac.cl).

I focused on the sites' textual, graphic, and multimedia content (575 graphics, thousands of texts, and dozens of songs, and so forth) as well as on the links between the sites (connectivity, hypertextuality), while also taking into account the structure (the number of pages, navigation options, or hierarchical order of pages etc.).

At the same time, I used the same content analysis technique to study Basque government's discourses in order to infer any possible influence on the Basque diaspora's discourses and to draw parallelisms between both set of discourses.[23] I analyzed dozens of speeches from online and offline newsletters of the Basque-diaspora institutions, from Basque governmental publications, such as the *Euskal Etxeak* magazine and World Congresses' Proceedings; from the Basque government's websites; and from local and national newspapers published since the 1980s. The analysis of the discourses yields insights into the role of non-state actors, such as the Basque government in international politics, foreign policy, and paradiplomacy, as well as insight into the mobilization of the Basque diaspora in achieving a certain institutional presence in the international political arena. The Basque diaspora's role in foreign politics will be exemplified by examining nation-

---

23 On diasporas and homeland governments' literature, see, for example, Ambrosio (2002), Constas and Platias (eds. 1993), Davis and Moore (1997), Duany (2004), Leonard (2003), Shain (1989, 1991), and Tölölyan (1996).

alist mobilization episodes in support of homeland nationalism and independence (see chapters 3 and 6).[24]

Hypertextuality or intertextuality is a central aspect of the web. That is to say, sites and their contents are implicitly or explicitly interconnected with each other—through reciprocity and interactivity—by *links.*[25] Consequently, I have conducted an analysis of the hyperlink network structure of the Basque diaspora webscape. I have analyzed nearly two thousand hyperlinks of ninety Basque diaspora websites in order to understand their preferential directionality and networking (see chapter 2).

Moreover, one hundred and five people from over twenty countries participated in two major and unparallel surveys exploring the Basque diaspora websites as well as the institutional relationship between the Basque government and the Basque diaspora. I designed an online self-administered survey for the Basque diaspora webmaster (as the person theoretically responsible for the technical and design aspects of the sites) and the website author (as the person theoretically responsible for the contents of the site, such as the composition of texts or the selection of images) in order to study the reasons for the establishment of the sites and the potential effect on their institutions and communities.

However, in practical terms, the division of roles between webmasters and authors was not so distinctive, as the majority of the respondents were simultaneously the ones responsible for the most technical aspects of the site, including its design, as well as for the creation of content—that is, authorship. In addition, I considered the creation of Basque diaspora websites, to a certain degree, the result of multiple or collective authorship due to the borrowing of contents—that is, file sharing—and the hypertextuality property of the web, which constructs a communal Basque webscape cyberspace. In other words, the sites' contents were not all produced by single webmasters, as they adopted and adapted borrowed material from the web (see chapter 2).

In summary, nearly 66 percent of the websites (fifty-eight) and 68.7 percent of countries (eleven) had participated in the web-based survey as of April–June 2005. Andorra, Germany, Switzerland, Chile, and Peru failed to participate in the survey. Over 37.5 percent (thirty-three) of those who participated were webmasters of *euskal etxeak*, and 28.4 percent (twenty-five) of the participants were webmasters of cultural, educational, political, portals, and federation sites. With the exception of the single federation type site (i.e., NABO), the political sites have the highest response rate by any type of site (85.7 percent), followed by the educational sites (81.8 percent), portal sites (66.6 percent), and cultural sites (58.3 percent).

---

24 See, for example, Aldecoa and Keating (1999), Arthur (1991), Legarreta (2001), Moreno (1999, 2001, and 2002), Lecours and Moreno (2001), Rudolph and Thompson (ed. 1989), Skrbis (1991), and Ugalde Zubiri (1996).

25 See, for example, McMillan (2000), Mitra (1999, online), and Mitra and Cohen (1999).

With the exception of Oceania, represented by a single site country and a response rate of 100 percent, the continent of North America has the highest response rate (80 percent), followed by South America (62.5 percent), and Europe (45 percent). With regard to countries, and with the exception of Australia and Italy with a response rate of 100 percent (single site countries), Venezuela and Mexico also have a response rate of 100 percent, followed by the United States (79.3 percent), Canada (66.6 percent), and Argentina (64 percent). France had a 57.1 percent response rate, while Uruguay and the United Kingdom each had a response rate of 50 percent. The lowest response rate belongs to Spain at 33.3 percent.

Some possible reasons for the low response rate of countries such as Argentina are related to the lack of spare time and/or lack of interest, universal to any type of research method, as well as, in particular, the impossibility of communicating with webmasters due to lack of proper contact addresses. In addition, the slow decision-making process of Basque clubs in Argentina is detrimental to a webmaster's finding the time to participate in the survey. However, this brings some reassurance about the role of a board of directors or a website's committee on overseeing the webmaster's work. For example, the Centro Vasco Itxaropena de Saladillo (Argentina, www.saladillo.gov.ar/centrovasco.htm) requested extra time to respond to the survey because it required the approval of the board of directors. I cannot conclusively determine the reasons for its failure to participate—that is, whether the board of directors did not authorize the participation or simply, if it did authorize participation, it did not do so in time to participate. Similarly, Gustavo Benegas, webmaster of the Centro Vasco Denak Bat de Mendoza (Argentina, www.denakbat.com.ar) stated, "[The Web page] and everything has to be approved by the Board of Directors," which consequently slows everything down.

Furthermore, I administered a survey questionnaire of the Likert-scale type to representatives, institutional leaders and congress delegates of Basque diaspora institutions who met at the Third World Congress of Basque Communities. This required the participants to either agree or disagree to a set of thirty-two statements using a scale in relation to the effect of the Basque government's support of the Basque diaspora's institutions and their future (see chapter 3; see appendix: tables A.6, A.7, and A.8). In sum, a total of 162 people took part in the research.

Organization of This Work

In the coming chapter, I shall introduce the Basque diaspora digital intelligentsia in order to explore their role in building an online presence for the Basque institutional diaspora. I shall also present an analysis of the hyperlink network structure of the Basque diaspora webscape in order to learn about its geographical and thematic directionality and social networking. Why does the Basque diaspora use digital technologies such as the Internet? And what difference do the technologies make? What impact do the new global communication technologies (such as the Internet) have on strengthening and maintaining Basque identity in the diaspora?

And how do the websites help to maintain Basque identity outside of the Basque Country?

In chapter 3, I shall examine the Basque government's ethnonationalist discourses on the Basque diaspora in order to assess the influence on the construction of identity discourses by the diaspora within the context of the historical relationships between the modern Basque nationalist movement and the diverse Basque diaspora communities since the end of the nineteenth century. Are there connections between Basque diaspora online discourses and those constructed by the Basque government? If yes, what are these connections? And why are there connections between both sets of discourses?

Furthermore, in chapter 4, I shall focus on the graphic and audio-visual content of the Basque diaspora webscape, while addressing the Basque diaspora self-discursive construction. What are the discourses produced by the Basque diaspora webscape? What are the goals, meanings, and characteristics of these discourses? Why does the Basque diaspora articulate those discourses? What do those discourses reveal about Basque diaspora identity? In what ways do diaspora institutions imagine the diaspora in general? And why does the diaspora define and imagine itself in such ways?

In chapter 5, I shall focus on the Basque diaspora online discourses related to homeland politics and to the Basque nation understood in terms of territoriality, commonality, uniqueness, and authenticity. In what ways do diaspora Basques re-imagine the homeland as the birthplace or ancestral land? And why does the diaspora define and imagine the homeland in such ways?

Finally, I shall also address political activism online, as a segment of the Basque diaspora has embraced online technologies of communication and interaction in order to advance its political goals. What do the online discourses reveal about their political ideology, symbolism, and definitions of nationhood and homeland? What attitudes toward the homeland and hostland are portrayed on the websites? Are they attitudes of opposition, neutrality, or support? And why does the Basque diaspora exhibit such attitudes? And finally, does the Internet empower diaspora Basques to get actively involved in homeland politics?

In conclusion, I shall summarize some of the main arguments highlighted in the previous chapters, while providing some new lines of future study on Basque diaspora web studies.

The Basque

(02)

Diaspora Webscape

Mapping the Basque Diaspora Webscape

As stated earlier, as of December 2005, the Basque diaspora webscape was formed by ninety-eight websites from sixteen countries. By June 2007, the number of websites increased to 123 (127 if we take into account the complementary online platforms built by diaspora associations with an established online presence), expanding geographically to nineteen countries throughout the Americas, Asia, Europe, and Oceania. Taking into account that there were 11.5 billion websites as of January 2005 according to Antonio Gulli and Alessio Signorini's (2005) analysis of the publically indexable web of the then-largest search engines—Google, Yahoo!, Ask, and MSN—the Basque diaspora webscape is a microscopic part of cyberspace.

As of June 2007, the Basque diaspora has a slightly larger presence on the web than other similar European diasporas, such as those of the Catalans and the Galicians. All of them share a common sociohistorical background and trajectory within the Spanish state. According to the Catalan Autonomous Community government's Foreign Office, there were 116 Catalan associations in thirty-six countries. However, only 69 associations (59.5 percent) from twenty-seven countries (75 percent of total countries) had established a presence on the web. The Galician Autonomous Community government's general secretary of emigration stated that there were 322 Galician associations in twenty-nine countries, but only 125 associations

(38.81 percent) from eighteen countries (62.06 percent of all countries) had a web presence.

The Basque diaspora is constituted by diverse types of associations that help us to establish a working, not mutually exclusive, typology applicable to the Basque diaspora webscape (see appendix for more information). The main Basque diaspora institutions are Basque clubs or *euskal etxeak* (EE), and they constitute 60.16 percent of the Basque diaspora webscape as of June 2007.[1] These clubs are recreational, sociocultural community-based organizations. Despite the existence of federations of Basque clubs in countries, such as Venezuela or Uruguay, NABO and FEVA are the only federations with a presence on the web as of June 2007. Those are followed by cultural associations (CUL), such as dance groups and choirs, which represent 13.82 percent of the Basque diaspora online, and by educational groups (EDU), with an online presence of 12.19 percent. They are formal or university-based institutions, such as the Center for Basque Studies at the University of Nevada, Reno (United States, http://basque.unr.edu) as well as informal or community-based associations, such as the Basque-language group Euskaltzaleak from Buenos Aires (Argentina, www.euskaltzaleak.org.ar).

A little over 4 percent of the Basque diaspora associations with a presence on the web are of a political nature (POL). Within this group, there are associations related to the current political conflict in the Basque Country. Those are advocacy and human rights groups related to Euskadi Ta Askatasuna ("Basque Country and Freedom" or ETA) refugees and political prisoners, such as the London-based Basque Campaign (United States, www.geocities.com/basquecampaign). There is also the London-based Basque Children of '37 Association (United Kingdom, www.spanishrefugees-basquechildren.org), which relates to old political conflicts, such as the Spanish Civil War.

There are also two Basque diaspora business associations on the web (i.e., 1.6 percent of total sites), such as the aforementioned Asociación de Empresarios de Origen Vasco (EmpreBask, Association of Business Owners of Basque Origin, Chile, www.empresariosvascos.cl). The cultural, educational, political, and business associations can be autonomous entities or just part of their local Basque clubs. Finally, the San Francisco, California, Boise, Idaho, and Mexico D.F., Mexico, Basque associations got together and established their respective portals (POR, 2.43 percent of total sites) or online directories or catalogues of Basque local associations.

As of June 2007, the majority of the Basque diaspora websites are found in the Americas (78.86 percent)—South America (46.34 percent) and North America (32.52 percent), Europe (18.69 percent), Oceania (1.62 percent), and Asia (0.81 percent). South America presents a larger number of *euskal etxeak* (44.6 percent) and

---

1 Although the literal meaning of *euskal etxeak* is "Basque homes," referring to Basque institutions within a physical structure, 25 percent of 111 Basque institutions abroad did not have a clubhouse as of May 2007 (Kerexeta, 2008). I decided to use the term *euskal etxeak* to refer to Basque diaspora associations, regardless of the existence of a clubhouse.

cultural sites (49 percent), while North America presents the highest number of educational institutions online (46.6 percent).

What can be said about the correlation of the number of sites per country and the Basque population and/or the existing number of Basque institutions? To some extent, there is an overrepresentation of some Basque institutions on the web—for example, from Switzerland or Italy—whose membership numbers are small, and they are fairly newly constituted compared to other Basque institutions—for example, from Argentina or Chile—whose membership numbers are quite large. These institutions have been established for decades and in some cases for over a century. The web magnifies the visibility of newly established institutions compared to other associations, old or new, that do not have any representation online. For example, all Basque institutions in the United Kingdom and in Canada have websites; however, this is not the case for the Argentinean *euskal etxeak* as of June 2007. That is, only 21 percent or twenty out of ninety-five *euskal etxeak* that form FEVA have established websites, while 63.15 percent or twenty-four out of thirty-eight associations that form NABO were online.

Digital Intelligentsia

The Basque diaspora webmasters constitute a digital intelligentsia and intellectual elite, which I define as those engaged in the development and dissemination of Basque culture by means of digital technologies such as the web. They act as the mediators between the Basque community at large and the information technology society.

The members of this intelligentsia are of Basque ancestry (90.7 percent), young adults (66.7 percent between thirty-one and forty-five years old), male (64.8 percent), university graduates (77.8 percent; 16.6 percent have master degrees and 7.4 percent doctoral degrees), and they have relative experience and/or formal education qualifications in information technology, computer science, or Internet studies (53.7 percent). Nearly all webmasters are members of Basque diaspora associations (98.1 percent) and volunteer activists (88 percent) within their local Basque associations.

According to the Basque government (Gobierno Vasco 2000), 83 percent of the Basque diaspora associations' members are born outside the Basque Country. Similarly, the majority of the webmasters (68.6 percent) are born outside the homeland. However, different generations of Basques are involved in the management of the sites, but their involvement varies, as follows: the more distant they are to the first generation to family member born in the Basque Country, the less active they are in their heritage association. This could entail a problematic future for the recruitment of new webmasters or, by extension, for recruiting any staff within their own organizations, as well as for the associations themselves, as the generations closer to the one born in the homeland will eventually vanish.

Functions: Design, Maintenance, and Authorship

Sixty-three percent of the webmasters are responsible for the design of their institutions' sites, while 88.9 percent of the webmasters are also responsible for maintaining and upgrading as well as for authoring the content of the sites. The webmasters are "jacks of all trades." Division of labor is almost non-existent in the Basque diaspora cyberspace. However, some webmasters showed their willingness to make their sites available, technologically speaking, to diverse members in order to have more collaboration. This delegation of responsibility not only alleviates the webmaster's work, but it somehow "democratizes" the site by bypassing the webmaster's function as the gate keeper and main authority allowing for various opinions and ideas to be expressed on the site. For example, Toni Sabarots, the webmaster from the Seattle Basque club (United States, www.seattleeuskal.org; EE) stated, "We are currently changing our site to be broader and user friendly. Soon all board members will be able to post information. This way the site can be updated constantly with current information."

Once the website has been designed, the content uploaded, and the entire site published on the web, the webmasters/authors stated that their main functions were maintaining the websites, informing, and communicating. Maintenance entailed updating the design, the links (e.g., troubleshooting links periodically) and also updating and creating the content (i.e., writing, editing, and/or searching for textual and graphic content) about the institution, its activities, and about Basque culture. Informing and communicating entailed sorting out e-mails, responding to inquiries, and creating awareness of the site to everyone in order to "become a link of unity and information about the diaspora Basques" (María Noel Irabuena, Salto, Uruguay, www.vascosensalto.tripod.net; EE), and "to increase the awareness of our existence as a People and as exiles" (Itziar Rodríguez, Caracas, Venezuela, www.kromasys.com/cvc; EE).

Are the Basque diaspora official websites a by-product of individual decisions by the webmaster/author, or are they a by-product of collective decisions by the board of directors, committees, and membership? The contents displayed on the sites were mainly selected and/or created based on "the personal interest of the webmaster/author" (48.1 percent), "the Basque organization board of directors' demands/requests" (38.9 percent), and "the members of Basque organization's demands/requests" (38.9 percent). That is, 77.8 percent of the contents are created by demands/requests originated within their own websites' associations and the Basque community versus the input of "outsiders" (14.8 percent).[2] The content is selected and/or created not only by the webmasters, but also by several entities within their own organizations, such as the board of directors, the associations' "website committees" (7.4 percent) and its members, and lastly by "non-members of the Basque community" (5.6 percent).

---

2 Total exceeds 100 percent as those responding could choose more than one option.

The webmasters' input as officers of their associations is obviously considerable. They are not only technicians but also content managers. They are active in the power structures of their associations, and they exhibit a great autonomy that allows them to select and/or create content, which, I argue, is reinterpreted following the goals of their associations and the desires of their board of directors.

I understand websites to be platforms from which the institutions voice their opinions and views. Consequently, I have not found a website whose content contradicts the goals of the association. If personal opinions are posted, the sites tend to display disclaimers stating that those opinions only reflect the views of their authors. For example, the Basque club Euzko Etxea de la Plata (Argentina, www.centrovasco.com; EE) states that, "The board of directors can demand the modification or elimination of any of the contents of the site. Articles, opinions, comments, guest books, or links, as result of the right of freedom of expression, are the exclusive responsibility of their authors, and they do not necessarily reflect the Basque club Euzko Etxea's way of thinking."

If conflict occurs between the webmasters and the board and/or the membership in relation to specific contents, there are two mechanisms for addressing the issue: the oversight role of the board of directors and/or web committees, and the registration of official complaints by the membership and general users. The webmasters stated that their sites, and by extension their work, were mainly overseen by "the Basque organization's board of directors" (48.1 percent), "the members of the Basque organization" (20.4 percent), and "the Basque organization's website committee" (11.1 percent).[3] In general terms, nearly 80 percent of the sites are subject to some sort of oversight despite the fact that the webmaster acts as the central individual who designs, maintains, and selects content.

In addition, the webmasters can receive complaints or disagreements about the contents posted on the websites from "the members of the Basque organization" (20.9 percent), "others" (14 percent; e.g., people from the Basque Country, Spanish nationalists), "the Basque organization's board of directors" (11.6 percent), and "non-members of the Basque community" (9.3 percent). Most of the complaints were related to the following contents posted on the sites: "political" (20.9 percent), "lack of content" (20.9 percent), and "others" (16.3 percent; e.g., the site was not available, or it was incorrectly functioning).

Are the websites superfluous, or are they trendy tools for the associations? If crises (e.g., lack of funding) occur, will the website project be at risk? Volunteerism plays a major role in constructing the Basque diaspora in cyberspace, meaning that the webmasters do not have the economic or financial incentive that other full-time webmasters might have. That is, the webmasters attend to their sites in their spare time. The webmasters report that they work on the sites monthly (33.7 percent), weekly (28.7 percent), once a year (23.1 percent), and daily (13 percent). Depending

3 Total exceeds 100 percent as those responding could choose more than one option.

on such volunteerism, however, could become a problem if future volunteers do not come forward.

In addition, the webmasters exhibit ambivalence regarding the significance of the sites for their respective associations and their Basque communities, which are their main target audience. The webmasters' perception is not overwhelmingly positive in terms of the feedback that they get from their associations and community-at large. For example, only 46.5 percent of the webmasters stated that, "The Basque organization and the Basque community express their interest or participate on the websites." Of the webmasters, 44.2 percent believed that "Their websites are vital for their local Basque communities," while 23.2 percent of the webmasters believed the opposite.

Goals: Information, Communication, and Online Presence

Of the webmasters, 96.3 percent stated that they had specific goals when they created their sites, and those were to provide information, to communicate, and to have an online presence. Seventy percent of the webmasters—mostly from *euskal etxeak* sites—stated that their major goal was to offer current information—"get the word out"—to Basques and non-Basques, to institutional members and non-members, both locally and non-locally, as well as to exchange factual information—that is, to use the web as a distributive medium.

The webmasters provided two levels of information. The first referred to the associations' day-to-day offline activities, while the second level referred to the opportunities that the Internet offers such as global accessibility and a global audience. Within the first level, the websites provided information about their associations' organized activities related to the nature or type of the site, and, in general, information about Basque culture and heritage. That is to say, the site provides a didactic narrative about the homeland and its culture, narratives of (self-) discovery.

> [Our goal] is to disseminate the activities of our club, inside and outside the Basque Country. (Luis Ángel Vidal, Madrid, Spain, http://euskaletxea-madrid.com; EE)

> Our main goal was to create a website to inform our members of our activities. Also to inform the world of our various links to other Basque websites, newspapers, radio, and forums and spread our culture. (Iñaki Ormaechea, British Columbia, Canada, www.bcbasque.com; EE)

The second level of information, with strong formal and informal educational components, was related to some of the peculiar characteristics of the Internet and the web. As noted earlier, the webmasters' goal was to provide information regarding not only the local institutions and their activities, but also regarding the Basque people and their ancient culture. Consequently, there is a manifest pride for their culture and an active commitment to spreading it around the globe. The goal was to disseminate as much information as possible about Basques and their cultural expressions. This could be read as: *We are very proud of our culture, and we want to share it with all of you. This is now possible, in part, due to the Internet.*

> [The goal is] to educate visitors about the richness and diversity of Basque dance traditions. (Lisa Corcostegui, Reno, United States, www.dantzariak.net; CUL)

> [The goal is] to disseminate the millenarian Basque culture [and] overall, to make the Basque language (Euskara) known. (Hernán Javier Yardin, Entre Ríos, Paraná, Argentina, www.vascos.8m.net/ibaiguren.htm; EE)

The statutes and by-laws of the Basque diaspora *euskal etxeak* and the cultural and educational institutions are defined by their apolitical and nonpartisan nature. Consequently, the majority of the Basque institutions display a cultural and educational dimension of Basque identity on their sites. Only 16.7 percent of the activities described by the webmasters are related to "discuss[ing] politics of the Basque Country," while merely 7.4 percent of the activities are related to "discuss[ing] politics of the country of residence of the local Basque organization." The links that the Basque diaspora websites provide also exemplify this. Significantly, only 2.46 percent of the total links referred to political organizations' websites.

Daniel Bilbao, the webmaster of the political association Asociación Diáspora Vasca–Euskal Diaspora Nazioarteko Elkartea (ADV, the Basque National Diaspora Association, Santa Rosa, Argentina, http://euskalherria.cjb.net; POL) was highly critical of the ethnic and cultural information disseminated by diverse Basque clubs and cultural associations. Bilbao argued that,

> It is essential to inform the Basques communities . . . Today, this does not exist. The information is remarkably 'official' and scarce. The Basque clubs must promote a greater involvement and must end with the fairytale that taking part in current issues is to 'do politics,' and therefore, they end up offering only one ethnic and cultural vision, camouflaged by the only allowed politics: the one promoted by the party that governs the BAC [the Basque Nationalist Party, EAJ-PNV in its Basque and Spanish acronyms].

In addition, Mikel de las Heras, the webmaster of the political association Asociación Venezolana de Amigos de Euskal Herria (AVAEH, the Venezuelan Association of Friends of the Basque Country, Caracas, Venezuela, http://earth.prohosting.com/avaeh; POL) stated that the main goal was "to disseminate the conflict that the Basque Country experiences." That is to say, Basque diaspora political websites not only had a critical role in the politics of ethnic identity promoted by Basque diaspora associations, but also attempted to publicly highlight the political dimension of Basque identity and culture.

In relation to the webmasters' goals, there is a significant issue related to the keyword "existence," which is often combined with other words, such as "awareness," "visibility," "recognition," "inclusion," and "presence." The issue refers to the strong desire expressed by the webmasters to make known their institutions, and particularly, the Basque people and their culture, while adopting an active role to counteract any negative stereotypes associated with the Basques, such as political violence/terrorism. In other words, the websites allow Basque diaspora institutions to gain a voice in a global public arena by counteracting negative stereotypes and presenting a positive image of Basque identity as well as promoting a committed and active role toward the Basque homeland. The Internet provides a platform for diaspora associations to define their own identities in positive terms: *We, the Basques, are not ETA; we are not a violent, but a peaceful people.*

> [The Internet is] a place where we can talk about the good of being Basque, because in countries such as this, the subject of ETA is very well known. (Jaione Arrieta, Mexico City, Mexico, www.centrovascomexico.com; EE)

> The main goal of the website is to emphasize the positive in reporting on Basque issues, culture, and the Basque people worldwide. (Luis Foncillas, New York, United States, www.eeny.org; EE)

Cathleen Acheritogaray, webmaster of the International Basque Organization for Human Rights (IBO, Corte Madera, California, United States, www.euskojustice.org; POL), stated that the main goal was "to be an alternate source of information, especially [negative] information that is reported in the United States news press." Consequently, the images that the websites intend to portray or to communicate to members, visitors, and/or users are positive, reinforcing the positive social status of the Basque community and its internal cohesion.

Moreover, the webmasters also attempt to neutralize any possible reading of diaspora Basques as "diluted" Basques in relation to the assumed "authentic" homeland Basques. On the one hand, diaspora webmasters sought inclusion and recognition from homeland Basques as they felt that diaspora Basques are being portrayed as minor players in promoting and maintaining Basque identity. On the other hand, the webmasters claimed or attempted to recover a central position within the overall discourse of constructing, promoting, and maintaining Basque identity in relation to the homeland's own identity discourse. The webmasters understood the Basque diaspora identity discourse as not being marginal or less significant than the homeland identity discourse.

That is, 27 percent of the webmasters attempted to articulate an image of commitment in the defense of Basque identity and culture in terms equal to those articulated, in theory, by homeland Basques.

> [The goal is] to offer an image about what we do about Basque [issues] from Argentina. Many people in the Basque Country do not know the existence of the Basque clubs, and they become emotional whenever they see the site. (Sebastián Caparros, La Plata, Argentina, www.centrovasco.com; EE)

> The idea was to create a site in order to let the members of [our Basque club] Toki Eder and all Basques in the Basque Country and the diaspora, know the activities that we do from here in order to maintain our roots beyond the frontiers. (Nekane Olázar, Villegas, Argentina, www.vascos-villegas.net; EE)

The issue of recognition was also related to newer and/or smaller diaspora associations, which are seeking a voice and a presence, and a more central discursive position in relation to older and/or larger associations. For example, Fabio Javier Echarri, the webmaster of the Basque club in Chaco (Argentina, www.ecomchaco.com.ar/centrovasco; EE) stated, "The goals were to let everyone know about the existence of the Basque club of Chaco, Kotoiaren Lurra, and its activities, and that anyone can have access to it [the site] from anywhere in the world [as well as] to let [them] know [of] the existence of Basqueness in this far place of the world."

As mentioned before, the web is a magnifying tool for many of the smaller diaspora institutions, as they are raised within Basque cyberspace to the same position as other larger and more historical offline institutions. In other words, the web has an equalizing effect. The central authority that offline organizations might assume is replaced by "de-centered participation" (Mitra, 1999, online) of other organizations that are building their own discourse. According to Mitra, the decentralizing characteristic of the web—in which no single text is more central than another, and there is no hierarchy of texts—allows the participants to acknowledge "each other's discursive existence in cyberspace" (idem) without anyone claiming primacy over any other. That is, cyberspace is understood as an egalitarian space.

Consequently, smaller associations' peripheral positions in the offline world is less relevant than in the online world, as there does not appear to be a hierarchical or ordinal structure of websites on the web. Furthermore, the preexisting offline social and historical context of some well-established associations is irrelevant in the online world. Well-established institutions with a long history prior to the Internet exist side-by-side with other institutions that have little history and/or are almost non-existent outside of the Internet. For example, Dario Artiguenave (Rauch, Argentina, www.ardanberauch.cjb.net; EE) argued that, "The goal was to make known the Basque club and the activities created in a small village of Argentina, and I know they are as important as other activities created in many other places in the country and in the world. And as a Basque from the diaspora, [the goal is also] to show the Basques from the Basque Country that we also contribute however we can from our places. Of course, [there is] also the fact of positioning the Basque club among the rest of the Basque clubs."

The second goal of the webmasters was to establish or reestablish effective channels of communication among the different individual or associative segments of the Basque diaspora and between Basques and non-Basques using interactive technology as a bridge. They pledged to utilize the opportunities offered by the networking of computers such as e-mail, chat rooms, mailing lists, or Internet teleconferencing programs. The purpose of most communication referred to the establishment and maintenance of ties and structures:

> The main goal was to fill a great empty gap in relation to the information and the possibility to interact with those who despite not being members of Basque clubs feel as Basque as anyone, but they are not connected, or they feel they lack information. (Magdalena Mignaburu, Avellaneda, Argentina, www.diasporavascarg.com.ar; EDU)

> [We wanted] the site to be a link for those Argentineans that want access to the Basque Country and to the Basque world, and for all those Basques who wish to get close to the Basque-Argentinean world. (Gonzalo Auza, Buenos Aires, Argentina, www.juandegaray.org.ar; EDU)

The webmasters also saw the Internet as a new and effective recruiting device. That is, there is a causal effect between the Internet and membership. Lisa Corcostegui, the webmaster of Ontario Basque club (Oregon, United States, www.ontariobasqueclub.dantzariak.net; EE) stated, "We have recruited new members through the site and have attracted Euskara students through it, too."

Finally, 10 percent of the webmasters argued that one of their main goals was to have an online presence not only for the sake of "existing" in the online world, but in order to conveniently reach a greater audience inside and outside of their immediate Basque and non-Basque community. The presence on the web breaks the physical barrier of the Basque diaspora associations' locality, and it exposes their existence to the world.

> We wanted the Center to have a place in cyberspace so people who surf the web could find us. (Robert Acheritogaray, San Francisco, United States, www.basqueculturalcenter.com; EE)

> [The goal was] to create an online home for the Basques of Kern County; a place where Basques and non-Basques who love the culture can share their experiences, meet, chat and exchange ideas. (Pierre Igoa, Bakersfield, United States, www.kcbasqueclub.com; EE)

This online presence is well exemplified by the following metaphor used by one of the respondents, Fabienne Prioux (Montpellier, France, www.eskualdunak.com; EE), "We think that a website is a sort of a 'window shop.' With it, we say, 'look, we are here, we do things, contact us.'" It is a visible place where people can log on and learn about the Basque culture. According to Blas Uberuaga (New Mexico, United States, www.buber.net/NMEE; EE), the Internet "is a place to put the new information about our club in an easy to access location." Webmasters also referred to the web as a potential meeting point for Basques, a place in a "placeless world," in a sense of togetherness, of building communities of interest—for example, through community-based sites or identity-based sites. In short, the re-creation of "an online ethnic corner" cliché. "We hoped to extend our presence with the website beyond the local area and beyond a Basque audience," Lisa Corcostegui stated (Ontario, United States, www.ontariobasqueclub.dantzariak.net; EE). Juan José Moreno, the webmaster of the association dedicated to the Spanish Civil War's Basque refugee children (London, United Kingdom, www.spanishrefugees-basquechildren.org; POL), stated that one of his particular objectives was "to bring exiles together" using the means of the Internet. In the same way, Daniel Bilbao (ADV, Santa Rosa, Argentina, http://euskalherria.cjb.net; POL) argued about the potential of the web in building a sense of community among members who share the goals of "independence and democracy for the Basque Country":

> I wished to create a space to unite pro-independence Basques dispersed throughout the world, [because] there was not any space . . . In the beginning, I was totally alone. Today, there is a community of hundreds of Basques dispersed throughout the world [over twenty countries] who know each other and we have given ourselves a small organization, we visit each other, and we have manifested ourselves about the situation of the Basque Country, claiming its rights and doing propaganda for it. There is a need to inform our Basque diaspora, [because] it is deeply uninformed and immobilized, which weakens the political commitment with the Basque Country.

The significance of having an online presence is particularly vital for those organizations that do not have a physical clubhouse where they can regularly meet. As of June 2007, in the United States, there were only twelve Basque clubhouses and nearly forty Basque associations. For some, the Internet has become their only "get-together" point. For example, in 2005, the Basque-language teaching association from Argentina, Euskaltzaleak, hosted for decades by one of the Buenos Aires Basque clubs, the Laurak Bat, was unfortunately evicted, thereby temporarily losing its physical meeting place (see chapter 6 for further details of this eviction and its political implications). Consequently, Teresa de Zavaleta, the webmaster of Euskaltzaleak's site (Buenos Aires, Argentina, www.euskaltzaleak.tk; EDU) highlighted not only the convenience but the importance of also "existing" online. She said, "Taking into account that at this moment Euskaltzaleak did not have a particular physical space, given the crisis with the Basque club Laurak Bat, the [web] page as well as the e-mail were the only way to locate the association."

Nearly 89 percent of the webmasters stated that their goals have not changed, as they are still the original webmasters. Only six out of fifty-five (10.90 percent) were new webmasters. There has been no replacement of webmasters in Australia, Europe, and the majority of the countries in South America since the creation of the sites. The reason for this low percentage of replacements is due to the recent creation of the websites. It is too early to comprehend the impact that a new webmaster and/or different overseeing committees and boards of directors could have on an existing site, previously authored by somebody else.

The six new webmasters argued that their sites are not static but evolving entities and that the changes on their associations' sites are related to new technological advances and to new members, visitors, or users and the needs of new boards of directors or new communication committees as part of the associations' agenda. More than adopting new goals, the sites are changing to reflect new purposes, activities, and services provided online, such as online shopping. New software for applications such as forums or blogs, that until recently were not available to the general public, are being incorporated into the sites.

> At the beginning it was only an informative site. Today, it is more interactive, therefore during the month of March it has served to register students into courses. (Teresa de Zavaleta, Buenos Aires, Argentina, www.euskaltzaleak.tk; EDU)

Despite the short history of the majority of the websites, 72.2 percent of the webmasters believed that they were reaching their intended goals. The accomplishment of their objectives were measured by the "hits" or visits to the site as a way to determine the awareness of the general public about the site, and the feedback provided by the visitors via e-mail, guest books, or forums:

> I think we are reaching our goals since I get feedback on the website from different areas. An example was when I posted an event for the showing of the Last Link [a 2004 documentary on Basque-American sheepherding] at a film festival last summer [2004], only a few weeks before the showing. There were only about eight people that showed up, but one of them I noticed had a Basque keychain. I spoke with the person and asked them how they found out about the film, and he said he saw it on the Basque club's website. He later joined the Basque club as well. (Philippe Acheritogaray, San Francisco, United States, www.basqueed.org; EDU)

On the contrary, 24.1 percent of the webmasters—80 percent of them from Basque clubs from South America and 70 percent from Argentina—considered that they were not reaching their goals owing to a lack of material and/or human resources, a lack of time to dedicate to the site, and a lack of technological knowledge, preventing them from developing the full potential of their websites, including their interactive dimension:

> [We are not reaching the goals] due to the lack of resources. That is to say, this type of activity is based on volunteerism, the same as the Basque clubs, suffers from ups and downs and depend, excessively, on the availability of volunteers. In the case of the web of the Basque club of Caracas, we never received resources to reinforce and keep the web up to date. (Mikel de las Heras, Caracas, Venezuela, www.kromasys.com/cvc; EE)

Budget and Funding: The Basque Government Support

Of the webmasters' annual budget, 46.3 percent varied between $10 and $3,000, with an annual average of $500. The Basque diaspora sites were mainly funded by the website's association (48.1 percent) and the webmasters' own funds (29.6 percent), while some of the sites were hosted by companies such as Yahoo!, Geocities, Lycos, or Wanadoo that offer free web hosting, or by other Basque diaspora sites.[4] Additionally, NABO and FEVA offer free space to their associated members. In the case of NABO, only one Basque club has taken active advantage of this free online space as of June 2007. The rest of Basque clubs in the United States have opted for the creation of their own online space outside NABO's site. In technical terms, the NABO clubs cannot upload any information without the NABO webmaster's direct intervention. This has most likely deterred the members from using this service.

Also in technical terms, FEVA's site has a greater advantage than NABO's, as the members can upload any information to their respective spaces without the

4 For example, the Basque clubs Gure Txoko (Valladolid, Spain, www.geocities.com/guretxoko; EE) and Euskal Etxea D'Andorra (Andorra, http://es.geocities.com/euskaletxea_andorra; EE). In addition, the Reno Basque-dancing association Zenbat Gara (Nevada, United States, www.dantzariak.net; CUL) hosts the Ontario Basque Club's site (Oregon, United States, www.ontariobasqueclub.dantzariak.net; EE) as both organizations share the same webmaster.

intervention of the webmaster. Therefore, theoretically, the central authority of the webmaster has already been bypassed in the Argentinean case but not yet in the United States. However, in practical terms, as of June 2007, only sixteen out of ninety-seven FEVA clubs (16.5 percent) have uploaded information to their respective spaces. That is, FEVA's site is barely used, and it has not become an online reference for its members yet. FEVA's clubs have opted for creating their own independent sites, paralleling the NABO clubs' online presence.

Hostland governments have provided 1.9 percent of the total financial help and 1.9 percent of the total technical help with setting up Basque diaspora websites and/or getting the diaspora associations connected to the Internet, while the Basque government has provided 9.3 percent of the total financial help and 1.9 percent of the total technical help. Of the webmasters, 48.9 percent agreed or strongly agreed with the following statement: "The Basque government's institutional help is not instrumental to develop the site," while 81.4 percent of them agreed or strongly agreed that "the Basque government has not (is not) significantly influenced the content of the website." That said, the governmental support to Basque diaspora sites is, therefore, minimal.

In relation to the incentives, goals, and objectives that the Basque government might have for funding Basque diaspora websites, 3.4 percent of the webmasters presented a negative attitude toward the Basque government's funding and its reasons for funding.[5] For example:

> The government of the Basque Autonomous Community has neither financed the page nor has given us any type of help. What's more, they have created obstacles, they have put us off, and they have brandished unacceptable excuses. (EE)

> I never asked or received any help from the Basque government. In the government's grants there are political clientele, manipulation, preferential treatment to friends, and partisan interests. (POL)

However, 8.7 percent of the webmasters presented a positive attitude toward the Basque government's funding. The webmasters believed that the Basque government's incentives, goals, and objectives for helping the websites were to increase communication and ties among the diaspora communities and between the diaspora and the Basque Country, to create an online Basque community, and to promote the Basque Country and its government's interests abroad (see chapter 3):

> [The Basque government incentives for funding us is] to create and maintain an online Basque community and to help Basque clubs to communicate. (EE)

---

5 In order to protect the anonymity of the respondents, particularly of those who expressed a negative view on the reasons behind the Basque government funding, no identification by website, name of the webmaster, or country of origin has been given. If needed, the responses have been translated into English, but the original text is not provided. These steps have been taken to prevent any possible consequence on future funding. The responses are only identified by the type of site.

> I think their incentives and goals are to advertise the Basque Country and its economy through the webs of the euskal etxeak around the world. (EE)

Finally, 10.5 percent of the webmasters had a neutral attitude toward the Basque government's funding. For example, one webmaster stated that "In 2003 we did receive some help to pay for the designing of the website. They [the Basque government officials] wanted the Basque clubs to have a website, and we thought that a news website about the Basques, the Basque culture and the achievements of the Basque people would be much more interesting than just having a web about the activities of the club." (EE)

During the 2003 World Congress of Basque Communities, I carried out a survey aimed at establishing the correlation between the future survival of the Basque diaspora institutions and the increasing flow of financial help, economic support, and political leadership guidance from the Basque government. That is, what is the degree of autonomy of diaspora associations and federations?

Thirty-six world diaspora institutional delegates (63.1 percent of total delegates) from seventeen countries (89.5 percent of total countries with representation at the congress) were asked to either agree or disagree with a set of thirty-two statements using a Likert scale.[6] The response options to assess the statements were: Strongly Agree (1), Agree (2), Not Sure (meaning not agreeing or disagreeing) (3), Disagree (4), and Strongly Disagree (5). Therefore, the median (Σ) was obtained from the response options. Once the median was obtained, I grouped the different median values into two groups according to the scale of agreement (or consensus, knowing that 1 means the highest level and 5 the lowest level) with the proposed statements. The total median by participant was 3.04. The statements lower than the total median showed a positive value, while the statements higher than the median showed a negative value. By countries there are no significant differences. The fact of being from one or another country is not a relevant factor. All participants regardless of their origin have similar opinions. However, the Dominican Republic, Canada, and Andorra presented the highest degree of agreement in relation to the overall number of statements. On the contrary, Chile, the United Kingdom, and Argentina presented the lowest degree of agreement in relation to the overall statements.

The statements that obtained the highest level of consensus or agreement (closer to 1) among the diaspora representatives refer to the positive relationship that Basque diaspora institutions maintain with the Basque government (consensus median of 1.78). However, diaspora representatives believe that the Basque government's policy toward the Basque clubs should be more efficient (consensus median of 2.74). On the one hand, according to the delegates, the Basque government's funding toward Basque diasporic institutions is *unsatisfactory* (consensus

6 Andorra, Argentina, Australia, Brazil, Canada, Chile, Colombia, El Salvador, Mexico, Peru, Puerto Rico, Spain, the Dominican Republic, the United Kingdom, the United States, Uruguay, and Venezuela.

median of 2.91). Nevertheless, the delegates agree that the Basque diaspora does not depend *totally* on the Basque government's financial help (consensus median of 2.91).

Consequently, it can be concluded that the Basque government's overall support had a positive effect or influence on the Basque diaspora, but this support was not essential for its future (consensus median of 3.56). Should the Basque government's support toward the Basque diaspora stop, it is unlikely that any Basque clubs would be affected to a great degree or even disappear (consensus median of 3.46). The absolute dependency of the Basque diaspora on the Basque government's financial support is not clear. Furthermore, it does not seem that the Basque government's financial support has been instrumental in the creation of newly established Basque clubs (consensus median of 3.69). However, at an individual country level, the picture is different.

For example, in the case of the United States, the grants that NABO receives from the Basque government only account for 17 percent of its annual total income as of 2011. The financial help goes toward the salary of two half-time paid positions—the Basque language coordinator and NABO's coordinator. In the case of Argentina, the Basque government is not only financially responsible for some of the specific sociocultural, linguistic, and recreational projects of the Basque-Argentinean federation, FEVA, but it is also responsible for approximately 78 percent of FEVA's annual total fixed costs as well as the salary of one of the two full-time paid positions. (HABE pays the salary of the other position, FEVA's Basque language coordinator.) In this regard, a FEVA representative stated that the federation has become "in reality a program of the Basque government." Without the financial support of the Basque government, "we would have to close FEVA," the representative admitted (EuskoSare.org, March 4, 2008). That is to say, there is an increasing financial, cultural, and political dependence on the Basque government. As we will see later, the Basque government has intensified its role in the maintenance and development of diaspora associations and federations. However, there is not any evidence that corroborates that this support implies a governmental imposition of any ideological or political agenda on the recipients of such a support or a sort of *quid pro quo*.

On the other hand, according to the diaspora representatives, the Basque government establishes financial and economical support according to technical criteria (consensus median of 2.26). However, the diaspora representatives believe that the Basque government is more likely to support financially those clubs who enhance Basque nationalist cultural projects (consensus median of 2.77).

Languages

The main languages of the sites used by the Basque diaspora webmasters are English (48.1 percent), Spanish (46.3 percent), Basque (38.9 percent), and French (14.8 percent). This is related to the language distribution on websites by the host country's official or co-official language/s as of December 2005. That is, thirty-eight sites (43.1 percent of total sites) are from Spanish-speaking countries, thirty-seven sites (42 percent) are from English-speaking countries, and nine sites (10.2 percent) are from French-speaking countries, while the rest are in German, Catalan, and Italian-speaking countries.

The reasons behind the selection of languages were similar to all countries and types of sites. Firstly, 65 percent of the webmasters used the official language/s of their host country because their major audience is believed to be local (e.g., associations' members). For example, Hernán Javier Yardin from the Basque club of Entre Ríos stated, "[We use] Spanish because it is the official language of Argentina, and the idea is to disseminate the Basque presence in the region through the activities of their descendants" (Paraná, Argentina, www.vascos.8m.net/ibaiguren.htm; EE). The second reason is related to the language/s spoken by the webmasters (20 percent of total responses): "All our members speak English, and it is the easiest language for me to work in" (Blas Uberuaga, New Mexico, United States, www.buber.net/NMEE; EE). The third reason is related to the official languages spoken by the Basques, at least, in the homeland—that is, Basque, Spanish, and French—according to 15 percent of the webmasters. For example, "All Basque people know at least 3 languages!" (Bourayne, Paris, France, www.anaiki.com; CUL).

Thus, the languages used on the websites were a rational or conscious decision made by the webmasters and their associations that depended on the use of the official language/s of their host countries; the availability of time and financial and/or human resources; the webmaster's knowledge of languages; and the act of thinking locally, for a local/private audience/sphere. However, the Internet and the web do not recognize geographical and/or political barriers, and therefore the audience is potentially global and public in nature, but not to the webmasters. For example, Mikel de las Heras argued that, "The goal is to reach the Basque community in Venezuela and Venezuela itself. Obviously, the language has to be Spanish. It's not worth it to spend resources and time, which are scarce, in translating the site into Basque" (Caracas, Venezuela, http://earth.prohosting.com/avaeh; POL).

What role does the Basque language or Euskara play on the Basque diaspora webscape? The Basque language performs a double role, as do many other languages; it is an effective identity marker that works as an internal element of group cohesion and at the same time as an external group differentiation element. It crosses all geographical, linguistic, and sociopolitical Basque diaspora communities. It is also a subjective symbolic marker. The knowledge of the language increases the strength of the identity as the language itself maintains and transforms the group's own daily cultural manifestations.

Despite the significance of the Basque language as part of today's Basque identity, the homeland Basques do not consider Basque essential to their self-definition. Sociological studies of respondents in the BAC population (Gobierno Vasco, 2003c: 26–27) state that the main conditions necessary for considering a person Basque are “to feel Basque” (64 percent), “to live and to work in the Basque Country” (50 percent), “to be born in the Basque Country” (28 percent), “to speak Basque” (11 percent), and “to have Basque ancestry” (10 percent). If we take into account studies that focus on the territories of the BAC, Navarre (Nafarroa), and Iparralde, the most important conditions for a person to be considered Basque continue to be the same, but the results are more balanced: “to feel Basque” (42 percent), “to live and to work in the Basque Country” (41 percent), “to be born in the Basque Country” (39 percent), “to speak Basque” (17 percent), “to defend the Basque Country” (16 percent), “to have Basque ancestry” (9 percent), and “to have Basque surnames” (4 percent) (Baxok et al. 2006).

Data from earlier Basque government studies (Gobierno Vasco et al. 1997a, 1997b) reinforce the argument that points out that the primordial marker of the Basque language is not an essential characteristic in defining Basque identity in the homeland. With the exception of Iparralde or the Northern Basque Country (40 percent), the rest of the territories' populations (BAC, 16 percent; Navarre (Nafarroa), 10 percent) do not consider the Basque language as an essential attribute for defining Basqueness (Baxok et al. 2006). Within this subjectivist tendency, “to feel Basque,” is increasingly positioning itself as the key definition marker of the Basque identity in the homeland, while other more objective markers, such as language, ancestry, or place of birth—territoriality—are losing importance (see Oiarzabal 2007b).

Certainly, the Basque language is highly regarded by the webmasters because of its unique and special character—that is, its “millenarian and mysterious origin.” It is symbolic and sentimentally charged, while being a reference for Basques across geographical borders and generations. In addition, over 35 percent of the services offered by the sites were intended to teach the Basque language.

> [We use] Basque to recall why we are doing this in the first place. (John Ysursa, New York, United States, www.basque.ws; EDU)

> [We use] Euskara because it helps to preserve part of the Basque culture. (Laura Tuyaret, Córdoba, Argentina, http://groups.msm.com/cordobatarrak/inicio/msmw; CUL)

However, the Basque language is only used by 38.9 percent of diaspora associations online. Euskara is barely used in combination with official host societies' languages, and it is used in a residual manner. The use of the Basque language is limited to a few sentences, isolated words, epigraphs, greetings, brief dictionaries, and lyrics of songs. Only 3 percent of associations, such as the ones in the United Kingdom (www.zintzilik.org) and in Switzerland (www.euskaletxea.ch) provide their entire sites in Basque. By September 2008, the Basque association of Bordeaux, France also began to offer its website, www.euskaletxea.org, in Basque. Significantly, the number of links that refer to Euskara sites—Basque-language promotion and Basque language teaching, not to be confused with Basque-language websites—was 9.21 percent of total links.

Nearly 12 percent of the webmasters, particularly from English-speaking countries, stated their enthusiasm to incorporate additional languages, and particularly the Basque language, into their websites.[7] For example, one webmaster stated, "We wanted the entire site to be in English, French, Spanish, and Basque, but we are a small group, and those of us who are most active speak English and Spanish only. We wanted to have the info in all the languages used by the people from the Basque Country, and that is still one of our goals" (Cathleen Acheritogaray, California, United States, www.euskojustice.org; POL).

Users

The intended audience of the Basque diaspora online was, by order of preference: the membership of the Basque association (83.3 percent), the local Basque community (79.6 percent; members and non-members), the Basques in the country of residence (68.5 percent), the Basques in the homeland (61.1 percent), the Basques outside the hostland (59.3 percent), and finally non-Basques in the local community (59.3 percent), and non-Basques outside the hostland (37 percent).[8]

This intended audience draws a geographical preferential map from a nucleus—proximity to the Basque association—to its periphery—separateness from the Basque association—as if it were concentric circles: from the Basque club, Basque community (members and non-members), Basque hostland, Basque homeland, to the Basque diaspora. It also draws a map of Basqueness that emerges from the Basque "in-group" ("us") to an "out-group" ("them"): from a Basque audience—in the association, community, hostland, homeland, and diaspora—to a non-Basque audience—in the local community and in the hostland—as well as to "anyone interested in the site."

The Basque diaspora is a prime example of the Internet as a communication tool at crossroads between the local and the global, the particular and the universal. Despite the borderless nature of the Internet and the web, Basque diaspora institutions continue reflecting the physical locality and thinking in local terms—such as languages used or potential users. Somehow, the Basque institutional diaspora does not show interest in the possible impact that the global reach of this technology might have on their associations.

Activities

The activities offered by the sites are intrinsically related to the intended users—members of the website's association and the local Basque community—following the goals of the site, such as providing information. Therefore, the four most important activities were to offer information about the website's association (74.1 per-

7 Total exceeds 100 percent as those responding referred to more than one reason for using the languages displayed on their websites.

8 Total exceeds 100 percent as the participants were asked to choose more than one option.

cent), to promote it (72.2 percent), to attract new members (61.1 percent), and to inform about the history, culture, language, or politics of the local Basque community (59.3 percent). At the bottom of the services offered by the webmasters were the ones offering to discuss homeland politics (16.7 percent) and to discuss politics of the country of residence (7.4 percent).[9]

Although the main activity offered by the Basque diaspora websites was "to provide information about the website's association," only 37 percent of the sites provided an electronic version of their association's newsletter—a central vehicle of communication between the board of directors and the membership. Eighty percent of associations provided a newsletter to their members. Consequently, the main vehicle of communication for Basque associations in the diaspora with websites continued to be the print newsletter as of April 2005. Timidly, associations such as the Basque club of Santiago de Chile are beginning to upload their newsletters to their websites. In June 2008, the aforementioned association created the digital magazine *Berriketari* to inform the Basque-Chilean community about their activities (www.euzkoetxeachile.cl).

Furthermore, there is no one site that clearly stated that it was providing, promoting, and/or carrying out activities that were not offered by the offline associations. This implies that those sites reflected exactly what they did in the physical world. There is a replica or reproduction of the associations' activities in their online version. For example, webmaster Julián Ojinaga of the Bolívar club stated, "In the site, you will find everything that the club can offer at the moment" (Argentina, www.centrovasco.tripod.com/informacion.html; EE).

However, many webmasters mentioned offering current information, feasible and fast communication, access to information, and e-learning as some of the exclusive online services provided on the sites but not available at the associations' physical location. There is no need for physical displacement of members, users, and visitors to an association's clubhouse, if one existed, to find information or join a language course, for instance:

> It [the site] is a convenient spot to get information without having to write or call the center if you want to know what is going on and coming up. (Robert Acheritogaray, San Francisco, United States, www.basqueculturalcenter.com; EE)
>
> Finding relatives. Services through the web without the need of traveling. Personalized answers to every e-mail. All enquiries are responded without being a member of any organization. (Magdalena Mignaburu, Avellaneda, Argentina, www.diasporavascarg.com.ar; EDU)

In relation to the specific goals of the sites, 70 percent of the webmasters would like to provide, in the near future, more textual and graphic content about the Basque language—once again, the language becomes central to the association's identity

9 Total exceeds 100 percent as the participants were asked to choose more than one option.

discourse—culture, history, genealogy, and e-learning opportunities. The content has an informational purpose, which, in turn, becomes educational:[10]

> Information about all means to learn Basque (methods, classes). (Mari-Andrée Ouret, Paris, France, www.eskualetxea.com/sustraiak/fr/intro.html; EDU)
>
> More information about: dances, history, physical environment of the Basque Country and of course the Basque language. Therefore, I am taking the course JAKINET [Basque online courses offered by Eusko Ikaskuntza, the Society of Basque Studies] so, I can know the place of my roots a little better, although I have never visited it. (Hernán Javier Yardin, Entre Ríos, Paraná, Argentina, www.vascos.8m.net/ibaiguren.htm; EE)

In general, the information that the webmasters wish to provide was primordially focused on the homeland, while only a very few webmasters, less than 3 percent, talked about incorporating content about their own history in their host countries. As an example of this, Oscar Nelson Bulacio and Fabio Javier Echarri from the Basque club in Chaco stated that they would like to provide "information about Basque culture, Basque language, dances, culinary, and tourism . . . History of Basque families from Chaco" (Resistencia, Argentina, www.ecomchaco.com.ar/centrovasco; EE).

The webmasters insisted on providing content that has to be "current"—one of the adjectives most used by the webmasters—as well as easily accessible, clear, and very specific in order to meet the needs of members, users, and/or visitors, and to improve the usage of the site.[11] Why is there a need for so much information? This is related to the need to educate the immediate Basque community, particularly club members and the emigrants' descendants on Basque related subjects. As an example, the contents displayed on the Basque diaspora websites tend to become useful channels of education about the main traces of Basque culture or the language. A quick look at any of the Basque diaspora websites, particularly the *euskal etxeak* sites, reveals large amounts of information about virtually anything related to Basqueness, from sports to cuisine, from history to geography.

Every single site attempts to cover as much information as possible, undermining the main purpose of hyperlinks, which is to connect a particular site or section of the site, text, or graphic to other similar sites or other similar texts, creating a cyberspace of flowing interconnected texts. These sites attempt to offer a sense of *completeness* in order to embrace as much content as possible in one single space. They become a one-stop shop where members, users, or visitors have all the information they might require. This sense of completeness often allows much repetition of information or "cross-fertilization."

Twenty-five percent of the webmasters would like to make their websites more interactive, using new software applications, such as blogs or forums, in order to increase the ties and the communication among the members or users of the asso-

---

10 Total sum equals more than 100 percent as those responding could choose more than one option.

11 As stated earlier on, 18 percent of the studied sites were not updated for almost a year.

ciations and sites. The most common interactive tools provided by the websites are traditional e-mail (in 64.8 percent of websites) and guest books (16.7 percent). Other websites provide more sophisticated tools, such as forums or chat rooms (11.1 percent; meaning interaction in real time), e-commerce (3.7 percent), blogs (1.9 percent), or Intranet—a network accessible only by its members—(1.9 percent), which are currently more easily available through inexpensive or even free software.

As of April 2005, 66.7 percent of the websites did not provide any interactive application to users or visitors, because the webmasters "do not have enough time" (66.7 percent), "do not have enough funding" (44.4 percent), and "there is not enough interest or demand" (22.2 percent). That is, the interactive capability of the Basque diaspora websites is minimized by the small number of interactive tools offered. However, we are witnessing an increase in the number of the Basque diaspora institutions choosing, for example, blogs as their online platforms.

The desire for interactivity clearly contradicts the low level of interaction or communication that exists between diaspora webmasters and other webmasters from the homeland and elsewhere, which is significant. Three percent of the diaspora webmasters said that they interact with webmasters from the Basque Country in relation to technical issues; 14 percent in relation to content issues, and 9 percent in relation to other issues. Twenty-four percent of the webmasters explicitly stated that they did not have communication with a homeland webmaster. Regarding the webmasters from outside the Basque Country—including intra-diaspora communication—5 percent of the webmasters interacted in relation to technical issues, 10 percent in relation to content issues, and 11 percent in relation to other issues. Twenty-one percent of webmasters showed no communication with a webmaster from outside the homeland. That is, despite the interactive and networking nature of the Internet and the Web, the Basque diaspora displays a minimal interactive capacity not only for their users, but with other webmasters.

Cybercommunities

According to the webmasters, cybercommunities offer their associations' members multifaceted up-to-date information (65 percent of total responses), facilitating interaction (40 percent of responses) and communication (35 percent of responses) among members, users, or visitors, while reaching not only those with similar interests or commonality, but with a global audience. In addition, the webmasters believed that the most important characteristics that make the Internet unique from other forms of telecommunication are "speed communication" (81.5 percent), "global connectivity" (66.7 percent), and "global audience" (53.7 percent).[12]

The webmasters understood interaction as participation and exchange of ideas and experiences, which facilitates the access to other perspectives and views from

12 Total equals more than 100 percent as respondents could choose more than one option.

all over the planet. Also, they understood communication in terms of accessibility, convenience, and connectedness, conveying notions of nearness and proximity. They acknowledged specific characteristics of the Internet, such as space and time shrinking:

> Virtual communities offer to the Basque organizations and its members a medium or locale where they stay connected and informed, communicate, collaborate and generally do everything they would do in other social settings: The difference is that they interact by computer and due to this many, many social barriers are broken down by the anonymous aspect of the medium. The Basque virtual community offers its visitors with common interest: a place to learn more about their culture; a place to share experiences and exchange ideas; a place to influence social change. (Pierre Igoa, Bakersfield, United States, www.kcbasqueclub.com; EE)

Moreover, 20 percent of the webmasters argued that cybercommunities helped to create a sense of community by bringing all the dispersed segments of the global Basque community together, although virtually. In their opinions, the existing physical distances between Basques dispersed throughout the world are increasingly being reduced. That is, cybercommunities help to create a cohesive community that builds, maintains, and strengthens identity—that is, a networked identity based on a cyber-imagination. For example, Blas Uberuaga explains that:

> They [virtual communities] allow for more communication amongst organizations, hopefully resulting in a tighter community and the exchange of ideas between groups. (Blas Uberuaga, New Mexico, United States, www.buber.net/NMEE; EE)

> Not everyone lives close to a Basque club/organization. [The] Internet lets them feel a part of the community, no matter how far away they live. It is also an important tool of communication for certain sectors of the Basque community, when their local centers do not provide resources on information they are interested in, then the virtual communities are important to fill this gap. (Cathleen Acheritogaray, California, United States, www.euskojustice.org; POL)

The Internet and Basque Identity Maintenance

There are two conflicting views of the Internet's role in empowering identity maintenance in the diaspora. Of the webmasters, 7.4 percent believed that the Internet does not help to maintain Basque identity in the diaspora. Over 22 percent of the webmasters were skeptical about the Internet's role in maintaining Basque identity in the diaspora because the Internet is just a tool, a medium that cannot compete against offline cultural manifestations, such as dancing or singing. The webmasters understood the tangible elements of the Basque culture and face-to-face interaction to be prerequisites for identity formation and maintenance. They believed that offline communities cannot be overridden by online aggregations of individuals, electronically networked by their connection to the Internet:

> The identity is alive when we are talking, singing, dancing; not on the website. (Fabienne Prioux, Montpellier, France, www.eskualdunak.com; EE)

> The Internet is just a medium, like the radio, television, or the cinema. What helps to maintain the Basque identity, are the projects, plans, programs designed with such a purpose. On the Internet, fortunately, there are spaces with cultural information and possibilities to learn about the Basque language, although there is a need to transform all that into a great project. (Daniel Bilbao, Santa Rosa, Argentina, http://euskalherria.cjb.net; POL)

Basque identity preexists the Internet. Therefore, its role in identity creation and maintenance is minimal, to say the least:

> The fact that we maintain the culture after various generations, and even when the great majority of us we have never visited the Basque Country, and thousands of kilometers of distance is totally independent from the Internet. (Hernán Javier Yardin, Entre Ríos, Paraná, Argentina, www.vascos.8m.net/ibaiguren.htm; EE)

However, the majority of the webmasters argued that the Internet has the potential to maintain Basque identity abroad. Similar to the role of online communities, the Internet has the potential to inform, and, once again, educate people and communities as indicated by almost 43 percent of responses.[13] It is understood as a platform for obtaining and providing information, mainly about the Basque Country and its culture, but also about its political reality—that is, about ethnicity understood as political means:

> There are many people interested to know about our identity, it [the Internet] is a fast tool to get the information to those people. Yes, people have very different ideas about the Basque identity and not all of them are good. The Internet helps people that are far away to get together, interchange ideas, and keep the Basque identity alive. (Elena Sommer, British Columbia, Canada, www.bcbasque.com; EE)

> We have to realize that in this global village that we live in, there are also many efforts on the Internet to crash the Basque identity. Conclusion: we have to redouble the efforts to multiply Basque sites on the Net. (Mikel de las Heras, Caracas, Venezuela, http://earth.prohosting.com/avaeh; POL)

The Internet offers the possibility for webmasters to provide information in real time, in a constant and current manner. Being connected and communicating are ways to articulate a translocal community of Basques abroad. That is, there is real time knowledge, a tendency to try for a synchronous knowledge between the Basque diaspora and the Basque homeland (see chapter 3). Thirty-seven percent of webmasters argued that "simultaneous interaction" is a definitive characteristic of the Internet.

The web works, theoretically, as a leveler of the information and knowledge gap that exists between the Basque Country and the Basque diaspora. The Basque diaspora can obtain via the web, in real time, the same information that is being produced in the Basque homeland, thereby leveling the knowledge between both of them. This, potentially, would "erase" the existing stereotypes created about

13 Total exceeds 100 percent as those responding could choose more than one option.

diasporas as merely nostalgic communities anchored in the past and fed by out of date information: "[The Internet] helps me because I can read [the homeland newspapers] *Berria*, *Gara*, [the news agency] Reuters etc., to find out what is going on in politics and *Sud Ouest* to get a little of the local feel from Iparralde. Sometimes, I think I'm more up to date with the information I gather on the Basque Country here in California than my cousins in Euskal Herria!" (Robert Acheritogaray, San Francisco, United States, www.basqueculturalcenter.com; EE).

In addition, the Internet, as a network of interlinked computers, has the potential to help to increase the connectedness (46.9 percent of responses), interaction (37 percent of total responses), and communication of individuals and communities of the Basque diaspora (81.5 percent of total responses), with those of the homeland, while emphasizing the possibility for community creation by empowering diaspora consciousness. The webmasters acknowledged the capacity of the Internet and the Web to reach beyond the immediate frontiers of their local communities, and consequently expand their communities and institutions to limits unknown prior to the Internet.

For example, Dave Green, webmaster of the Cenarrusa Foundation for Basque Culture (previously known as the Cenarrusa Center for Basque Studies, Boise, United States, www.cenarrusa.org; EDU), stated, "It [the Internet] keeps people connected . . . There are people of Basque descent within the U.S. and around the world that feel disconnected until they find the resources and people via the Internet who are willing to educate, support and promote the culture and heritage throughout the world and to insure the language and culture are always available."

That is to say, the majority of the webmasters believed that the Internet also has the potential to help maintain a collective identity, while reconnecting individuals with their identity and with a larger global Basque community—homeland and diaspora. They believe that the Internet has the potential to maintain Basque identity in terms of information, interaction, and communication. Between 24.1 percent and 38.9 percent of the webmasters believed that "identity creation" and "community creation" respectively are the main characteristics of the Internet. The webmasters attribute the Internet with accessibility, ease, speed, and fluidity in comparison to other communication tools, such as ordinary mail or the phone, though all reach people beyond borders.

> [The Internet] reestablishes connections to people, events, and traditions that a person may have lost touch with or not have access to in their daily life. (Luis Foncillas, New York, United States, www.eeny.org; EE)

> The Internet is an essential tool for the diaspora, now more than ever the Basques can be more united and communicative through it. It is not a coincidence that relatives have reunited through our site after almost eighty years of not knowing each other . . . In one year more people have gone through our page than through any Basque club, there were around 6,500 people, this presents an excellent stage. (Magdalena Mignaburu, Avellaneda, Argentina, www.diasporavascarg.com.ar; EDU)

Theoretically, the Basque diaspora intelligentsia understands and is aware of the Internet's potential for offering updated information and facilitating interaction and communication. However, in practical terms, members of the intellectual elite fail to take advantage of those potentialities or perhaps they have no interest in doing so. As mentioned earlier, websites are not updated regularly, preventing current information from being accessed by their associations' members and general users. In addition, the websites' interactive tools are minimal, while their communication with co-webmasters is almost non-existent. And finally, the ability to reach a global audience is almost totally ignored because the webmasters focus on the immediate physical locality and the local members as their target audience. There is a wide gap between theory, based on webmasters' recognition of the potential benefits of the Internet, and practice, based on the actions taken by webmasters to reach such benefits. In this sense, the webmasters have a long way to go in order to bridge such a gap.

The Hyperlink Network: Toward the Homeland

Folding the Web

The Basque diaspora is a network of transnational migrant and exile communities comparable to nodes such as individuals, groups, or organizations in a social network connected by a set of affiliations. Similarly, the Internet is also a network of computers or electronic nodes that tend to facilitate or cultivate social networks that people may currently maintain in the offline world (see Boase et al., 2006). As already mentioned, I define the Basque diaspora webscape as a networked landscape produced by the Basque diaspora institutional websites. The hypertextual nature of the web text allows for the aforementioned networking and for analyzing the relationship among websites, which represent organizations as well as the discourses constructed by Basque diaspora institutions online. The online text provides the opportunity to interconnect the diverse Basque text-sites with specific "hyperlinks" or "links" allowing the reader to move from one text to another.

I have applied hyperlink network analysis based on traditional social network analysis in order to identify the diverse networks among Basque diaspora sites. How and why is the Basque diaspora webscape interconnected? Social network analysis focuses on the social relationships or ties between nodes—individuals or groups—within a network. Similarly, hyperlink network analysis attempts to reveal social structures among websites in terms of their hyperlink relationship or connectivity in order to infer the social structure among individuals, groups, or organizations that have created those websites.[14]

---

14 See Galaskiewicz and Wasserman (1993); Garton, Haythornthwaite, and Wellman (1997); Henzinger (2001); Park (2003); Park and Thelwall (2003, online); and Wasserman and Faust (1994).

As we will see, the Basque diaspora webscape is interconnected, via common hyperlinks, and exhibits a high level of ties that bind (online) institutional sites together, at least theoretically. However, can the study of the Basque diaspora hyperlink network reveal a social networking in the physical world? Han Woo Park (2003) suggests that the possible answers to this question would imply not only hyperlink network analysis but also in-depth interviews with webmasters in order to examine their reasons for choosing to link with certain sites as well as social network analysis of the physical organizations in order to determine their relationships with diaspora organizations. That is to say, the existing online interconnectedness does not imply that at a non-online level, the associations know each other or maintain any relationship inside and/or outside of cyberspace, particularly across continents (see also Van den Bos, 2006).

According to Antonio Rodríguez de las Heras, hypertextuality is "a way of folding a text, a new geometry of the text [in cyberspace]" (1999, online). Imagine an ordinary piece of paper filled with words that we are then asked to read through a small window such as a computer screen. The area of the written paper is obviously larger than the screen; however, the technology offers you an unlimited depth. The author states that there are two ways to solve this discrepancy. First of all, if the page is too large, we need to "chop" it down to the size of the screen. Then, the technology offers us links to tie the pieces of the "chopped" page together.[15] This is the most common solution, indeed almost the only solution, provided by Basque diaspora webmasters. Nick Fox and Chris Roberts state that, "electronic writing such as World-Wide Web . . . provides the possibility for hypertextual links [or hyperlinks] to other blocks of [html] texts [within and outside the site], ad infinitum" (1999, 644). Secondly, instead of cutting the page, we fold it. Rodríguez de las Heras concludes, "As we fold it, the text is disappearing under the creases while emerging as an origami figure, an interface that fits on the screen. Then, the reader will unfold the text by touching it. The hypertext is an origami work, although what is being folded is not the paper but the text" (1999, online).

Categorization of Links and Overview

I was able to study seventy-five Basque diaspora sites out of a total of ninety-five sites—79 percent of the total sample; and 100 percent of the operational sample—from fifteen countries, with a total of 1,910 external links as of July-August 2005 (see appendix). The site that displayed the most links, nearly three hundred, was www.eskualdunak.com from Montpellier, France. Fifteen sites (15.7 percent of the total sites studied) presented no links, failing to utilize the hypertextual nature of the web. In addition, two sites were under construction, and three other sites had long since "vanished." I did not specify internal links that refer to relevant pages or sections within the site itself in the study. Nor did I specify "deep" hyperlinks to

15 The aforementioned technology refers to the hypertext transfer protocol (or http://) that allows files (or sites) written in the hypertext markup language (or html) to link to each other, thereby constructing a network of interlinked files or sites, which might contain textual, audio-visual or graphic content.

a website other than the site's homepage. I took them as a whole without differentiating between the homepage's links and deep links. I did not study either the reciprocity of links between the homeland, the hostland, and the diaspora due to time constraints. I focused on one-way links from diaspora sites to homeland and hostland sites, and the extent of intra-diaspora's interconnections.

I took into account the continent, country, and type of site—*euskal etxeak* or Basque clubs and federations of Basque clubs, cultural, educational, political, portals, and business—as well as type of thematic links and their directionality. The sites themselves already provided some degree of thematic link categorization. I added new categories in order to provide a more clear and concise picture of the Basque diaspora webscape's link network. The categories and subcategories of links created are the following: Business (shops, import-export, ethnic marketing, etc.); culture (Euskara, music, dance, sports, art, or cuisine); Basque diaspora sites by country; education (universities, museums, history, libraries, or genealogy); government (parliament, institutional or departmental entities); media (newspapers, television, or radio stations); non-governmental organizations; personal sites; political organizations; search engines; tourism; youth organizations; and weather.

The links were categorized and compiled in four directional groups: homeland, hostland, diaspora, and other countries. The homeland was divided into four specific subgroups according to its current administrative division: in the Spanish state, the Basque Autonomous Community (BAC) constituted by the provinces of Araba (Álava), Bizkaia, and Gipuzkoa, and the Foral Community of Navarre (NAV); in the French state, Iparralde (IPAR) constituted by the provinces of Lapurdi (Labourd), Lower Navarre (Nafarroa Beherea in Basque; Basse-Navarre in French), and Zuberoa (Soule); and a Non-Identified (NI) category in cases in which it was impossible to determine the geographical origin of a website.

Those subgroups provide a very useful tool for identifying which preferential "homeland" the Basque diaspora webmasters link to in the absence of a politically unified and independent state. There are few cultural and political organizations' sites that represent the whole of the Basque Country as a political and/or cultural administration—that is, as an administratively divided "homeland." On the contrary, the BAC is the most populated area, which, in turn, could imply a higher number of websites than other areas such as Iparralde. The webmasters show their homeland preference by intentionally choosing links that I group into any of the subgroups created—BAC, NAV, or IPAR—or a combination of them. This combination might reflect not only a choice of links but, for example, the regional/provincial origins of their associations' membership, particularly in the case of the Basque clubs.

The European Basque diaspora websites presented the largest percentage of total links of the websites (37 percent), despite their modest number of websites (twenty-one) compared to the American continent (seventy-five). This is due to the exacerbated number of links offered by the aforementioned Basque club's site from Montpellier. Europe was followed closely by the South American websites with 35.2 percent of the total links, and the North American websites with only 27.4 percent. Oceania with Australia as its only representative had only 0.3 percent of the total links (see figure 2.1a). The majority of the Basque diaspora websites were linked to cultural sites (28.1 percent of total links), telling us about the social and cultural nature of the majority of the Basque diaspora sites' organizations. This was followed by diaspora (17.3 percent), educational (15.9 percent), media (14.8 percent), and government sites (8.3 percent) (see figure 2.1b).

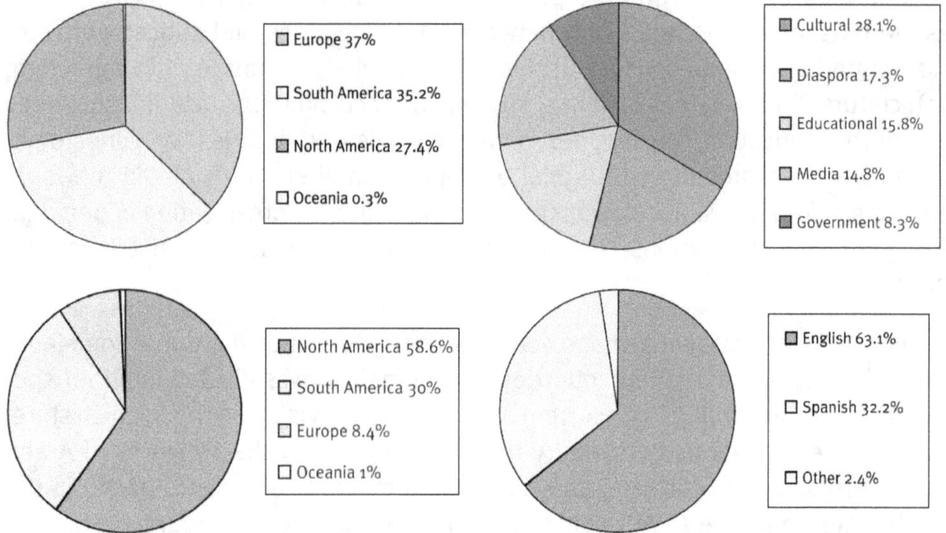

Figure 2.1. The Basque diaspora webscape: (a) links by continent; (b) type of links; (c) geographic connection; (d) linguistic connection.

Geographically, the Basque diaspora online was connected to North American Basque sites (58.6 percent), South American Basque sites (30 percent), European sites (8.4 percent), and Oceania sites (1 percent), establishing a correlation between the existing number of websites and their geographic dispersal (see figure 2.1c). Linguistically, the Basque diaspora online was consequently connected to English-speaking countries (63.1 percent), then to Spanish-speaking countries (32.3 percent), and to other countries (2.4 percent; see figure 2.1d). That is, the Basque digital diaspora is not separated geographically, as territorial boundaries are not an issue online, but linguistically into English- and Spanish-speaking countries. However, the Basque diaspora offline is segmented both geographically and linguistically.

The self-proclaimed apolitical and nonpartisan character of the Basque institutional diaspora is a relevant issue and also vividly present in cyberspace. In this regard, for example, *euskal etxeak* websites, from five countries, offered twenty-five links to political organizations' sites. This represented 53.2 percent of total political links and merely 1.3 percent of total links. Forty-four percent of the total political links were from South American Basque sites, 36 percent from European Basque sites, and 20 percent from North American Basque sites. Eighty percent of the total political links referred to homeland political organizations—particularly to Basque nationalist and proindependence associations with representation in all Basque homeland territories—and 20 percent to hostland political organizations. That is, despite their assumed apolitical and nonpartisan nature, they facilitated political links for users/visitors (see see chapter 5 for a detailed analysis of the Basque diaspora's apolitical and nonpartisan nature).

The Basque diaspora political websites showed a higher degree of connection to similar sites (from homeland to other countries) than to other types of sites such as the *euskal etxeak* ones, demonstrating a "hyperlink-affiliation network" based on the similarity of their aims and activities rather than geographic location (Park and Thelwall, 2003, online). In other words, the level of intra-diaspora networking among *euskal etxeak* was lower than the level of networking among political sites, which formed a small tight community of a few similar sites, all of which were interlinked. This is significant for raising awareness about particular political issues among similar political organizations throughout the planet—a network ideology (see Flichy, 2001). This emerging political activist community within the Basque diaspora online and offline will be examined in more detail in chapter 6.

Directionality

As we will explore in chapter 4, by order of priority, the Basque diaspora webscape constitutes discursive domains in relation to the homeland with regard to connection with the place of origin, diaspora with regard to connection with other Basques, and hostland, which translates into a tendency to acknowledge dual allegiances. Similar to other diasporic groups, such as Indians (see for example Mitra 1999, online), the main Basque discursive domain is also based on the place of origin. This prioritization is exemplified by the diaspora's hyperlink network. In regards to the directionality of the Basque diaspora links, a striking 68.6 percent of the total links were directed at the homeland, showing a pattern of proximity, priority, and a hierarchy of links. That is, the Basque diaspora is primordially homeland-centric. The different associations' sites in various countries had in common their connection to homeland sites.

Significantly enough, the second-highest number of links (17.4 percent) were directed at the Basque diaspora itself (dual/multiple intra-diaspora connections; particularly to the United States, 54.4 percent and Argentina, 26 percent), while only 10.4 percent of the total links referred to the hostland's educational, cultural, government, and media sites. Four percent of the total links were directed to other countries (figure 2.2).

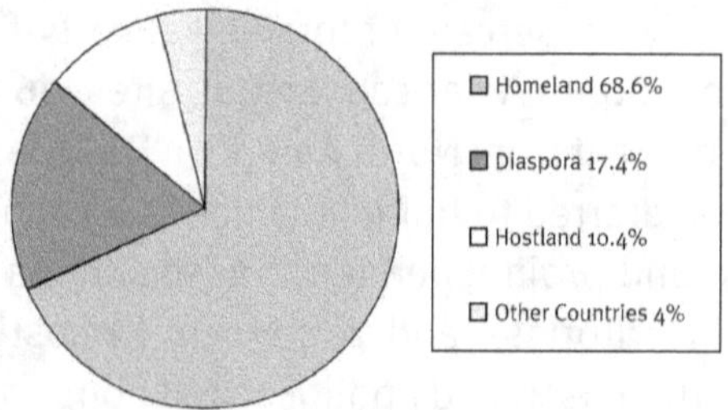

Figure 2.2. The Basque diaspora webscape links: directionality.

The majority of the Basque diaspora institutional websites were directed toward the homeland. For example, 50.5 percent of total links were directed at *euskal etxeak* sites. The diaspora identified a common homeland despite the fact that its members are geographically dispersed and sociohistorically, culturally, and generationally separate from each other. The links were aimed explicitly at a Basque historical homeland, not at the states of Spain, France, or any other country where Basques obtained their national citizenship. Presumably, those countries lack significance to the Basque communities abroad as represented on their organizations' sites. In this sense, hyperlinks are not only informative, but also meaningful. The particularly low percentage of links (less than 1 percent of total links) to Spanish and French websites is quite significant.[16] According to the links analyzed for this project, the Basque diaspora websites portrayed a community of Basques territorially defined by boundaries that shift from the current autonomous communities of the Basque Country and Navarre and the territory of Iparralde to any combination of all of those provinces by reconstructing a unified (cyber)imagined homeland delineated by seven historical provinces.

The majority of the Basque diaspora hyperlinks (21.3 percent) were primordially connected with the BAC's political organizations 70.2 percent, media 58.3 percent, government 55.6 percent, and educational sites 28.4 percent (if we do not take into account the number of non-identified homeland sites), followed by Navarre (5.3 percent) and Iparralde (1.5 percent) (see figure 2.3).

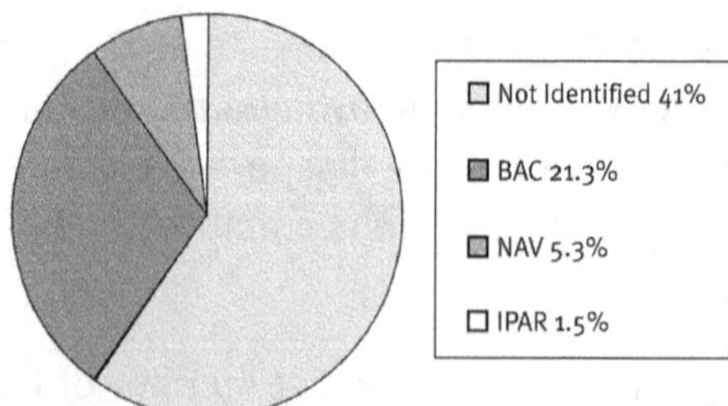

Figure 2.3. Basque diaspora webscape links: homeland.

16 For example, two Basque Clubs' sites in the United States referred respectively to the French Consulate in Los Angeles and the Spanish newspaper *El País*.

The fact that the majority of the links connecting with the homeland referred to BAC sites had to do with the reality that there are more sites in the BAC than in Navarre or in Iparralde. However, I argue that there is still a preferential choice in the election of the BAC sites over the Navarre or Iparralde sites. For example, the two existing Navarrese clubs' websites (see below) were exclusively linked to Nafarroa despite the fact that there are fewer sites in Nafarroa than in the BAC. However, the combination of links to the BAC, Navarre, and Iparralde were the norm in the majority of the sites, implying, for example, the widespread regional origin of their institution's membership. In general terms, according to diaspora institutions' statutes and by-laws, membership is open to all Basques from the seven homeland provinces. This could indicate the webmasters' willingness to provide links for their membership and visitors to homeland sites with which they have a strong connection, and that might be useful to them as part of their organizations' agenda.

The BAC's institutional presence is quite noticeable in the diaspora, as its government has played an increasingly significant role in the international sphere or in non-state paradiplomacy, and particularly in diaspora policy-making. This is exemplified by the number of Basque diaspora hyperlinks connecting with the BAC's governmental sites, which accounted for 21.6 percent of total BAC links and 55.7 percent of total links, overall. Additionally, the BAC has played the role of institutional mediator not only between its immediate administrative constituency, which includes three of the four southern Basque provinces in Spain, but also between the entire Basque "imagined" homeland (formed by Navarre and Iparralde) and the diaspora.

The BAC government has undeniably been the main homeland institutional reference for the Basque diaspora for the last twenty years, just as it was during the period of the Basque government-in-exile (1937–1978). This characteristic role of the Basque government is closely related to the goals and principles of the Basque Nationalist Party (EAJ-PNV), such as territorial unity and political sovereignty of the seven Basque territories. The EAJ-PNV has been the main governing party of the BAC since the return to democracy in the late 1970s. Consequently, the EAJ-PNV, in charge of the department of foreign affairs and diaspora matters within the President's Office or Lehendakaritza, has never discriminated against any Basque individuals or institution of the diaspora on the basis of their national and/or provincial origin (i.e., Basques from Basque areas other than the BAC) in relation to any of the BAC's diaspora policies, grants, and/or subsidy programs.

That is to say, the Basque government, in its policy-making and its grant programs, interacts with the diaspora in a homogeneous manner, without differentiating or giving preference to Basques from one province or another. For example, in July 2003, the Basque Government introduced Atzeus, a registry to identify the socioeconomic situation of Basques abroad. Reflecting on the issue of territoriality and political competence of the BAC, Josu Legarreta, then–director for the relations with the Basque communities, stated, "On the one hand, the direct help can only be obtained by anyone who judicially is Basque, that is, who has [Spanish] nationality and was born in Bizkaia, Araba, or Gipuzkoa. [On the other hand] according to the Law of Relations with the Basque clubs [Law 8/1994] there is a decree of subsidies to Basque institutions, and through this mechanism Basque Navarreses or Basques from Iparralde who are in extreme economical necessity could benefit from such a support" (*Deia,* July 16, 2003; see chapter 4).

The assistance offered by the Basque government targets Basque associations abroad, meaning outside the BAC territory, and their members regardless of their provincial (i.e., BAC, Iparralde, and Navarre) origin. However, according to Law 8/1994, the Basque government is allowed to assist and recognize Basque associations regardless of their geographical location, even if those are in Spain. Consequently, Basque associations in Spain are organized in a federation called Euskal Herria and attend the world congresses of Basque communities abroad as representatives of their "country of origin"—that is, Spain. Similarly, the Basque associations in France claim France as their country of residence. The Basque club in Barcelona has requested that the Basque government recognize their right to declare Catalonia, rather than Spain, their country of residence (Gobierno Vasco, 1994, 2004).

Furthermore, as stated earlier, I highlight the existence of two online Navarrese clubs or *nafar etxeak,* both from Argentina, as separate entities within the overall Basque diaspora, online and offline, based on the Navarrese websites' demonstration of a clear sense of identity that differs from the overall Basque diaspora identity. Aside from the historical cases of the French-Basque club from Buenos Aires and the aforementioned Navarrese associations, there are no clubs created by emigrants from other Basque provinces such as Araba, Bizkaia, or Gipuzkoa. That is, there are no Araban, Bizkaian, or Gipuzkoan clubs in the diaspora. The existence of this clearly identifiable "internal element" of the Basque diaspora online in relation to other Basque online institutions, such as the *euskal etxeak* websites, allows us to study and compare the diverse identity markers of the Basque diaspora online and offline.

For example, one of the most distinguishable characteristics of the *nafar etxeak* online is the directionality of their links and their definitions of homeland. While the *euskal etxeak* sites were mostly linked to the BAC, as well as Navarre and Iparralde, the *nafar etxeak* sites were almost exclusively linked to the Foral Community of Navarre. At the same time, the inter-connectivity, via hyperlinks, between the *euskal etxeak* and other educational and cultural sites, and the *nafar etxeak,* and vice versa, was almost non-existent. Only one *euskal etxeak* site from France provided a link to one of the two *nafar etxeak* online.

The Basque and Navarrese diaspora intelligentsias have constructed two parallel Basque and Navarrese cyberspaces that ignore each other's reality, or at least do not acknowledge it, failing to provide online bridges of communication and understanding. On one hand, a visitor to any of the *nafar etxeak* sites would find no reference to the Basque Country or to the Basque and Navarrese common history;

if this visitor knew of Basque history or geography, nothing would be missing from the site. On the other hand, an uninitiated visitor to any of the *euskal etxeak* websites would find multiple references to Navarre, not as an autonomous community of the Spanish current political and territorial structure, but as a part of an imagined unified Basque Country delineated by seven provinces of one common origin (see chapter 5). This also reflects the plurality of the *euskal etxeak* memberships, many of which are from Navarre.

According to Han Woo Park and Mike Thelwall, "The literature [on hyperlink network analysis] suggests how hyperlink networks may in some circumstances reflect offline connections among social actors, and be unique to online interactions in other cases" (2003, online; see also Park, 2003, online). However, I cannot infer, conclusively, from the data analyzed that there is no communication and/or cooperation between *euskal* and *nafar etxeak* in the physical world.

As examples of the directionality of the Basque diaspora webscape, all links from Oceania were to the Basque homeland, representing 0.5 percent of total links to the homeland. European links to the homeland represented 45 percent of total links to the homeland, while South American links to the homeland represented 34.4 percent of total links to the homeland, and North American with 20.1 percent of total links to the homeland (see figure 2.4).

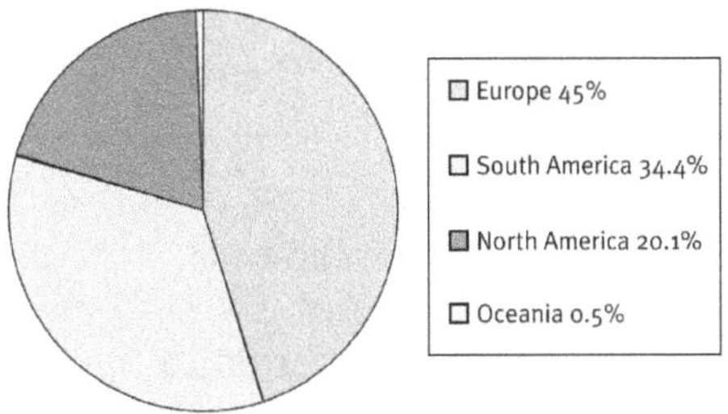

Figure 2.4. The Basque diaspora webscape links: homeland.

According to the European webmasters, the high percentage of links connecting to the homeland was due to their knowledge about homeland sites and their potential usefulness for the organizations' members. In addition, the South American webmasters indicated that their desire to reconnect to the homeland was a way to learn about it. This is also related to the different membership composition of both European and South American institutions. The membership of the European institutions, mainly Basque clubs in this case, is primordially formed by the emigrant generation that has the potential to travel to the Basque Country more often than their counterparts from more distant lands. The membership of South American institutions such as the Basque clubs is composed of a variety of generations, many of whom may never have traveled to the Basque Country. North American webmasters argued that the reasons for connecting to homeland sites were the availability of knowledge and the desire to keep their community and membership informed.

Only four *euskal etxeak* sites and one educational site from Argentina, Canada, the United States, and Venezuela provided a parallel hyperlink structure formed by similar link categories, which connect with both the homeland and the hostland. That is, the sites offered similar homeland and hostland thematic links to their users or visitors, reflecting a double identification and consciousness of belonging to both the homeland and the hostland. In a sense, the sites and their institutions become cyber-mediators or cultural brokers between both dimensions of one reality—the home of their cultural heritage and the place of their adopted residence. Nevertheless, most of the websites provided links to both the homeland and the hostland, but in a less structured and visible manner.

South American links to hostland sites represented 47 percent of total links to hostland sites, North American links to hostland sites represented 39.4 percent of total links to hostland sites, and European links to hostland sites represented 13.6 percent of total links to hostland sites (see figure 2.5).

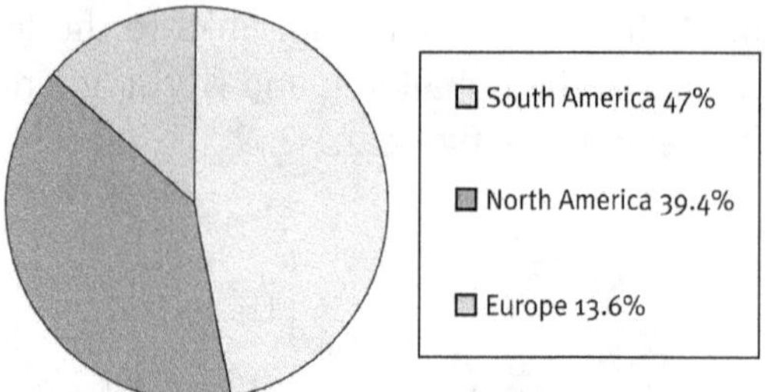

Figure 2.5. The Basque diaspora webscape links: hostland.

In relation to the specific links that referred to the Basque diaspora—that is, intra-diaspora connectivity—the sites from North America presented the highest percentage of relational links, 28.8 percent of total North American links or 45.6 percent of total diaspora links, followed by South America with 16.6 percent of total South American links or 33.2 percent of total diaspora links, and Europe with 10 percent of total European links or 21.1 percent of total diaspora links (see figure 2.6).

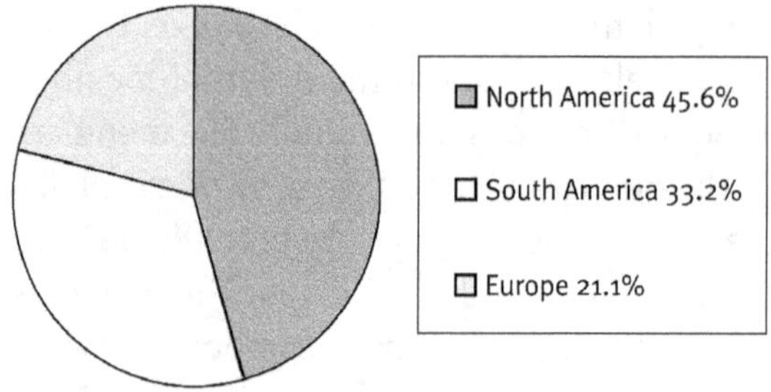

Figure 2.6. The Basque diaspora webscape links: diaspora.

Finally, the links that referred to "other countries" were minimal. North American links to other countries represented 44.3 percent of total links to other countries' sites. European links to other countries represented 28.6 percent of total links to other countries' sites. South American links to other countries represented 27.1 percent of total links to other countries' sites (see figure 2.7). That is, there was a minimal presence and linkage to any site outside the "triadic relationship"—homeland-diaspora-hostland—in Gabriel Sheffer's words (1999). Another extremely suggestive fact is that there was not a single link found related to either different ethnic, regional, or minority groups' sites nor other diasporas' sites.

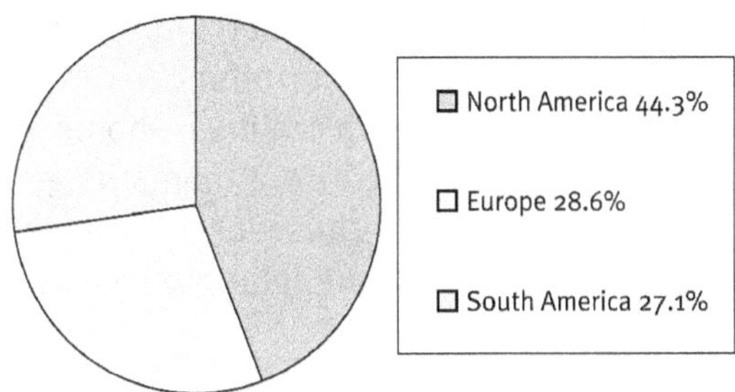

Figure 2.7. The Basque diaspora webscape links: other countries.

Conclusions

As of June 2007, nearly 90 percent of the institutional websites that comprise the Basque diaspora webscape had been established in the new millennium, while only a few sites dated back to the mid- and late-1990s. The Basque diaspora webmasters constitute an incipient voluntary digital intelligentsia with considerable input regarding the creation and development of the Basque diaspora presence online. In this regard, the webmasters understand the utility of the websites as tools for strengthening the Basque communities, but they believe they are not essential for the future or for the survival of their associations. The webmasters do not only need to acknowledge the significance of the Internet as a networking and distance-shrinking technology, but they need to implement the mechanisms to allow their users to take advantage of it. I argue that the Internet is a tool for interaction, communication, networking, and for socializing; however, the utilization of the Internet cannot maintain an identity by itself. It definitely needs to complement offline world activities.

The web is a compendium with an "infinite" number of pages, where none is the first and none is the last. The visitor/reader does not turn the pages, but uses its hypertextual organization to unfold the text. Basque diaspora websites offer a number of selected external links that connect with other similar or related sites on the Basque webscape. As we have seen, the links provided by the diverse Basque diaspora websites offered a sense or degree of commitment to the homeland, the hostland, and the diaspora. The diaspora sites' links were related to the specific purposes and goals of the other websites and offline associations, as well as to their positionality—the bridge between homeland and hostland. They emerged from a motivation or desire to connect while enhancing the diasporic tendency of connecting and networking the different segments that constitute the Basque diaspora.

The links imply networking and an awareness of the websites' existence, and in many cases their offline associations as well as a geographic and linguistic "proximity"—the illusion of closeness—have the potential to open channels of communication and networking. Consequently, these links work as informational points of entry into a "greater" Basque webscape, including the homeland and the diaspora webscape, which re-creates a networked topography of Basque communities on the web as well as a network of cybercultural brokers or ambassadors between the homeland and the hostland. They offer basic information allowing anyone to become an informed person in both realities—homeland and hostland. The links work as a preference directional figure—a thematic, geographical, and ideological network among Basque diaspora sites—or as a web of attachments and as a conscience of diasporicity—intra-diaspora relational connections.

The hyperlink network analysis of the Basque diaspora webscape reveals an online world that displays a vibrant and constantly changing community transforming itself relentlessly. As if it were a galactic nebula, the Basque diaspora webscape is constantly being constructed by individual stars that we can trace using imaginary lines called hyperlinks.

The Mirror of

(03)

Euskal Herria[1]

> Today, if we are a nation, to a large degree it is thanks to you as well—that's to say, the Basques who live far away from Euskal Herria—because you are, without any doubt, the mirror of the true Euskal Herria. Although so many have tried to destroy the true image using the unacceptable violence of ETA in a rotten and evil organized spider's web.
>
> — Joseba Azkarraga, 2004

The Basque government of Euskadi, established under the 1978 Spanish Constitution and the 1979 Gernika Statute of Autonomy, is the heir to the historical Basque self-government established in October 1936 at the outburst of the Spanish Civil War (1936–1939). Forced into exile until the restoration of democracy, that government instituted early ties with Basque communities throughout America. As the only government that deals with diaspora Basques, regardless of their provincial origin—the BAC (Euskadi), Navarre, and Iparralde—it has designed and implemented a legal and financial framework since the mid 1980s, such as Law 8/1994 and subsequent policies in order to strength those historical ties with Basque communities and institutions abroad.[2]

---

1 A version of this chapter was published as "We Love You: The Basque government's Post-Franco Discourses on the Basque Diaspora," *Revista Sancho el Sabio* 26 (2007): 95–132.

2 Azkarraga is the former Minister of Justice, Employment, and Social Security of the Basque government. He gave the talk at the San Francisco Basque Cultural Center in February 2004. Azkarraga's speech was reproduced at the San Francisco Basque Club's site, www.basqueclub.com.

In 1984, the government established the figure of a councillor for relations with the Basque diaspora communities and clubs, and two years later it set up the Service for Relations with the Basque Centers within the Department of Culture, which was, in 1991, renamed as the Directorate for Relations with the Diaspora and was placed under the General Secretariat for Foreign Action. The Secretariat was established the same year within the Lehendakaritza or President's Office. In 1995, the Directorate was once again renamed as the Directorate for Relations with the Basque Communities, and in 2009 it became the Directorate for the Citizens and the Basque Communities. Since 2012, it carries the name of the Directorate for the Basque Community in the Exterior (i.e., outside the territorial confines of the BAC).

From 1986 to 2006, the Basque government has provided over 17.5 million euros (approximately over 24 million dollars) in financial help—subsidies, grants, and so on—to one hundred and fifty diaspora centers and federations—meaning outside the BAC borders (Ugalde Zubiri 2008). For example, from 2004 to 2007, the Basque government gave nearly 4.5 million euros (over 6 million dollars) to diaspora institutions. Nearly 46 percent of that help went to Basque institutions in Argentina, nearly 14 percent to Basque institutions in the United States, nearly 11 percent to Venezuela, and over 10 percent to Spain (Oregi and Martín 2008). The Foral Community of Navarre passed Law 2/2004, which offers financial assistance exclusively to Navarreses and their descendants and Navarrese associations abroad, meaning outside Spain.

Since the transition to democracy in the Basque Country and until March 2009, nationalist parties and coalitions have dominated the Basque government. In addition, during the aforementioned period, the President's Office, the General Secretariat for Foreign Action, and the Directorate for Relations with Basque Communities Abroad have been in the hands of the EAJ-PNV. The EAJ-PNV won the March 2009 elections to the Basque Parliament. However, it did not have enough parliamentary seats to form a government by itself or in coalition. Consequently, the Socialist Party of Euskadi (PSE by its Spanish acronyms), the chapter of the Spanish Workers Socialist Party (PSOE by its Spanish acronym) in the Basque Autonomous Community, formed a government in minority with the support of the Popular Party (PP by its Spanish acronym) in May 2009.

The Basque Government's Discourses

Homeland Ethnonationalism

Taking into consideration the suggestions made by Walker Connor on his seminal work on nationalism, I conducted an analysis of Basque governmental officials and leaders' political speeches, conferences, and lectures delivered to and for the Basque diaspora since democracy up to 2009 in order to understand the emotional depth of the ethnonational identity.

Connor (1994) defines a nation as a group of people who believe they are ancestrally related (i.e., an ethnic or ethnonational group), while nationalism connotes identification with and loyalty to one's ethnonational group (see also Smith 1992; Gellner 1983; Hobsbawn 1990). A common ancestry means an intergenerational link to common ancestors, maintaining and transmitting traditions and heritage to the next generation. That is to say, there is a preservation and continuity of past tradition in the present and the future. The preservation, maintenance, and promotion of tradition—a forward orientation—become central to diaspora communities, such as that of the Basques.

Following Connor, an ethnonational group is a tangible, rational identity phenomenon—that is, a nation with a common language, religion, territory, or ancestry based on myths of common descents or kinship—that "contribute to this notion or sense of the group's self-identity and uniqueness" (1994, 104; see also Smith 1981). And it is also a non-tangible, less visible phenomenon, more physiological and emotional, and therefore subjective. Connor concludes that the both rational and emotional ethnonational dimensions maintain national consciousness.

Consequently, ethnonationalism is an assertion of being and belonging to a people, a territory, a heritage, and a culture. Diaspora, on the other hand, is an assertion about not being in the homeland—the permanent absence from the place of origin. As we will explore in Chapter 5, the Basque diaspora identifies almost exclusively with a Basque homeland, defined as a country made up of seven provinces spread over the states of Spain and France. (This seven-province nation is one of the historical claims of the Basque nationalist movement.) The study of the content of diaspora websites also invokes a strong emotional aspect, which reinforces in-group solidarity, uniqueness, cohesiveness, empathy, and commonality, while at the same time reinforcing out-group differentness and even antipathy.

As we will see, the Basque government is emphasizing its institutional and symbolic legitimacy—central aspects of state loyalty—in order to politically socialize its population, including those Basques living abroad.

Past-Oriented Discourses: Origins and Authenticity

The Basque government's past-oriented discourses are structured around three recurring themes: an *illo tempore* nation, a territory, and a historical golden age, which suggests the Basque nation's antiquity and continuity. These discourses recreate a community of history based on a common ancestry, language, and territory. That is, the government defines Basques in terms of their past—a retrospective imagined discourse.

Evidence shows that the current Basque nationalism re-imagines and reconstructs a pre-existing Basque identity by mystifying its history and culture, just as was done in the nineteenth century. Arguments about Basque singularity, authenticity, and historical continuity are not new but draw on previous scientific and ideological discourses. For example, since the mid-nineteenth century, international and local social scientists have been immersed in addressing the Basque people, language, and history by creating and reproducing a great number of icons, which have become defining canons of Basqueness, such as the "particularity" of the Basque language, the "exclusive" physiognomy and blood type of the Basque people, or "perennial" Basque history. Those icons or canons were used to differentiate the Basque people and culture in relation to other cultures and helped to re-create a culture of continuity, purity, isolation, and resistance (see Douglass, Lyman, and Zulaika 1994, 90–93; Zulaika and Douglass 1996; and Zulaika 1998).

Basque authenticity is believed to be based on a remote past, which justifies the existence of the Basque nationalist ideology, as its goal is to create a politico-territorial state in order to ensure the protection of Basque identity and culture. There is a projection of the nationalist ideology and its raison d'être into the past through the assertion of certain direct links to what are considered Basque nationalist common myths of ancestry, origin, and election: direct descent from the Cro-Magnon people—first inhabitants of Europe, mysterious origins of the Basque people and the language, or racial pride and biological differentness (see Smith 1992, 21).

Over the last three decades, the diverse Basque administrations have re-created an ethnonationalist "emotional" discourse directed at the diaspora. At the same time, the Basque government views the diaspora as a vivid proof of Basqueness. The existence of Basques abroad is a proof of the authenticity of Basques in the homeland. Consequently, the government celebrates the perpetuation of Basque identity, values, and cultural traditions abroad, which survive despite not having always experienced the right conditions. This psychological and emotional dimension of identity flows easily across geographical, sociopolitical, cultural, and generational contexts, creating a strong affection-based adscription to the individual to the collective identity.

The sense of the "singular" and "authentic"—real or imagined—character of Basque heritage provides pride and self-esteem to individuals and community, which in turn make them feel special and unique. In other words, government officials evoke emotionally charged arguments by re-creating a mysterious and perennial Basque nation, which might generate in an audience an automatic pride of an invaluable identity and culture that unquestionably deserves to be preserved and nurtured. I argue that the self-perpetuation of Basque identity in the diaspora is very much based on the pride and affection for assumed characteristics, such as uniqueness or singularity of such an identity. Those characteristics are maintained, defended, and transmitted as part of one's heritage due to the positive social status associated to them.

In very general terms, the positive social identity theory considers that the purpose of identification of individuals within a group or "in-group" is to obtain a positive social identity different from that of the outside group or "out-group." Therefore, the theory focuses on the in-group individuals' self-perception, their positive self-esteem based on the characteristics of the group, in comparison with other individuals and/or groups within the same society. Consequently, the maintenance of an ethnic identity and an affiliation to a group is directly related to the desire to increase comparative social status (see Tajfel's 1978, 1981, ed., 1982, ed., 1984; see also Oiarzabal and Oiarzabal 2005, 119).

For example, the Basque government's site, www.euskadi.net, provides a section dedicated to the Basque diaspora titled "Basque Clubs and Communities."[3] Under this section, the government offers an electronic document titled "The Basques in History," which exemplifies a Basque historical golden era by highlighting "universal" Basques, while referring also to the future as a culture of continuity:

> Over the centuries, the Basques have produced a number of great men who have left their mark on history: men like Juan Sebastián Elcano, first man to sail around the world between 1519 and 1521; [Andrés de] Urdaneta and [Miguel López de] Legazpi, pioneers of the Pacific route between Mexico and the Philippines; Juan de Garay, founder of Buenos Aires; Simón Bolívar, liberator of much of colonial South America; Ignatius of Loyola, founder of the Jesuits; and Francisco de Vitoria, one of the forefathers of international law, and the Navarrese Francisco de Javier [Francis Xavier] . . . In more modern times, the same kind of drive and initiative led to the creation of highly respected industries and banking houses . . . Today, industry and finance remains a solid combination, guaranteeing the Basque Country's prospects for the future.

The Basque diaspora also establishes a nearly identical discourse. For example, 60 percent of Basque diaspora sites also provide sections that re-create a glorious past by highlighting famous or prominent Basque personalities who have contributed to global history and culture—such as, by order of popularity, Saint Ignatius of Loyola, José María Iparraguirre, or Juan Sebastián Elcano—as well as the colonization, independence, and formation of the host country during the nineteenth century. For example, the Basque club of Chaco (Argentina, www.ecomchaco.com.ar/centrovasco/default.htm) and the educational association Diáspora Vasco Argentina from Buenos Aires (Argentina, www.diasporavascarg.com.ar/) published articles titled, respectively, "St. Ignatius of Loyola: The Most Universal of the Basques," and "St. Ignatius of Loyola: A Basque Emigrant Saint." José María Iparraguirre was a poet, bard, and a political exile from Gipuzkoa who lived from 1848 to 1853 in several European countries, including Switzerland, Italy, Germany, and the United Kigdom, and from 1858 to 1876 in Argentina and Uruguay. He is the author of the song *"Gernikako Arbola"* (The Tree of Gernika), considered by many the Basque national anthem.

Members of the diaspora also view Basque culture as an essential component of their respective hostland's culture—particularly in countries that received a massive Basque migration, such as Argentina, Chile, and Uruguay. For example, the diaspora uses topographic Basque names and the names of Basque historical figures, of migrants and their descendants, as examples to claim the host countries' history and culture as its own history, as well as to measure the degree of Basque-

3 This page was last updated in 2004, and it was last retrieved on February 21, 2006.

ness of those histories and cultures. The Buenos Aires educational foundation Juan de Garay measures this influx of Basqueness into Argentina by the number of presidents of Basque origin between 1854 and 2002 (a total of eleven) and the many Argentinean localities named after Basque founders, such as Necochea, Ezeiza, and Olabarria. Also, 80 percent of Basque websites in Argentina estimate that there are between three to five million people of Basque descent (between 10 percent to 15 percent of the total population) and approximately fifteen thousand Basque surnames in Argentina as a way to underpin the significance of the Basque collectivity there. This presence may be more symbolic than factual if we take into account that approximately only eighteen thousand Basques or Basque-Argentineans are members of Basque associations as of July 2007.

In sum, diaspora associations as well as the Basque government reproduce a historicist vision of the Basque people and convey a positive message about their splendid shared past by enumerating names of Basque historical or charismatic personalities who had excelled in life, while instilling a sense of pride amongst their current membership and community at large. The fascination for the past and for origins encourages diaspora associations—particularly from Argentina, Chile, Uruguay, and the United States—to build databases of Basque surnames in their hostlands in order to offer genealogical services as well as services to search for lost Basque relatives, while providing information on Basque heraldry and the meaning of those surnames. For example, 20 percent of Basque websites offer some of the above-mentioned services. The positive values embedded in touted historical figures and in their enterprises and contributions are transmitted through the present Basque community by linking a golden past to the present. Diaspora institutions appeal to such figures in order to overcome the negative values of terrorism and political violence associated with the Basque identity for the past decades.

Future-Oriented Discourses: Endurance and Positiveness

The Basque government is not only producing past-oriented discourses—a community of memory—but also a future-oriented, postmodern discourse by presenting Basque identity and culture as a guarantee of survival, a community of destiny based on a common future. The Basque government sends contradictory images or messages in relation to the homeland's current reality to the diaspora. However, the government sees those discourses as complimentary, re-creating images that tend to depict the Basque Country as both traditional and postmodern—a symbiosis between tradition and innovation. On the one hand, for example, the covers of the books on diaspora matters *Euskaldunak Munduan—Vascos en el Mundo* (Basques Around the World), published by the Directorate for Relations with the Basque Communities, depict traditional images of the Basque Country, such as farmhouses, fishing ports, or children dressed in typical dancing or rural costumes. On the other hand, simultaneously, some issues of the magazine *Euskal Etxeak* are monographic portrayals of a postmodern Basque Country based on science and technology, tourism, or contemporary Basque music, cinema, or architecture.[4]

In addition, the Basque government has sponsored cultural and educational programs for the Basque diaspora since 1989, which tend to be more "contemporary" and eclectic than traditional activities, such as Basque rural sports. Every four years since 1995, the Basque government has organized diaspora congresses, following the dictates of Law 8/1994 and the *Gaztemundu* annual workshop aimed at diaspora youth since 1996.[5] All those programs attempt to promote a particular postmodern homeland-centered culture, while somehow dismissing other more traditional aspects of Basque culture.

The government constantly invokes the diaspora to participate in a postmodern, non-traditional, or non-essentialist Basque Country. Governmental speeches introduce a "new" view of Basque society, culture, identity, and values embedded in a process of globalization and postmodernity. Consequently, the government repeatedly invites the diaspora to promote this newly crafted image of the Basque Country to their communities and countries of residence, as they are considered the "true ambassadors" of the homeland. The promotion of a postmodern image of the Basque Country is somehow related to the promotion of an assumed "true" image of the Basques: peaceful, serene, innovative, and industrious.

There is no doubt that the institutional diaspora is assuming the role of being the Basque government's ambassadors. For example, at the Fourth World Congress of Basque Communities (Bilbao, July 2007), Mariluz Artetxe, then-president of FEVA (April 2006–March 2008), enthusiastically argued, "If the Basque Centers are the Basque Country's image in the world, we have a great commitment, spreading the other side of the truth to counteract distorted and manipulated information [about the Basque Country]. Demonstrate the values of this peaceful and hard-working People and be able to make the qualitative jump from being 'known' to being 'recognized as a People,' as our President, Juan José Ibarretxe, says" (in Ayesa and Orbaiceta 2008, 137).

Basque Identity Endurance

The discourses promoted by Basque government leaders attempt to convey the idea that the Basques are not all about the past but also about the future by highlighting the fact that the antiquity of the Basque people guarantees their survival in a near or remote future. That is, the Basques, while remaining faithful to their history and language, are an enduring and restless people "open to globalization" and internationalization. The Basque language becomes, once again, a prominent defining element of Basque identity.

---

4 For example: Issue 69 (2005): "A Shot in the Arm for Science in Euskadi"; Issue 66 (2005): "Basque music today"; Issue 60 (2003): "A Country on the Move: Social Well-being for All"; Issue 59 (2003): "Discover the Basque Country. It's Out of this World"; and Issue 35 (1997): "Museum Guggenheim: Symbol of the New Euskadi."

5 From 1996 to 2006, 451 young people from fourteen countries took part in Gaztemundu (Bilbao, 2008).

For example, during an official visit to the United States, then–Minister of Justice Azkarraga delivered a series of lectures on the proposal for a New Political Statute of the Community of the Basque Country—the so-called Ibarretxe Plan, a bill to reform the Statute of Gernika. The Proposal for a New Political Statute was sponsored by then-President Ibarretxe's coalition government and was passed by an absolute majority by the Basque Parliament on October 25, 2004, but rejected by the Spanish Parliament in February 2005. The proposal is based on the following principles: the recognition of Basque identity, the recognition of the right of self-determination, and the freedom to form relations with Navarre and Iparralde. The two branches of the two main Spanish political parties with representation in the Basque Parliament—the conservative PP and the PSOE—voted against the New Political Statute as they considered it an exclusive project for the Basque nationalist community. The preface defines the Basque people as "A People with its own identity within the community of European peoples, repository of a singular historical, social, and cultural heritage, distributed geographically in seven territories, currently articulated in three different legal-political regions and located in two different states."

In the lecture given at the San Francisco Basque Cultural Center in February 2004, Azkarraga stated:

> Our Euskal Herria is one of the oldest nations in Europe—old, historically speaking, but young in spirit. At the footsteps of this newly born twenty-first century, ours are a people with the doors open wide. However, always holding on to their identity . . . above war, repression, dictatorship or partition of the land; just as until now, our people have known how to keep their identity—like Euskara, their beloved language . . . And, that nation, Euskal Herria, if she keeps alive is thanks to today's efforts. But most of all, thanks to the work carried out by those who came before us: our parents, grandparents, and forefathers. (Basque club of San Francisco, www.basqueclub.com/)

Juan José Ibarretxe, Basque president from 1998 to 2009, delivered a powerful inaugural address at the Third World Congress of Basque Communities (Vitoria-Gasteiz July 2003), which was widely echoed by the press:

> No one . . . in the name of globalization has the right to ask us to stop being what we are: Basques. No one in the name of globalization should be allowed to strip naked a nation that has been around for more than 7,000 years. No one in the name of globalization has the right to deprive the world, not only of the Basque people, of Euskara, the oldest language in Europe . . . I once heard a highly acclaimed Basque linguist [Koldo Mitxelena] say that 2,000 years ago different languages, such as the Romance languages, were spoken in the world. But here in Euskadi, there was a small group of Basque men and women who communicated with each other in Euskara. Today, 2,000 years later English and Spanish are the world's dominant languages . . . but here in the Basque Country we still speak our own language, Euskara . . . I don't know what languages might be spoken in another 2,000 years' time, but I am absolutely certain of one thing . . . we will still be communicating with each other in Euskara. And there will be a Basque nation. (Gobierno Vasco 2004, 31)

At the opening ceremony of the inauguration of the Cenarrusa Center for Basque Studies (Boise, United States, July 26, 2005) within the context of the celebration of the Fifth International Basque Cultural Festival, Jaialdi, Ibarretxe summed up the central argument of the discourse on identity and globalization by once again arguing that "The Basque people is one of the oldest people in the world; the Basque language is one of the oldest in the world; nevertheless, we are open to globalization." Ibarretxe also delivered similar speeches at Jaialdi's closing ceremony (July 31, 2005) and the opening ceremony of the Fourth World Congress (Bilbao, July 8, 2007) (*Deia,* August 2, 2005). These arguments are not exclusive of governmental leaders but also are commonly found in the Basque diaspora. For example, Mark Bieter, a second-generation Basque author from Boise, Idaho (United States), wrote an article titled "A Distant Mirror" for the homeland Basque-language newspaper *Berria* (August 10, 2005): "Many years ago, an old Basque man told me a story that every Basque knows. When he was a boy, his grandfather took him to a bridge built by the Romans, somewhere in the Basque Country. His grandfather pointed to the bridge and said 'The Romans are gone but the Basques are still here.' . . . I have a one-year old daughter. When I returned from Jaialdi, the best surprise was realizing that someday I can take her to the Roman bridge."

A Postmodern Basque Country: Satellite Television and the Internet

I argue that the Basque government assumes that the Basque diaspora is outdated culturally and identity-wise, living in a past detached from today's homeland—in other words, a "Jurassic park" of identity (Iñaki Egaña, *El País,* July 23, 2004). In this regard, Josu Legarreta, former Director for Relations with the Basque Communities, argued:

> The history of the world is a continuum search for renovation and change . . . Traditions is what persists; it's what we hold on to as an emblem of our cultural roots, a sign of identity which keep us united. It is which shows others that we belong to a certain group of people. [At the same time] we must live for and create the future; we need to modernize and move forward or allow ourselves to fall behind . . . Without roots there can be no trees. But trees cannot exist without branches and leaves and new fruit. The Basque centers see to preserving these roots, disseminating Basque folklore as part of their activities . . . We are all the makers of history, but today's reality is much more than a struggle to keep our past alive. Remembering the past is essential, but we must do so while looking towards the future and setting our sights on the new reality. (*Euskal Etxeak* 2002, 3)

I agree with the argument that portrays diasporas as "mythologizing" agents of homelands that reproduce ideal, nostalgic, and timeless images and memories from an inherited lost past—that is to say, narratives of migration created from a sense of loss, separation, and crisis from the homeland and consequent yearning. By the same token, diaspora Basques are not mere reproducers of homeland culture, but they also produce their own sense of Basque identity based on their migration experiences and adaptation to the hostlands. This transnational, diasporic, or hybrid culture re-creates a different sense of Basque identity, which, consequently, differs from the one in the homeland.

In the case of the Basque diaspora, this constitutes a reconstruction of an image of the Basque Country "in the distance" and "disconnected from the real appearance of the actual Basque Country" (Alonso 1998, 288). That is, there is an apparent disjuncture or disconnectedness between the diaspora and the homeland notion of Basqueness according to the discourses constructed by the Basque diaspora via its webscape (see chapters 4 and 5). The diaspora displays a more essentialist interpretation of Basque identity based on a re-creation of the past and its idealization, while the homeland's subjective criteria on defining Basqueness are gaining ground (see Gobierno Vasco, 2003a, 2003b, and 2003c).

However, the existence of a spatial and temporal dislocation does not necessarily imply that the diaspora is completely detached from the current homeland's reality. Basque diaspora communities are evolving identity-based communities, and they are far from isolated. The increase of communication and the flow of daily information work against the assumption that they are stagnated, frozen in time, like postcards from the past.

Consequently, the Basque government is resolute on "bringing up to speed" the Basque diaspora into the "current" reality of the Basque Country. The government is keen to "sell" abroad, particularly to the diaspora, an extremely innovative and prosperous image of the Basque Country as a way to show the well-being of Basque society in comparison with its neighbors. Mass media facilitates the construction and dissemination of such an image into the diaspora through its institutions. This Basque postmodernity based on socioeconomic and technological progress is taken as a differentiating factor in relation to neighboring societies by reinforcing the in-group borders and its positive social status while encouraging a sense of pride amongst diaspora Basques.

For example, President Ibarretxe told the audience congregated for the centennial of the Buenos Aires Basque club Laurak Bat (November 29, 2002): "Today we are one of the most advanced societies, with a better quality of life in Europe and in the world. Euskadi is one of the ten first countries of the world ranked in relation to the UN [United Nations] human development index; the one that does not only take into account economic growth, but also other elements that are part of the integral growth of the people" (Centro Vasco Eusko Etxea de La Plata, www.centrovasco.com).

In addition, the Basque government's discourses attempt to reproduce the benchmarks of Basque homeland identity for the diaspora. That is, Basque diaspora identity needs to be defined according to the homeland's identity parameters. The government's constant references about the postmodern identity of the Basque Country tend to push the diaspora toward a more "civic" and subjective dimension of Basque identity as expressed in the homeland. Certain questions arise from various elements, such as the diaspora's exposure to the aforementioned Basque government's politics of identity and culture, personal visits by government officials, homeland musicians and other cultural performers, homeland media, and, particularly, the Internet. These questions include: Will this exposure and contact between the homeland and the diaspora lead to a synchronization of both the diasporic and homeland cultures? Or on the contrary, will this exposure and contact between the homeland and the diaspora lead to an increasing awareness of "differentness" and separateness from homeland Basques?

For example, on May 12, 2000, at the Buenos Aires Laurak Bat clubhouse, former Minister of Culture Mari Carmen Garmendia gave a lecture that clearly summed up how the Basque government views the diaspora, while encouraging the diaspora, without departing from tradition, to embrace a more current understanding of today's Basque identity. Garmendia stated:

> We the Basques, those who stayed there, and those who, today, live dispersed around the world, cannot limit ourselves to the roots. . . Basque society is a changing society. . . We still feel Basque like our ancestors, but, we hardly look like them. . . We don't relate to the image of the Basque that your elderly transmitted to you. . . I want to say to you that new "branches" are growing from the roots that we share, from our collective memory; that we all, Basques who live here and Basques who live outside here, need to incorporate to our common cultural heritage. We cannot content ourselves with sharing memories, but we have to share also the projects. Our cultural community cannot remain anchored in the past, but we have to open it to the future. In other words, a time will come, in which we could fail to recognize each other. We have to achieve that every time that a Basque, from abroad comes back to her land, recognize us as part of her community, and recognize also herself as a member of this cultural community. . . In order to obtain such a bond, in order to avoid that our sense of belonging and community be broken, there is no other better tool than to keep alive in a constant manner our communication . . . for example, through the Internet. (Juan de Garay Foundation's site, www.juandegaray.org.ar)

Communication, according to Garmendia, is the key to eliminating the existing disjuncture between the diaspora and the homeland by promoting, developing, and disseminating the contemporary Basque Country reality abroad, and particularly throughout the diaspora. Law 8/1994 was the facilitator of the first satellite television broadcasts for the Basque diaspora. Indeed, Law 8/1994 is intended to "project knowledge of the reality of the Basque Country in the places where Basque communities are settled" (Gobierno Vasco, 1994, Article 1c).

The different satellite television experiments carried out by Basque Public Radio and Television (EiTB) resulted in the creation of Canal Vasco for Latin America in 2000, which is currently the only Basque satellite television. Josu Amezaga (2004) found two main attitudes toward the use of Canal Vasco by diaspora Basques from Argentina and Venezuela and its influence on identity maintenance and formation. On the one hand, for viewers with a well-"established" and well-defined Basque identity, Canal Vasco would obviously either contradict or assert their preconceived definitions of Basque identity. These viewers tend to have a more critical attitude toward the channel if the discursive images shown contradict their definitions of what Basque culture and identity are. On the other hand, viewers in the process of constructing their Basque identity do not have any problem with what the programs have to offer because their expectations are minimal. This second group of viewers believes that the television channel is showing the unquestionably *true* Basque Country.

Amezaga argues that Canal Vasco helps diaspora Basques to visualize, imagine, and re-create the most tangible aspects of the Basque homeland. The television channel introduces a current Basque homeland dimension in their living rooms, consuming an immediate and quotidian "digital experience" of Basqueness. However, the author concludes that this digital experience alone is not sufficient for an individual to maintain her Basque identity. There is also a need for real life experience, for example, by participating in Basque diaspora community gatherings or by visiting the Basque Country.

If in 1995 the diaspora institutional delegates at the First World Congress of Basque Communities called for the need of a Basque television channel for their communities as a way to get close to the Basque homeland reality, in 2003 the delegates at the Third World Congress suggested, "that EiTB [should] include news of the diaspora in its habitual programs and news." At the same time, they urged "all journalists and media in Euskal Herria to get involved in the habitual coverage of news from the diaspora" (Gobierno Vasco 2004, 254).[6] That is, the Basque diaspora would like to become an integral part of the Basque homeland's day-to-day experiences. The institutional delegates advocated for a two-way communication channel, where both current realities from homeland and diaspora could be shown in each other's living rooms as a way to narrow the existing differences between both realities, not just as a way for the diaspora to become more *like* the homeland.

Finally, learning from the Turkish diaspora, Asu Aksoy and Kevin Robins conclusively argue that new media technologies, such as satellite television, *enhance* a synchronization of diaspora's culture and identity with homeland's culture and identity and consequently enhance a de-ethnicization of the diaspora. According to their research on Turkish migrants in London, the authors argue that although "television may nourish warm and nostalgic feelings," satellite television "brings the ordinary, banal reality of Turkish life to the migrants living in London. . . The 'here and now' reality of Turkish media culture disturbs the imagination of a 'there and then' Turkey –thereby working against the romance of diaspora-as-exile, against the tendency to false idealization of the 'homeland'. We might say, then, that Turkish television is an agent of cultural de-mythologisation" (2002, 10–12).

---

6 EiTB offers, through its news site, EiTB24 (www.eitb24.com), a specific news section on the Basque diaspora called "Basques around the world," in Basque, English, and Spanish. Since February 2007, the news section on the Basque diaspora is complemented by blogs on Argentina, the Dominican Republic, Venezuela, and the United States. By the end of 2008, EiTB24 site was replaced by www.eitb.com, and the blogs were placed under the ETB Sat section.

Therefore, satellite television, marketed primarily for the audience in Turkey, creates a united audience, a common national imagined community without marking differences between Turks in Turkey and Turks abroad. However, Aksoy and Robins (2002, 18) argue that in the Turkish case, the viewers might not feel at home in the "we-ness of Turkish broadcasting culture"—that is, satellite television is embedded in a national imaginary that works toward the creation of a national imagined community rather than a diasporic imagined community.[7]

What are the implications of new technologies, such as the Internet for resolving the estrangement between the Basque Country and the Basque diaspora? Is the Basque diaspora perceived by the Canal Vasco's board of directors as part of a Basque imagined transnational community constituted by both homeland and diaspora? Or is the Basque diaspora just an audience that is willing to consume programs that were originally aimed at the homeland?

The Internet as a channel and particularly the web as a medium allow for diaspora Basques to access and distribute a vast number of resources and information for material and symbolic re-creation of some aspects of the Basque culture, such as history, games, sports, or language. Those technologies also provide diaspora Basques with the ability to construct social ties among individuals and communities, allowing them to *interact* with each other as well with homeland Basques in an immediate way on matters that might be core to their identity. When one considers the specific characteristics of the Internet and the web, their potentiality for enhancing or strengthening identity maintenance in the diaspora is higher than other media, such as Canal Vasco, where the viewer is a mere receptor or consumer of a culture produced or tailored not only for Basque viewers but for the general Latin American population. On the web, diaspora Basques are not only consumers of a predetermined culture, but also producers of culture.

The existing gap between homeland and diaspora, for example in the different interpretations on Basque identity, could well be narrowed by the communication and interaction provided by the web, but not by these alone. Diaspora Basques can access this Basque "reality" in an unprecedented manner via the Internet and the web. But in this equation, the offline dimension is key if diaspora Basques and their institutions wish to implement this "new" Euskal Herria into the communities' imaginary, thereby building bridges to the homeland.

However, it is up to the diaspora Basques and their institutions to close the aforementioned gap. At the same time, it is also up to the Basque government to understand the uniqueness of diaspora identity characteristics, and the reasons behind its exclusiveness and continuous allusions to primordial identity markers, such as language or ancestry. In this way, the Internet and the web are great windows of opportunities for government officials to learn in a fast, immediate, and inexpensive manner about Basque diaspora identity.

7 See also Milikowski 2000, 443–68.

Politics of Self-Determination

Heartwarming speeches by government leaders and officials produce strong emotional connections with diaspora Basques by utilizing ethnonationalist arguments, which reinforce not only cultural uniqueness but also political uniqueness. The Basque government not only defines Basque identity and culture in symbolic, cultural, or historical terms but also in political terms, where national differences provide a new perspective in the construction of Basque singularity. To some extent, the Basque diaspora is an ideological community—an extended family that spans the planet—enhanced by the Basque government and fueled by a nationalist agenda.

According to Law 8/94 and successive decrees, diaspora Basques have rights similar to those enjoyed by the BAC citizens/taxpayers, but what about their duties? Which roles does the Basque government assign to the diaspora?

Law 8/94 defines the role of the diaspora in the following terms: "In an environment of continuous globalization and internationalization of modern societies, Basque communities [abroad] can play the part; there is no doubt, of stimulators of social, cultural, economic, and political relations" (Gobierno Vasco 1994). That is, Law 8/94 provides certain legitimacy for diaspora institutions to get involved in homeland matters, if not in real terms at least in a symbolic way. Furthermore, the General Secretariat for Foreign Action included the Basque diaspora's roles identified by Law 8/94 in its Strategic Plan (March 8, 2005) as part of the development of the BAC's foreign policy. The Proposal of the Four-Year Plan for Institutional Action 2008-2011, drawn up during the celebration of the Fourth World Congress of Basque Communities (July 2007), identified the following goals, among others, for the diaspora: the promotion of Basque identity in the world and the projection of the knowledge of the current reality of Euskadi (Oregi and Martín 2008; Gobierno Vasco 2008). That is to say, the Basque diaspora and its institutions constitute another dimension of the international projection of the Basque Country and the Basque government.

According to a survey I carried out during the Third World Congress of Basque Communities abroad (July 2003), diaspora institutional leaders from seventeen countries believed that the diaspora should have an active participation in homeland matters, such as, in order of importance, culture, politics, and the economy. Political participation would include direct political representation in the Basque Parliament and role in the resolution of violent conflict. Diaspora representatives believed that for the Basque government the Basque diaspora is, mainly, a tool for promoting Basque culture abroad. However, they tend to be indifferent about the Basque diaspora's active participation in the government's international relations, in paradiplomacy, or in the Basque government itself.

Although, diaspora institutional leaders do not consider that the diaspora has much weight in homeland politics, the government feels differently. The level of the government's political (nationalist) discourses on diaspora have gradually increased in relation to the homeland's political momentum, particularly since 1998—a year marked by ETA ceasefire,[8] following the so-called Lizarra Agreement,[9] and the formation of a short-lived Basque government nationalist coalition (1999–2000), which also included ETA's alleged political arm, Euskal Herritarrok (former Herri Batasuna). Consequently, the direct calls for the diaspora to take action and be part of the homeland political process have become more overt than in previous eras.[10]

The government has openly called upon the political support of the Basque diaspora in any exercise of the right of self-determination in the near future, including the so-called Ibarretxe Plan, in order to guarantee the future of the Basque identity, culture, and ancestral homeland, which could directly affect the diaspora's "survival" (see for example, Gobierno Vasco 1996, 19).

Particularly within the context of campaigning for the New Political Statute, various government officials went to different diaspora communities to convey the political messages embedded in the proposal.[11] For example, during a visit to Buenos Aires, the then–Minister of Education, Anjeles Iztueta, openly asked the Basques in Argentina for their support of the Ibarretxe Plan "in order to exercise our right of self-government, because we want to be the masters of our own future" (*Deia*, October 10, 2003). Similarly, Minister Azkarraga strongly and bluntly invoked the audience and the diaspora: "You . . . will continue to defend your father's house . . . you need to become active agents [to obtain] peace and freedom for Euskal Herria" (at

8 ETA's ceasefire began in September 1998 and ended in November 1999. Since then, ETA has declared two partial truces—an end of violence in Catalonia on February 18, 2004, and an end of violence against elected politicians on June 18, 2005—and a "permanent" ceasefire on March 24, 2006, which ended on June 6, 2007. Finally, ETA declared the definitive end of its "armed activity" on October 20, 2011.

9 The Lizarra Agreement was signed in September 1998 by the Basque nationalist parties—EAJ-PNV, Eusko Alkartasuna (EA), and Herri Batasuna (HB)—Izquierda Unida/Ezker Batua (IU/EB), and another nineteen organizations, which included trade unions and social associations. These political parties obtained 60.1 percent of the total results in the Basque elections in October 1998. The PP and PSOE voluntarily excluded themselves from such an agreement. The agreement identified the Basque conflict as an historical and political one; therefore, the resolution of the conflict should also be political through dialogue and negotiation without limits and exclusions, in a context of total absence of violence. It also recognized the self-determination of the Basque people and the unification of all Basque territories, as key elements to resolve the so-called Basque conflict, which was defined not in terms of violence, but in terms of a historical political conflict between the Basque Country and Spain.

10 For example, political news and editorials as well as monographic issues on homeland politics that were displayed on the Basque government's diaspora magazine *Euskal Etxeak* have become the norm for the past few years: Issue 39 (1998): "Euskadi Chooses its Future," editorial titled "To Vote: Right and a Duty also for Basques living Abroad"; Issue 40 (December 1998): "Euskadi Faces the Legislature of Peace"; Issue 41 (1999): "Time to Talk: Euskadi holds out Hope for the Peace Process"; Issue 42 (June 1999): "Historic Agreement: EH [Euskal Herritarrok] committed to Democratic Procedures," editorial titled *"An Agreement for History"*; Issue 48 (December 2000): "Declaration of Gernika: An Ethical Engagement in Defense of the Right to Life and the Freedom of All Persons"; Issue 49 (May 2001): "The Lehendakari Call for an Election in the Basque Country on May 13th"; Issue 50 (September 2001): "Euskadi Votes for Peace: the PNV-EA Coalition Wins the Election"; Issue 51 (October 2001): "A Commitment to Euskadi," editorial titled *"To Life, Peace, Respect for the Basque People and Solidarity"*; Issue 53 (March 2002): "Where there isn't Life, there isn't Freedom; Where there isn't Peace, there isn't Freedom"; Issue 54 (June 2002): "The Idaho State Legislature Unanimously Approved a Declaration in Favor of the Basques Right to Self-determination"; and Issue 67 (March 2005): "New Political Statute, A Proposal for Coexistence," editorial entitiled *"A Proposal for Coexistence."*

11 For example, Joseba Azkarraga (minister of justice, February 2004, United States); Anjeles Iztueta (minister of education, October 2003 and March 2004, Argentina); Idoia Zenarruzabeitia (vice president, June 2004, Argentina, Chile, and Uruguay); Miren Azkarate (minister of culture, November 2003, Argentina, Chile, and Uruguay; and June 2004, Mexico); and Sabin Intxaurraga (minister of environment, August 2004, Argentina).

the Center for Basque Studies, University of Nevada, Reno, United States, February 11, 2004).

As a result of the increasing politicization of the government's discourses on the diaspora over the years, the 2002 Idaho Joint Memorial No. 144 responded to those direct calls. The Idaho Joint Memorial No. 144 was passed unanimously after being submitted by local Basque-Americans to the Idaho State Legislature.[12] The Memorial declared the State of Idaho's support for the Basque people to exercise their right to self-determination, while calling for the end to violence in the Basque Country perpetrated by ETA, as well as to that committed by the Spanish government.[13] The Idaho Memorial created an international dispute with Spain as the latter understood the memorial as a statement of support for ETA. It also provoked an internal clash with the U.S. State Department, which argued that "foreign policy is a presidential prerogative" (CNN, March 11, 2002; *Gara,* March 8, 2002). The Basque homeland nationalist and pro-independence press (*Deia, Gara,* and *Egunkaria*) welcomed the Idaho Memorial declaration, while the Spanish press (*ABC, El Mundo,* and *El País*), the Spanish government, and the PP criticized the initiative for its interference into domestic politics, while also ridiculing diaspora Basques, including one of the promoters Pete Cenarrusa, former Secretary of the State of Idaho, for being so ignorant of the homeland reality (see *Gara,* March 6 and March 12, 2002; *Deia,* March 12, 2002; *ABC,* September 5 and 6, 2002; *El Semanal Digital,* September 1, 2004). Basque historian José María Portillo, who had been threatened by ETA, stated, "I would like to propose to our representatives in the Parliament of Vitoria [the home of the Basque government] first of all, to send quickly educational material, particularly on history, geography, and anthropology of the Basque Country to the Idaho Congress" [because of] "the manifest ignorance of those Americans" (*El Correo,* March 9, 2002; *El País,* March 10, 2002; *Deia,* March 20, 2002b; Savater 2004, 69–72).

Following the Idaho Memorial and during President Ibarretxe's visit to Argentina in November 2002, FEVA presented him with a document in favor of peace, freedom, and self-determination for the Basque Country, while manifesting its adherence to the Idaho Memorial declaration. Similarly, the Chamber of Deputies of the Province of Santa Fé (Argentina) issued a statement in May 2002, endorsing the Idaho Joint Memorial and FEVA's respective declarations on a future peace process and the self-determination of the Basque Country by peaceful means, while rejecting ETA's methods.

In addition, Guillermo Canut, the then-president of the Basque club Zazpirak Bat from Rosario (Argentina) and former vice president of FEVA (2002–2004), wrote an article titled "El Camino hacia la Libertad" (The Way to Freedom), in the homeland newspaper *Gara* (January 21, 2005) defining the Ibarretxe Plan as "an irrevers-

12 Idaho's involvement in Basque politics is not new. For example, in 1972, the Idaho Joint Memorial No. 115 condemned the Franco's regime and urged peace and democracy in the Basque Country.

13 See Totoricagüena 2005, 265–87.

ible process" and the best way to achieve more freedom and peace: "There are not threats, decrees, tribunals, or jails that could contain the process of self-determination of a people who wishes more freedom and more quality of life for far too long." Other public figures, such as the Basque-American Mayor of Boise, David Bieter, have publicly expressed their support for the Ibarretxe Plan (*Deia,* December 13, 2003). Moreover, during an official visit to the Basque Country, the president of the Buenos Aires Province's Chamber of Deputies, Osvaldo José Mercuri, stated his personal support for the independence of the Basque nation, while recalling the historical ties between the Basques and the Argentineans as well as the significant number of Argentineans of Basque ancestry—an estimate of 15 percent (*El Adelantado de Salamanca,* July 29, 2004).

In October 2004, the Chamber of Deputies and the Senate of the Province of Buenos Aires received President Ibarretxe according to protocols reserved for heads of state. Deputies and Senators officially expressed their support for the Ibarretxe Plan (*Deia,* October 27, 2004). Similarly, in October 2006, the Senate of the Republic of Chile unanimously passed an institutional resolution supporting a Basque peace process in relation to the then latest ETA ceasefire (2006–2007) as well as the right of the Basque people to decide their own future by respecting their "democratic sovereign will" (*Gara,* October 20, 2006). Additionally, the document reflected Chilean history and the significance of Basque immigrants in the construction of a modern nation: "The assimilation of Basques was essential to contribute, without any doubt, to shape our national identity" (idem).

More recently, since October 2007, President Ibarretxe and members of his cabinet have toured Basque communities abroad (e.g., Argentina, Chile, Colombia, the Dominican Republic, Puerto Rico, and the United States) to rally support for a new political proposal or "road map" designed to bring an end to the Basque conflict after the collapse of the latest peace process. This peace proposal was first incorporated in the *lehendakari*'s address to the Basque Parliament on September 28, 2007 (Gobierno Vasco, 2007). The road map, sponsored by the Basque government, included the offer of a political agreement with the Spanish government and the holding of elections following a plebiscite or consultation in Euskadi on October 25, 2008.

For instance, during the last day of the Basque National Week that took place in Rosario, Argentina on October 7, 2007, Ibarretxe invited the Basque-Argentinean community to participate actively in building the future of the Basque Country: "Those who live in Euskadi have to decide the future, and also those Basques who live abroad" (EuskalKultura.com, October 9, 2007). Similarly, at the Basque clubhouse of Santiago de Chile, on October 9, 2007, Ibarretxe proposed his road map as the best possible way to achieve peace and invited the Basque-Chilean community to get involved in the process because "the diaspora is the eighth province of the Basque Country."

On October 6, 2007, FEVA issued a declaration that endorsed the Basque government's new proposal for peace and democracy "as the only ethical and possible way to resolve the political problem of the Basque People, being conscience that as a People, we, the Basques have the right to decide our own future . . . without being intimidated by the violence of those who wield a Constitution that has been imposed upon us or by those who believe that something valuable can be built by armed violence." The declaration ended with the slogan *Gora Euskadi Askatuta* [Long life to a Free Basque Country] (FEVA, October 6, 2007).

Meanwhile, the Spanish government not only refused to discuss the new political proposal, but also rejected the celebration of the Basque plebiscite.[14] Furthermore, the Spanish Supreme Court declared the plebiscite illegal. During NABO's 2008 convention (Chino, California, August 29–September 1, 2008), its delegates endorsed a new declaration on support of the October 25, 2008, plebiscite that FEVA had previously issued. The authors of the text argued that "The Basque People is one of the oldest in Europe. It is a mature People, with its own identity, and it has the right to be consulted in order to be able to decide its own future. In the twenty-first century, projects of cohabitation between different Peoples cannot be planned from imposition but from free adhesion while taking into consideration the opinion of its citizenship, expressed democratically and free" (*Deia,* October 23, 2008).

This is one of the first times, if not the first time, that NABO has passed—though not unanimously—a political declaration regarding homeland affairs. Representatives of the Basque government as well as of the EAJ-PNV were present at the meeting during which the discussion took place, which clearly might have coerced the freedom of expression of some of the delegates. The declaration was also ratified by the Federation of Basque-Uruguayan Institutions and the Federation of Basque Centers of Venezuela as well as the Basque clubs of São Paolo (Brazil), Santiago de Chile and Valparaiso (Chile), Bogota (Colombia), Mexico, D.F. (Mexico), Asuncion (Paraguay), Lima (Peru), and Montevideo (Uruguay). Finally, the Basque government respected the decision of the Spanish Supreme Court and decided not to convoke the consultation.

Significantly, FEVA and NABO as well as the aforementioned Basque clubs define themselves as apolitical and nonpartisan institutions. Do FEVA and NABO consider, for example, self-determination and the achievement of peace and freedom to be Basque nationalist partisan demands? Or do they consider them instead to be intrinsic rights of the Basque people, and consequently, nonpartisan? I leave the question open for the moment, as this issue will be addressed in more detail in

---

14 If the plebiscite had taken place, the citizens of the Basque Autonomous Community of Euskadi would have been asked the following questions: "Do you agree to support a negotiated end to violence, if ETA declares unequivocally its wish to put an end to violence once and for all?" and "Do you agree to the initiation by all Basque political parties, without exclusions, of a negotiation process to reach a Democratic Agreement on the right of the Basque People to decide their own future, and to the holding of a Referendum on the aforementioned Agreement before the end of 2010?"

chapter 5. This self-proclaimed apolitical and nonpartisan dimension of the Basque institutional diaspora constitutes, if not a cornerstone of Basque diaspora identity discourse, an official rhetorical stand that has little to do with the reality of many diaspora institutions abroad as we will see in the coming chapters.

A Peaceful and a Positive Image Abroad: The World Congress Declarations

Basque political violence becomes central to the discourses created by government representatives in relation to the Basque diaspora. The Basque government attempts to circumvent the consequences of ETA's violence by promoting a peaceful image abroad (see Watson, 2008). ETA is seen as a major obstacle to this goal, according to different sociological opinion polls carried out by the Basque government (e.g., see Gobierno Vasco 1983, 2005a, and 2005b) and by Eusko Ikaskuntza, the Society of Basque Studies (Baxok et al. 2006). That is, according to those sociological studies, there is an ever-present over saturation of the political dimension in the homeland over other aspects—for instance, cultural or economical.

The Basque government establishes direct correlations between promoting peace abroad and achieving a positive social image and status abroad, as well as between achieving peace and achieving a new political framework, such as the New Political Statute, for the future political relationship between the Basque Country and Spain. Consequently, one of the goals of the Basque government is for the diaspora to convey to their countries of residence a peaceful and socioeconomically modern society. The government invites the diaspora not only to proclaim its commitment to the homeland's right to self-determination, but also to have an active role in international politics by promoting the "true" Basque Country's self-image as postmodern, peaceful, and tolerant.

For example, the post-Francisco Franco Basque president, Carlos Garaikoetxea (1980–1984), was one of the first Basque leaders to provide a statement regarding the role of the diaspora in promoting a peaceful Basque image while also conveying the wish of the Basque people to achieve peace: "I want to proclaim before you all that the reality of the country is one in which the immense majority of men and women ardently desire peace and detest violence, and they pursue with equal earnestness their national liberties" (at the First Basque American Congress, Donostia-San Sebastián, September 1982, *Basque Studies Program Newsletter,* 1982). In 1983, President Garaikoetxea then traveled to Panama, Venezuela, and Colombia within the framework of the bicentennial birth anniversary of Basque descendant Simón Bolívar, the Liberator of Latin America. The purpose of his trip was to renew ties and to express gratitude to those countries that have received Basque migrants, while conveying a peaceful message: "The oldest nation of Europe, the Basque Country, fights for its national liberties . . . However, minority groups of our country still think that Basque national liberties can only be obtained through violence . . . In contrast to the image of violence that minority actions could project . . . there is a reality of a country that has chosen the weapons of peace and the democratic fight to obtain the self-government of the Basque nation . . . There is a reality of a peaceful and solidarian country" (Gobierno Vasco 1983). Garaikoetxea was received by the three American countries with the same honors of a head of state (Gobierno Vasco 1983, 11).

Later on, during the 1999 Second World Congress of Basque Communities, President Ibarretxe stated that "We have to get across to the world that the Basque people are a hard-working and peace-loving people, over and above all the cliché's that are being branded about us around the world . . . You are extraordinary ambassadors of this value that the Basque society has" (Gobierno Vasco 2000, 23). More recently, in January 2007, the government signed an agreement with the BAC Association of Basque Municipalities to channel a process of citizens' participation to contribute to the resolution of the Basque conflict. Within this framework, the initiative of Citizens' Participation for Building Peace or Konpondu (To solve) provided an online space at the government's site, www.konpondu.net, for the Basques abroad to articulate their opinions—an e-participatory democracy—regarding a peace process, which later would be taken to the Basque Parliament for consideration (*Euskal Etxeak,* 2006, 22–24).

The government's calls for the diaspora to play the role of the Basque Country's ambassadors have been answered on multiple occasions as diaspora Basques are confronted by daily news that almost exclusively associates Basques with violence. There has been a common interest for both homeland and diaspora to overcome such a negative identification and stereotype by promoting a collective positive image. According to Jolanta A. Drzewiecka, labels "are used strategically to assert different positionalities and rights of the collective 'we' in specific situations . . . to accomplish a variety of goals" (2002, 8). In this sense, diaspora Basques and homeland Basques perceive "terrorist label" as an obstacle for establishing a constant positive collective identity. This has provoked the reaction of diaspora Basques from an individual level to a more organized defense to confront those assumed false public accusations by portraying the Basques as "peace lovers" while disengaging the collectivity of Basques from the violent actions of a minority.

According to several authors (e.g., Tajfel 1978, ed., 1982; Calhoun, ed. 1994), the acquisition and maintenance of a positive social status and self-image for emigrant groups is essential for their identity promotion within their host societies and the potential affiliation of the members to a specific group. For example, the Basque club of North Queensland (Australia) states its frustration by acknowledging that "Unfortunately for our club very few people in the wider community are aware of the Basque people and our culture. Most of the Australian media coverage regarding Basques focuses on a negative extremist minority group ETA and their terrorism in Spain" (North Queensland Basque club, http://basqueclubnq.com).

After the terrorist attacks in Madrid on March 11, 2004, which resulted in nearly two hundred deaths, the Spanish government rushed to blame ETA, and continued to do so, even after a group linked to Al-Qaeda claimed responsibility for the terrorist attacks. The *New York Times* opened the following day's front page with an article titled, "10 bombs shatter trains in Madrid, killing 192: 1,400 are hurt—top suspects are Basques and Al-Qaeda," while on Page 1 a report stated, "Rush-hour blasts kill 192 on Madrid trains: Basques first blamed, but Al-Qaeda role claimed" (March 12, 2004). On March 13, 2004, the newspaper carried similar headlines: "Bombings in Madrid: Spanish officials divided of whom to blame for train attacks: Basques or Islamists." The use of the term "Basque" instead of the term "ETA" created certain public distress in the Basque-American community. New York–based Basque organizations—the Society of Basque Studies in America (1979–2013), the Basque International Cultural Center, and the Eusko Etxea of New York (the oldest Basque club in the United States, established in 1913; see Oiarzabal, Sebastián and Aguirre, forthcoming)—sent a letter to the editor of the paper, but it was never published. The letter reads as follows, "It's time to stop maligning Basques . . . Let's get it straight: Basques are NOT terrorists, Basques are a peaceful people . . . Please do not confuse Basques with ETA, nor Irish with IRA [Irish Republican Army], nor any other culture with a terrorist group . . . We wish the media would show the true response of Basques to ETA, to Al-Qaeda and to the bombing of Madrid" (Eusko Etxea of New York, www.eeny.org; emphasis in original).

Moreover, the California-based International Basque Organization for Human Rights (IBO) also sent a letter to the *New York Times* editor in protest for the use of the generic term "Basque" to refer to a particular group "ETA," while rejecting the use of ETA by the Spanish government as a tool to discredit the Basques in the homeland and in the diaspora: "What the Spanish government is trying to do is to strip the Basques of their right to self-determination, a right enshrined in the UN's charter" (IBO, www.euskojustice.org). Significantly, NABO maintained itself outside this polemic and did not state an opinion on the matter (for further discussion on the *New York Times* coverage on the Basques, see Zabaleta 1999).

On a previous occasion, in a public event in Oklahoma on January 31, 2004, Senator John Kerry, and former Democratic candidate to the 2004 U.S. Presidency, while referring to the IRA, compared the Basques and Sikhs to terrorist organizations. IBO also sent a letter to Senator Kerry seeking a public apology for defining Basques as terrorists. IBO representative Alejandro Eguia-Lis stated that "Nothing could be further from the truth; the majority of Basque people both within the Basque Country and abroad reject ETA's violence, and it is unfair to bundle all of us Basques under the label of 'terrorist supporter" (February 9, 2004; IBO, www.euskojustice.org). The Basque government also requested that Senator Kerry rectify his statement on the Basques (*El Correo,* February 11, 2004; *Deia,* February 15, 2004). Senator Kerry sent an apology letter, stating, "It has [been] brought to my attention that remarks I made . . . gave the false impression that people of Basque heritage condone terrorism. I regret that the imprecision of my statement led to this misunderstanding. I should have referred more specifically to Basque Fatherland and Liberty (aka ETA), a U.S. State Department designated foreign terrorist. I realize that, like me, the vast majority of Basques in the United States and worldwide abhor terrorism, and I am sorry for the offense caused by my comment" (February 24, 2004, IBO, www.euskojustice.org).

Finally, the government's demands for promotion of a peaceful image of Basque society reached a high point when institutional leaders of the Basque diaspora issued an Institutional Declaration that explicitly condemned ETA and its actions for the first time ever, at the Third World Congress of Basque Communities (Vitoria-Gasteiz, July 14–18, 2003), which was attended by one hundred and fifty institutional diaspora leaders from nineteen countries. At the inaugural ceremony, President Ibarretxe requested a direct response from the diaspora to ETA's "terrible and inhumane violence" in order to prevent the image of the homeland abroad from being further distorted. Ibarretxe stated:

> You are Euskadi's face to the world. We are judged internationally by the efforts that you carry out. The image of Euskadi in the world has been torpedoed, manipulated, and twisted. How is it that such a peaceful and hard-working nation like the Basque people has been so viciously depicted as a nation of controversy, a nation wrecked by the savage violence of a senseless few? You've seen the harm brought about by ETA violence. What an enormously damaging and unjust international image this gives to Euskadi and the Basque people. You are the image of Euskadi in the world and it is our job to let the world know who we really are: a peaceful hard-working people, not the other conflictive stereotype which some self-interested people seem to want to spread, based mainly on the terrible and inhumane violence perpetrated by ETA. (Gobierno Vasco 2004, 32)

On the last day of the congress, an Institutional Declaration, theoretically endorsed by "all" delegates, was issued. The initial draft of the declaration was introduced by the Argentinean/FEVA delegation. FEVA had already issued a similar declaration in June 2003 condemning those who used violence—that is, ETA—and those who persecuted the Basque Country, closed down newspapers, and illegalized political parties—a reference to the Spanish government—while supporting the Ibarretxe Plan: "We don't want through violence neither the freedom for Euskadi not the unity of Spain; not only the goals have to be just but also the means" (Centro Vasco Euzko Etxea, www.centrovasco.com). However, as it will be discussed below, the majority of the delegates did not confer, vote, or endorse the declaration. The declaration addressed the main concerns raised by Ibarretxe's inaugural address:

> Our condemnation of violence of all types; naturally, this includes ETA perpetrated violence, to which we demand an immediate end. As delegates to this Congress, we stress that violence inflicts enormous damages to the personal and social life of Basque women and men and to the image of the Basque people as a whole in our countries of residence. With the same responsibility, we ask people in positions of authority in Euskadi to initiate dialogue—the only valid instrument for resolving differences and conflicts—in order to achieve democratic and peaceful coexistence, as well as economic and social development for our people . . . We look forward to a peaceful future, economic and social development, and recognition as a nation by all international institutions. (Gobierno Vasco 2004, 261)

The diaspora took on the role of promoting the "true" image of the Basque Country by going a step forward and explicitly condemning ETA and demanding its end, for the first time ever—though the 2003 Declaration was not the first overtly political declaration made by the Basque diaspora as an institutionally organized "entity."[15] Even more, the diaspora representatives positioned themselves in favor of dialogue in order to end the Basque conflict, while favoring the right to self-determination of the Basque nation. The diaspora representatives believed that the Basque conflict was a political conflict that went beyond ETA's violence. Consequently, dialogue was the key to the resolution of a political conflict.

However, what about the so-called apolitical and nonpartisan character of the Basque institutional diaspora? The politicization of the Basque diaspora was clearer than ever. The 2003 declaration associated peace with the dismantling of ETA and a negotiated political end to the historical conflict, recurrent demands of the EAJ-PNV. In theory, the diaspora, as a whole, consequently sided itself not only with the vast majority of the Basque society, but also with the moderate Basque nationalist movement, while turning away from the most radical wing of Basque nationalism, which overtly supports ETA's goals. In the eyes of the Basque society and the rest of the world, this declaration was the diaspora's unequivocal disapproval of ETA as a whole. Irremediably, the diaspora became another participating voice in relation to the so-called Basque conflict.

The declaration finally incorporated into the congress's proceedings was never a product of a common consent agreed upon by the majority of the participants. In fact, many did not welcome the draft, and some delegates were angered by it.[16] In particular, the delegates' objections were directed to the "political nature" of the document because of the inclusion of the reference to ETA. Some delegates stated that they did not have authorization from their board of directors to sign a "political document." However, there were no objections raised about the demands for political dialogue as a means of attaining peace, while respecting the will of the Basques to decide their own future and understanding that there were many more sides to the violence besides ETA—and thereby implicating Spanish state. Were those not considered political enough in nature?

Furthermore, other delegates believed that the draft was a political endorsement of the Basque government and particularly of its main party, the EAJ-PNV. These delegates did not want to get involved in partisan politics, manifesting their

---

15 The 1999 World Congress Institutional Declaration, endorsed by representatives from eighteen countries, was also imbued with political connotations. It also addressed the need for peace and self-government, but it did not make any reference to ETA. It recognized the Basque people as a sovereign nation, without a state, but with the right to decide its own future. At the same time, the diaspora requested that the international community support the rights of the Basque people: "We wish for the Basque Country to reach at the beginning in this new century a situation of coexistence in peace and freedom with the level of self-government that the Basque people wish to obtain. Many of us are a result of two centuries of political conflict and we want to be the last children of Basque exile . . . With the same end in mind we require from state governments, supra-state institutions and international bodies, respect for the individual and collective rights of the Basque Country and support for the decisions that Basque society may make regarding its future, making it possible in the mean time to have a direct presence in these institutions and efficient overseas projection to guarantee the defense of its identity as a nation in the international arena" (Gobierno Vasco, 2000, 127).

16 The different positions are not identified by name or delegation in order to protect the anonymity and confidentiality of the participants. As an observer, I took part in the working commission, where conversations took place regarding the institutional declaration.

concerns about the diaspora becoming an exclusive or nearly exclusive patrimony of the Basque government and the EAJ-PNV. Finally, some delegates believed that signing the declaration meant going against the spirit of their institutions—the *homes* for *all* Basques, including ETA political refugees. Delegates, particularly from South America, had a long history of welcoming any Basques, regardless of their political orientation and background into their associations.[17] According to some delegates, signing the declaration would be like "hanging a 'not welcome sign' at our *euskal etxeak* doors. It would mean discriminating against Basques for seeking an independent homeland." Facing the reluctance of most of the delegates, the representatives from Argentina, promoters of the draft, strongly stated, "If we don't approve it unanimously, it will damage the diaspora greatly. If we don't sign it, it will go against us. We are not guilty for signing the document but those who promote violence. Violence is the worst problem for the Basques abroad as Basques are increasingly identified with violence."

Finally, the initial draft was presented as the final declaration, and consequently published in the congress's proceedings. At the closing ceremony, Ibarretxe told the diaspora delegates, "For the next four years, [your] main goal must be to transmit to the world that we are a peaceful, hard-working nation, and that we want to live in peace . . . Thanks to you, we'll be recognized in the world as people with good hearts" (*Deia,* July 19, 2003b).

On the one hand, the Basque government and the Basque nationalist parties EAJ-PNV and Eusko Alkartasuna (EA in its Spanish acronym) welcomed the declaration. The Basque Minister of Justice Joseba Azkarraga publicly praised the Basque diaspora for taking an active approach "as agents of justice and freedom." Azkarraga added, "So, the Basque nation becomes synonymous with well-being and hope in the future; not of violence and resignation. So, you can tell our historic truth . . . With your testimony you will help your countries of residence to have a more exact view of the Basque nation. You will offer, from your personal and collective experiences, the real version of what we are and what we want to be" (*Deia,* July 19, 2003c).[18]

On the other hand, representatives from the pro-independence political coalition Sozialista Abertzaleak (inheritor of the historical Herri Batasuna) accused then-President Ibarretxe and Josu Legarreta, then director for relations with the Basque communities, of "manipulating" the Basque centers and "utilizing the diaspora

---

17 According to ETA prisoners and refugees' associations, such as Presoen Aldeko Taldeak or Amnistiaren Aldeko Mugimendua, and Spanish security forces, the number of refugees could be in the low thousands.

18 Nearly three years later, in an interview by Federico Borrás (Asociación Vasca Urrundik from Paraná, Argentina) for his veteran Basque Radio Program Presencia Vasca (Basque Presence) (February 2, 2006), Azkarraga was once again asked about the role that the Basque diaspora needed to play in relation to the Basque conflict. He insisted on his previous arguments: "The Basque diaspora attitude has to be the one of continually transmitting the real image of our country, outside of our [homeland] borders: To continually transmit to Argentina that the Basque people are a hardworking and peaceful people who wish peace and prosperity for their citizens . . . The best ambassadors that we have, and I will encourage them very much to keep up with this work, because it is essential at this moment."

politically."[19] Consequently, they called for the resignation of Josu Legarreta as they argued that the Institutional Declaration was never approved or signed by the majority of the delegates (*Gara*, July 19, 20, and 27, 2003).[20]

What are the potential implications of the 2003 declaration for the diaspora and for its relationships with the Basque government? First of all, the declaration demonstrates an unbalanced equilibrium of powers within the institutional Basque diaspora, where FEVA has attempted to place itself in a privileged position by displaying a great strategic strength within the diaspora. (Nearly 50 percent of the government's financial help was directed to Basque centers in Argentina from 2004 to 2007. However, it is also true that the majority of the Basque associations abroad are in Argentina.) Certain leaders in FEVA have become tactical allies of the then Directorate for Relations with the Basque Communities, and by extension allies of the EAJ-PNV, which controlled both the Directorate and the General Secretariat for Foreign Action until May 2009. However, this tactical alliance is related to who controls the presidency of FEVA as the policies and the relationships with the Basque government and with a non-nationalist administration depend on it.

Second, the declaration demonstrates the political divisiveness of the diaspora. The institutional diaspora is not a community free of tensions and disagreements. This divisiveness is not black and white. That is to say, it is not as much about being in favor of ETA or against ETA, but rather about ETA being used explicitly for partisan purposes, which goes against the principles of many of the diaspora associations—inclusiveness, openness, and, in theory, nonpartisan allegiances and apolitical principles. These divisions tend to neutralize any preconceived inter-

19 Sozialista Abertzaleak has had a long nationalist political history under previous names. On May 23, 2002, the Spanish government passed the Law of Political Parties in order to outlaw Batasuna, as it was considered part of ETA. On March 28, 2003, the Spanish Supreme Court outlawed Herri Batasuna (created in 1978), Euskal Herritarrok (created in 1998 as a substitute of Herri Batasuna), and Batasuna (created in 2001 as an internal renovation of Herri Batasuna). The Basque government has constantly opposed the illegalization and the disbandment of Batasuna's Basque Parliament Group. Batasuna became known as Sozialista Abertzaleak in order to retain parliamentary representation. This group occupied its seats at the Basque Parliament until new elections were called on April 17, 2005. As an illegal organization representing an outlawed party (Batasuna), a new coalition was formed, inheritor of the Basque nationalist-left ideology, called the Communist Party of the Basque Territories (EHAK by its Basque acronym). EHAK obtained nine seats, two more than Sozialista Abertzaleak. EHAK and the historical political party, Basque Nationalist Action (ANV by its Spanish acronym), which participated in the 2007 municipal elections, were banned for their links with Batasuna in September 2008. In 2009 another two parties, Democracy Three Million (D3M by its Basque acronym) and Askatasuna (Freedom), representatives of the Basque nationalist-left movement, were forbidden by the judges to take part in Basque Autonomous Community Parliamentary elections (March 1, 2009) for their links with ETA and Batasuna. This was the first time that the Basque nationalist-left movement did not take part in those elections. The Spanish Court System has also outlawed between 1998 and 2005 other Basque nationalist-left or pro-independence associations, such as the youth organization Jarrai and its successors Haika and Segi, as well as Gestoras pro-Amnistia in 2001 and its successor Askatasuna—a group that was created in 1976 to advocate for the amnesty of ETA prisoners. Furthermore, the Spanish Court System has closed down Batasuna's newspaper Egin (created in 1977-July 1998; today's Gara), the Ardi Beltza magazine (March 2001), and the only Basque-language newspaper *Egunkaria* (February 2003) under allegations that they are part of ETA.

20 On October 23, 2003, in a session of the Basque Parliament, Joseba Álvarez, member of the group Sozialista Abertzaleak, requested an official explanation about the polemics surrounding the declaration. On behalf of the Basque government, Josu Jon Imaz—the then minister of industry, trade, and tourism—concisely explained that the declaration was approved by the congress, and that "only one person disagreed [with it]" (Parlamento Vasco, Official Transcript 031024).

pretation of the diaspora as a homogeneous and passive entity. It shows that the Basque diaspora is as plural, even politically, as the Basque homeland itself.

Diaspora Basques with Spanish citizenship, for example, have exhibited trends in voting patterns similar to those of homeland Basques at the time of homeland elections, such as the BAC Parliamentary elections. The number of registered diaspora voters as of the 2005 BAC elections was 38,270. Since the return to democracy to Spain, the EAJ-PNV has been the single most voted-for party in both the diaspora and the homeland (see *Euskal Etxeak*, June 2005).

Basque political representatives often campaign "abroad" seeking the vote of diaspora Basques. For example, during the 2009 BAC Parliamentary elections pre-campaign events, members of the EAJ-PNV, PSOE, and PP travelled to the Spanish Mediterranean city of Benidorm to meet with the local Basque community, which is estimated to be around eight thousand members. Those members are still registered with their respective Basque town councils, and, consequently, have the right to vote in the different Basque elections. Within the Spanish state, Benidorm is one of the largest enclaves of Basque voters outside the BAC. The number of registered diaspora voters as of the 2009 BAC elections was 43,546.[21] In close dispute for a parliamentary seat in the province of Álava/Araba between the PSE and the nationalist EA, the diaspora vote gave the seat to the PSE, allowing Patxi López to be the new lehendakari or president of Euskadi with the support of the Popular Party and PSE members of parliament.

The 2003 declaration and all the surrounding events that took place during and after its approval symbolize a potentially destabilizing episode of the recent intra-diaspora institutional history, as well as of the short history of the relationship between the Basque government and the diaspora. However, no official complaints were raised against the government and the directorate. Whether the particular benefits that the declaration might have generated overcame the potential risks of issuing such a disruptive declaration could only be measured with time—for example, in the 2007 congress.

During the celebration of the 2007 World Congress, which was attended by eighteen countries, the Peruvian delegation presented a draft of a declaration to be discussed by the delegates. The draft endorsed five points: to support peace; to reject violence while expressing solidarity with victims; to support "the right of the Basque nation to determine and develop its historical destiny freely and responsibly"; to support President Ibarretxe, as there was back then an open judicial case against him for his talks with the banned political party, Batasuna, during the lat-

21 According to the Spanish Electoral Census of Absent Residents (i.e., Spanish Citizens residing abroad) as of January 1, 2009, there were 43,546 Basques (3,467 from Araba; 23,287 from Bizkaia; and 16,792 from Gipuzkoa) residing in twelve countries (Argentina, Australia, Canada, Chile, France, Germany, Italy, Mexico, the United Kingdom, the United States, Uruguay, and Venezuela) with the right to vote. Only 6,857 (i.e., 15.74 percent) voted in the BAC Parliamentary elections of March 2009.

est ETA ceasefire; and to transmit to their countries of settlement the reality of the Basque Country—"peaceful, democratic, and hardworking inclusive society."[22]

Delegates did not reach any consensus regarding the declaration's draft, and it was not approved. The delegates opposing the draft thought of it as being too political, while stating that they did not have any mandate from the board of directors and membership to sign such a politicized document. However, the proposal of the Four-Year Plan for Institutional Action 2008–2011, which included a commitment of Basque centers to promote peace, was approved. Iñaki Aguirre, then general secretary for foreign action, manifested his "uneasiness" to the convention delegates for failing to reach an agreement on the declaration's draft, which defended and promoted peace, freedom, and coexistence along the lines of Ibarretxe's strategic goals. But Aguirre respected the decision that the delegates took.

Therefore, I can conclude by saying that the 2003 declaration was a timely though experimental diaspora incursion into homeland politics, and if there were any plan laid out for continuance in the future, it did not seem to have worked at the 2007 congress or for that matter at the 2011 congress. On this occasion, similar arguments were raised and similar and bitter discussions among delegates ocurred at the time of including an institutional declaration during the 2011 World Congress. Finally, the declaration was not approved due to the lack of consensus (see Gobierno Vasco 2012; Oiarzabal 2012b).

Conclusions

For nearly three decades, the different Basque administrations—all dominated by nationalist parties and coalitions—have constructed a set of past and future-oriented discourses in relation to the Basque diaspora, which aimed to maintain national consciousness among Basques abroad by playing into an emotional dimension of collective identity. Those discourses have re-created and delivered a nationalist interpretation of Basque identity and culture to the diaspora. However, the diaspora has already been reproducing to some extent and in similar terms, consciously or not, a nationalist perspective of Basque identity, territorial homeland, nation, and traditions inherited from previous waves of Basque migration, particularly related to the Spanish Civil War and Basque nationalist exile.

In a sense, Basque government's discourses fall on a fertile diaspora soil, where Basque nationalism is not unknown to many Basque individuals and institutions. Particularly in Basque communities of countries such as Argentina, Chile or Venezuela, there is a widespread idealization of the EAJ-PNV as today's main or even *sole* guardian and guarantor of Basque liberties as it was once during the Spanish Civil

---

22 In this regard, FEVA issued a declaration in support of Ibarretxe and against any criminal investigation (*Deia*, October 29, 2006; *Euskal Etxeak*, 2006, 24). In February 2010, Ibarretxe was cleared of any wrongdoing for talking to Batasuna representatives by the Spanish judicial system.

War and Franco's dictatorship. Although, political activism in the institutionalized diaspora and Basque nationalist influence is evident as early as the late nineteenth century, the impact of the discourse of the Basque government and homeland political parties has been exponentially accelerated by the utilization of rapid technologies of transportation, such as the airplane, and communication, such as the Internet and e-mail.

Government's discourses re-create the idea of a unified territorial homeland as a seven-province nation, with a right to self-determination as paramount for the protection and promotion of Basque identity, Basque culture, and the ancestral homeland, while enhancing the imagination of diaspora Basques as part of a wider imagined Basque community: that is, a Basque "long distance nationalism," understood as "the ideology of belonging that extends homeland politics into transnational social fields," which "links together people living in various geographic locations and motivates them to action in relation to an ancestral territory and its government" (Anderson 1991, 327). This long-distance nationalism is the direct impact of technological advancements that contribute to connect the diaspora and the homeland across space and time.

The government also promotes a postmodern, peaceful, and positive image abroad as an attempt to close the "knowledge gap" and the existing disjuncture between homeland and diaspora. New telecommunication technologies, such as satellite television and the Internet, are taken as prime instruments to eventually close such a gap. In a way, those technologies facilitate the renewal of collective memory of diaspora Basques. Consequently, the government bestows upon the diaspora the role of an active agent for the promotion of a peaceful Basque Country and for the defense of the right of its people to self-determination. Thus, the diaspora becomes an instrument guaranteeing the survival of the identity, culture, and homeland of the Basques. The declarations made at the world congresses are diaspora attempts to establish one institutional voice by addressing issues almost exclusively related to the homeland.

The formation of a new administration by the Socialist Party of Euskadi (PSE), supported by the Spanish nationalist PP, might modify the relations and policies toward the Basque communities abroad and its institutions. Would the Socialist government actually reinforce Basque "nationalist" imaginaries in its dealing with the diaspora? Or would it reinforce the Basque imaginary as a region of Spain and reinforce the Spanish national identity of the diaspora? In Paddy Woodworth's words, "the present moment offers a test of maturity for Basque democracy. Can the EAJ-PNV be pluralistic and plastic enough in their definition of identity to see the new government as simply a different expression of Basqueness, and not demonize it as an imposition of Spanishness? And can the new government be generous and sensitive enough to recognize and respect the nation-building achieved by the EAJ-PNV? Instead of attempting to dismantle that nation, can it give it a fresh infusion of broader and deeper life?" (2009, 26). These open questions call for a deeper analysis of the relation between the PSE and the diaspora, which goes beyond the goal of this book. Having said that, for the past years, the public statements made by the Socialist administration, which ended in 2012, called for continuing support Basque communities abroad, while emphasizing the (Basque nationalist) "de-politicization" of those communities and institutions as the new administration was not in the business of identity politics (*El Correo,* May 28, 2009). The Socialist administration has been highly critical of the Basque Nationalist Party for its assumed "patrimonization" of the Basque society and the diaspora as a way to homogenize the perception of Basque identity. But, if anything, the Basque diaspora is about identity. Was this "de-politicization" in fact a new "politicization" of the diaspora?

(04)

Digital and

Nationalism Online Self-representation

In this chapter, I address Basque diaspora discourses as displayed on their institutional websites. I focus particularly on the construction of a Basque nationalist discourse and on the Basque diaspora organizations' own self-representations by examining the sites' audio-visual and graphic content. In a sense, those discourses also re-create, to some extent, some of the main aspects of the Basque government's discourses on identity, homeland, and nation as analyzed previously. In what ways does the Basque institutional diaspora's use of the Internet help to foster an online digital nationalism? What is the image that the Basque diaspora portrays online? And what does the Basque diaspora attempt to express and promote?

Digital "Banal" Nationalism

Diasporic Symbolism: Designing Identity[1]

Michael Billig's influential study on national identity introduced the concept of "banal nationalism" as the "ideological habits which enable the established nations of the West to be reproduced." He states that "National identity in established nations is remembered because it is embedded in routines of life, which constantly

---

1 A version of this section was published as "Basque Diaspora Digital Nationalism: Designing 'Banal' Identity," in Andoni Alonso and Pedro J. Oiarzabal (eds. 2010), *Diasporas in the New Media Age: Identity, Politics and Community*. Reno: University Nevada Press.

remind, or 'flag', nationhood" (1995, 6, 38). That is to say, *banal nationalism* refers to mundane daily and nearly subliminal events that promote national identity without people really thinking about it. However, being mundane or subliminal does *not* equate to being insignificant or meaningless.

Banal nationalism also applies to diaspora communities. For example, everyday objects and commodities from "back home," or from the "old country," re-create familiar nostalgic images while helping to evoke memories of belonging and identity (see Cohen 2004; Davis 1999; and Geisler 2005). They are "unconscious" and "unnoticed" reminders of nationhood, "preventing the danger of collective amnesia" (Billig 2003, 133). Symbols, particularly national symbols (*the* flag, *the* anthem, *the* language, monuments, clothing, or food), play a role in creating, maintaining, and expressing individual and collective identity, as well as providing a sentimental or emotional attachment and identification of individuals with the group. In other words, as Anthony D. Smith (1992, 77–78, 160) argues,

> National symbols, customs, and ceremonies are the most potent and durable aspects of nationalism . . . that evoke instant emotional responses from all strata of the community . . . By means of ceremonies, customs and symbols every member of a community participates in the life, emotions and virtues of that community and through them, re-dedicates him or herself to its destiny. By articulating and making tangible the ideology of nationalism and the concepts of the nation ceremonial and symbolism help to assure the continuity of history and destiny . . . Through ceremonies and symbols the individual identity is bound up with the collective identity.

According to authors such as Richard D. Alba (1985), Herbert J. Gans (1979, 1994), and Peter Kivisto and Ben Nefzger (1993), symbols are the last vestiges of ethnic identity among assimilated groups to their hostlands. For example, Gans describes the phenomenon of consumption of ethnic symbols by third-generation individuals born in the United States as "symbolic ethnicity" or "leisure-time ethnicity." According to the author, they look for "easy and intermittent ways of expressing their identity, ways that do not conflict with other ways of life," such as the celebration of festivals, commemorations, cuisine, and parades (1979, 6).

Regarding diaspora Basques and particularly the descendants of the emigrant generation, Lisa M. Corcostegui argues that diaspora Basques "increasingly rely on symbols to formulate and bolster their ethnic identity" (1999, 250). Focusing, for instance, on Basque dance as one of the key elements of Basque identity in the diaspora, the author argues that dance "as physical movement is itself indicative of vitality, an image of Basque cultural vitality is conveyed through dance. Images of Basque dancers are often used to signal Basqueness. The website of the Ventura County Basque club [Thousand Oaks, California] is an example of this. Pictures of dancers figure prominently on the page, although the club does not have a dance group" (ibid., 251).

Symbols help diaspora Basques to express or externalize publicly and privately their own identity showing individuality but referring to a collectivity. Festivals are a visible public expression, while private expressions might include homeland decorations, such as Pablo Picasso's *Guernica* painting, or personal adornments, such as Basque-themed tattoos. For example, Basque and Basque-American identities are represented by the use of a large inventory of symbols (see Douglass and Zulaika 2007). In the Basque-American diaspora one can observe *ikurriñas* (Basque flags); *lauburus* (four-headed crosses); bumper stickers with messages such as, "Thank God I'm Basque," "Living with a Basque builds Character," "Basque-Euskalduna," or "Proud to be Basque"; and Basque custom license plates. If there is any public space in the United States where the Basques have re-created an identity landscape saturated with Basque symbols, it is without a doubt Boise, Idaho's "Basque Block."

An examination of these symbols may assist in showing their emotional impact. The *lauburus*—four-headed crosses or solar swastikas—are not exclusive Basque symbols, but are shared by other cultures. However, it is considered one of the most popular and universal Basque symbols. In addition, the lauburu symbolizes the four Basque provinces that lie within Spain according to current Basque nationalists (see figure 4.1).

Figure 4.1. Examples of *lauburus* and Basque (waving) flags displayed on diaspora sites.

Since 2005, the Basque club of San Francisco has provided a space on its website, www.basqueclub.com/Plates.htm, where it displays "Eusko Plates" or Basque motor vehicle license plates. They refer to names of cities in the Basque Country, first names, surnames, and slogans. Dirk Kempthorne, the then-governor of the state of Idaho, even authorized a license plate to honor the Basque heritage in Idaho, becoming the first of its kind in the history of the country. The plate refers to an almost vanished rural American West sheepherding industry where Basques played a significant part for many decades. From April 2006 to July 2011, the license plate was available to the public, but it was discontinued as it failed to meet minimum sales. A portion of the Idaho Basque plate's fee went to the Cenarrusa Foundation for Basque Culture.

Figure 4.2. Basque license plates or "Eusko Plates."

On the "Basque Block," a central mural is a good example of the saturation of Basque symbols. This descriptive case will introduce the reader to the symbols of banal nationalism that will be discussed in the subsequent passage on banal nationalism in the webscape. The mural combines both Basque and Basque-American history—particularly in relation to Boise and Idaho. "The Basque Mural" was designed by Bill Hueg and sponsored by the Basque Museum and Cultural Center of Boise in 2000 (see figure 4.3). From left to right are references to the Columbus voyages and the involvement of Basques in the "discovery," conquest, and colonization of America; a homeland *baserri* or farmhouse on the top of a green mountain; a fragment of Pablo's Picasso *Guernica* painting—a great majority of Idaho Basques are originally from the province of Bizkaia, particularly the Gernika area; the Tree of Gernika and the Assembly House; the Uberuaga/Aguirre's boardinghouse established in 1903 in Boise; a portrait of Juanita Uberuaga Hormaechea who began teaching Basque dancing in 1947; the Oinkari dancing group of Boise created in 1960; the Boise Saint John's Catholic Cathedral, which illustrates the main religion of the Basque population; a celebration, at the center, of the Basque community of Boise is the San Inazio Festival (July 31) in honor of Basque saint Saint Ignatius of Loyola; Jim Jausoro playing the accordion (he played for the Oinkari from 1947 to 2005, when he passed away); a man lifting a quadrangular stone, a reference to Basque rural sports; and finally, a sheep camp (sheepherding was one of the main occupations of those Basques who emigrated to the United States. In spite of the powerful message conveyed by the mural and its significance for local Basque history, no Basque association website in Boise displays it.

Figure 4.3. Mural by Bill Hueg. Photo by author.

In 2005, the Vale Historic Mural Society in Vale, Oregon, commissioned artist Colleen Mitchell-Veyna to paint four murals dedicated to Basque, Chinese, Hispanic, and Japanese peoples. It depicts Basque symbols, such as the Basque flag, the *lauburu,* a Christian cross, dancers, and a sheep camp, taken as quintessential "Basque" elements in the American West.This banal nationalism is also present on the Basque diaspora webscape. Although the main format of the web is textual, the text cannot be analyzed in isolation while one is exploring and examining the discourses of the Basque diaspora. Consequently, I have examined the textual, audiovisual (i.e., songs that can be listened to online), and graphic (symbols, photos, and maps) aspects of the sites, including their "decoration," a sort of digital banal nationalism that portrays and reinforces certain Basque national representations of identity, nationhood, and homeland. This banal nationalism is evident in 95 percent of Basque symbols displayed on the sites, including the maps, *lauburus,* and *ikurriñas.* In a sense, image-based narratives define the landscape of the Basque diaspora online and help to reconstruct a Basque imagined community by displaying information about "themselves." Arjun Appadurai (1991) calls these image-based narratives "ideoscapes."

Basque nationalist iconography, historical symbols, mythological imagery, and banal ideology, once exclusively identified with a particular homeland party, such as the EAJ- PNV, have passed into the heritage of the Basque people, at home and abroad. The Basque flag and anthem, for instance, which were created in the homeland during the late nineteenth century by Basque nationalists, were made the official flag and anthem of the first Basque government in 1936. They were once again ratified as the official flag and anthem of the government of the BAC in the early 1980s.[2] In the same way, other iconographies forged by the Basque Nationalist Party, such as Aberri Eguna (Day of the Homeland) also passed into the broader Basque nationalist patrimony and to some extent into the general heritage of both the homeland and the diaspora.

In the case of the Basque diaspora online, the multimedia character of the web is exemplified by Flash presentations on homepages. These Flash presentations combine high-quality graphics, music, and text that serve to introduce the various associations' websites. For example, the main upper banner of the Basque club of Valencia's homepage (Carabobo, Venezuela) is represented, in the left corner, by the name of the club and the web address, and the *ikurriña* and the Venezuelan flag with poles crossing, and is flanked by the coats of arms of the Basque Country, Venezuela, and Carabobo, as well as a postal image of the Guggenheim Bilbao Museum and a lauburu. In the right corner, there is a photo of San Juan de Gaztelugatxe—a church on a small island that is joined to the coast by a bridge—and a superimposed Basque word that reads *etxean* (at home). On the upper right side of the banner are another ikurriña and a silhouette of the map of the BAC. At the bottom of the banner there is an image of the Basque clubhouse and a Spanish legend that reads *Bienvenidos al Centro Vasco* (Welcome to the Basque Club; see figure 4.4).

2 Eighteen percent of the sites reproduce the BAC anthem, "Eusko Abendaren Ereserkia."

Figure 4.4. Banner of the Centro Vasco de Valencia's homepage (www.valenciakoeuskoetxea.com/) as of 2006.

Users easily grasp the nationalist displays, which visualize diverse representations of identity. In fact, words, photos, and sounds emphasize each other in the construction of identity discourses throughout the Basque diaspora webscape. The use of particular fonts is quite effective. Early Basque typefaces have been found dating back to the late Middle Ages, and some of those typefaces were recovered in the 1930s. Here there are three examples of different Basque typefaces used by the Basque diaspora online (e.g., Vasca, Vasca Berria TT, and Basque Country 2.0).

Music, images, and colors abound as ornaments, backgrounds, and wallpapers, especially the green, red, and white colors of the Basque flag. For example, the background of the web pages of the Valladolid club's site (Spain, www.geocities.com/guretxoko/) is made up of *ikurriñas* and *lauburus*. Similarly, the wallpaper of the Parisian choir association's site, Anaiki (France, www.anaiki.com/), is a concatenation of *lauburus*. Functional link buttons in the shape of *etxeak* or homes, *baserris, lauburus,* and *ikurriñas* and Navarrese flags, layout styles, and even Basque emoticons[3] or smiley faces, all help to express a specific Basque collective identity online, and by extension a collective identity offline. They embed a Basque particularity and uniqueness into the banal design or decoration of their associations' sites, which set them apart from other communities. The *etxea* and *baserri* symbols are used as the homepage or index page buttons in 15 percent of the total Basque diaspora websites. Figure 4.5 features some examples of Basque symbols: a Basque flag in the shape of an oak tree leaf in reference to the Tree of Gernika—and the Navarrese flags, and Basque coat of arms. Figure 4.6 shows emoticons from the Basque club in Calgary (Canada, www.muturzikin.com/euskalgary.htm), which includes Basque emoticons wearing berets and even a balaclava!

The past and the idyllic rural homeland symbolized by the *baserri* are central to diaspora identity discourse, as evident in 80 percent of the websites I studied. Figure 4.7 provides some examples of images that evoke a much-romanticized view of Basque identity by depicting scenes of the past related to an almost vanished agrarian world.

3 Emoticons or smiley faces are emotional graphics, facial expressions made by the combination of certain keystrokes and used to express feelings visually without words in e-mails and instant messaging.

Figure 4.5. Examples of Basque symbols used as buttons: a Basque flag in the shape of an oak tree leaf in reference to the Tree of Gernika, the Navarrese flags, and Basque coat of arms

Figure 4.6. Emoticons from the Basque club in Calgary, Canada (www.muturzikin.com/euskalgary.htm).

Figure 4.7. Images evoking a much-romanticized view of Basque identity by depicting scenes of the past related to an almost vanished agrarian world.

In addition, 80 percent of Basque diaspora websites offer the visitor a section dedicated to the Basque Country, and a gallery of photos is usually available. Ninety percent of those photos reconstruct a bucolic Basque Country, far from the most modernized and urban aspects of Basque society.

At the same time, the sites also offer images of Basques in "traditional" garments, particularly in dance costumes, which evoke an earlier Basque culture, as shown in figure 4.8.

Figure 4.8. Images of Basques in "traditional" garments, particularly in dance costumes, which evoke an earlier Basque culture.

Contemporary assertions of identification are also found but in a very small proportion, that is, only in 5 percent of all diaspora websites. The image of the Guggenheim Museum in Bilbao monopolizes the contemporariness of Basque identity for the Basque diaspora online. No other contemporary images seem to represent Basque identity as well as Frank Gehry's 1997 museum does. The website of the Basque Educational Organization of San Francisco (United States, www.basqueed.org) displays the following image of the museum (see figure 4.9).

Figure 4.9. Guggenheim Museum, designed by Frank Gehry, in Bilbao, featured on the website of the Basque Educational Organization of San Francisco (United States, www.basqueed.org).

Diaspora Basques are symbolically connected not only to the homeland, but also to their respective hostlands' specific dates, places, names, activities, and events. Eighty percent of the websites portray the "in-betweenness" of the diasporic condition of Basques abroad. They reflect on the dual and non-competing allegiances to homeland and hostlands and on the amalgamation of Basque symbols with the hostlands' symbols (see figure 4.10).

Figure 4.10. Amalgamations of Basque and hostland symbols.

In 2005, the Mexico City Basque club created a new "mascot" called "Coatlitxu" (the Little Snake) in order to merge both millenarian symbols—*coatl* (or snake) from the Aztec culture and *txu*, a Basque-language diminutive. Also, the logo of the first Basque association in China integrates both Basque and Chinese characters and symbols (see figure 4.11).

Figure 4.12 shows the NABO emblem designed by Glenn Heinmiller in 1978. According to *Voice of the Basques*, "The central element in this emblem is the lauburu (green), the universal Basque symbol . . . The top band within the circle is red, center band white and bottom, blue. This symbolizes the importance of being both Basque and American and the nature of the NABO as a grouping of Basque-American Organizations" (*Voice of the Basques* 1977, 8). The emblem symbolizes FEVA as a bridge between the Basque and the Argentinean cultures. However, it does not incorporate any Argentinean symbols. Within the context of the 2008 FEVA elections, Alejo Martin, the candidate of "Basque Clubs for an Alternative" to the presidency of FEVA, argued about the need to add to the federation logo the white and blue colors in representation of Argentina. Figure 4.13, FEVA's new logo, which was created in 2005.

Figure 4.11. Logo of the first Basque association in China integrates Basque and Chinese characters and symbols.

Figure 4.12. NABO's emblem, designed by Glenn Heinmiller in 1978.

Figure 4.13. FEVA's 2006 logo.

Gernika

If any symbol is "universally" recognized as Basque, it is the Tree of Gernika. Gernika, in the province of Bizkaia, has become a symbol of multiple meanings from a local to a global context. It hosts the "sacred" Oak Tree and the Assembly House of

Gernika where the representatives of the Bizkaian territory met for centuries under the rule of consuetudinary laws or fueros until their abolition in 1876 (see Monreal 2005). Pauliina Raento and Cameron J. Watson argue that "by the late nineteenth century, then, Gernika not only came to represent 'Basqueness' or a Basque ethnic identity, but also its political expression, Basque nationalism" (2000, 714). Different representations of the Tree of Gernika and the Assembly House are displayed on Basque diaspora sites (see figure 4.14).

Figure 4.14. Representations of the Tree of Gernika and the Assembly house from Basque diaspora sites.

During the Spanish Civil War, Gernika became the target of one of the first intentional aerial bombings of a civilian population in Europe, achieving substantial human loss and urban destruction. Previously, Francisco Franco's allies had targeted Basque villages and towns such as Durango and Elorrio. Gernika in particular became the single most important event in contemporary Basque history. The event is recognizable on a global scale not only by Basques but by non-Basques as well. The destruction of Gernika and up to some thirty-seven villages and small towns by Nazi Germany in 1937 is constantly used as an identity marker that defines Basqueness and recent Basque history within the context of Franco's victory, dictatorship, and subsequent political and cultural repression against republicans and nationalists.[4] It is estimated that 150,000 Basques, including 25,000 children, went into exile, while an estimated 100,000 were imprisoned, 30,000 were forced labor, and 50,000 died. In 1936, the total population of the Basque provinces in Spain was 1.3 million. Thus, approximately one-fourth of the population was killed, imprisoned, or displaced during the Spanish Civil War.

Sixteen diaspora organizations online re-create Gernika as an enduring historical testament of contemporary collective victimhood and as a space that embodies the historical continuity of Basque liberties, autonomy, political determination, and nationalism. The diaspora discourse on Gernika follows to some extent a romanticized reading of the proto-democratic and egalitarian Basque society symbolized by the Gernika Assembly House and the Gernika Oak Tree, where some representa-

---

4 Among the bombed localities were Amorebieta, Bilbao, Eibar, Galdakao, Mañaria, and Munitibar (Arbatzegi-Gerrikaitz). Sixty years after the bombing of Gernika, Germany officially recognized its involvement in the destruction of Gernika and other Basque localities.

tives of the society met to decide their own future. For example, the Centro Vasco del Chaco site states:

> On the evening of April 26, 1937, the Nazi-fascist air force bombarded during three long hours the defenseless town of Gernika; the heart of the oldest democracy in the world. But the symbol of the Basque nation, perhaps, because of the eternal Oak Tree's divine fate, kept standing amongst the ruins. The 'blessed tree' and the Assembly House were the only things that were saved from the disaster . . . And the spirit, with more strength than ever, screamed from the eternal Oak Tree that the Basques were immortal. (www.ecomchaco.com.ar/centrovasco/default.htm)

In 1937, Pablo Picasso painted *Guernica,* which would become a famous symbol immortalizing the horrors of the war, while universalizing the name of the Basque town as the Basque people's collective suffering (see Cava Mesa 1996). As of August 2005, the *Guernica* painting was displayed on three Basque websites—the Gernika Euskal Alemaniar Kultur Elkartea, Berlin (Germany, www.geocities.com/gernika_kultur), and the associations' sites from La Plata and Rosario, Argentina.

Gernika has become an expression of collective memory, identity, and belonging in both the homeland and the diaspora. For example, there are several oak trees planted abroad from seedlings taken from the Tree of Gernika. They represent the old traditions transplanted into a new soil, the taking root of identity and alleged historical continuity between the past and the present.[5] The Basques from Elko, Nevada, commissioned a mural of a young man in front of the Gernika Oak Tree (figure 4.15). The mural is on the exterior wall of the Basque handball court in a park in Elko. Significantly enough, there is no single image of the above mural in the Elko Basque club's site, despite its being a symbolic cornerstone of Basque community identification. A commemorative plaque for the mural reads as follows:

> A young man stands one last time before the Tree of Gernika to say good-bye before leaving his homeland to start a new life in America. He will carry on the Basque tradition to be free, responsible only to himself, his family, and God . . . [W]e Basques who are American born dedicate this mural to all those Basques living and dead who left their homeland to carry on their traditions. We honor them with our belief that all Basque, living and dead, are one . . . As we salute them let us cry '*Ama, aita, euzkaldunak, inoiz ez dugu ahaztuko*' . . . mother, father, Basques everywhere, we shall not forget! Our roots run deep.

5 There are seedlings planted in several countries including Argentina (e.g., at the Basque clubs in Buenos Aires, Necochea, planted in 1944, and Bragado); Chile (e.g., at Plaza Vasca, Santiago, planted in 1931); the United States (e.g., at Cyrus Jacobs-Uberuaga boardinghouse, Boise, San Francisco, California, and Ontario, Oregon, planted in 2007); and Uruguay (e.g., at La Plaza Gernika, Montevideo, planted in 1944) (EuskalKultura, August 17, 2005, online). There are also Basque diaspora associations named after Gernika. Those associations are Gernikako Arbola Centro Vasco, Junin (Argentina), Gernika Taldea, Paris (France), and Gernika Euskal Alemaniar Kultur Elkartea, Berlin (Germany).

Figure 4.15. Mural depicting a young man in front of the Gernika Oak Tree, Elko, Nevada, United States. Photo by the author.

Political homeland and diaspora associations related to the defense of ETA political prisoners and refugees (for instance, the Josu Lariz Askatu Campaign in Argentina, (www.josu-askatu.org) and 6 de México (www.6demexico.org), and to the defense of human rights (such as the International Basque Organization of Human Rights in the United States (www.euskojustice.org) have deconstructed or fragmented the painting into individual icons, appropriating them as powerful logos (see figure 4.16). By using those logos, these associations attempt to claim the message embedded in the original painting itself as well as the historical legitimacy of the Basque struggle against fascism (see chapter 6 for a further analysis of this argument).

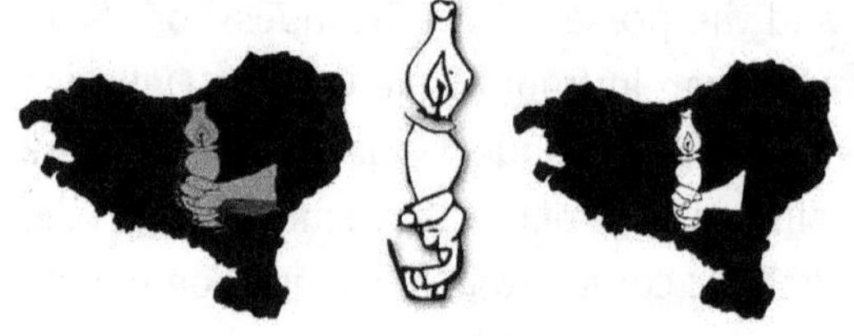

Figure 4.16. Logos based on fragments from Picasso's *Guernica*. From left to right: IBO, Josu Lariz, 6 de México.

Furthermore, according to the contents displayed on 60 percent of diaspora associations' websites, Gernika is undeniably a focal discourse on the reconstruction and maintenance of the Basque politics of identity in the diaspora. This discourse pertains not only to political associations, but it is widely accepted by different types of associations across geographical and linguistic barriers. Discourses on the Spanish Civil War, Franco's dictatorship, and mostly the Gernika bombardment are emotionally charged issues that bring significance to "the other" as a part of the diaspora's own identity construction.

Diaspora associations have interpreted Gernika as a rhetorical construction of Basqueness not being the same as Spanish, which has been politically articulated since the inception of Sabino Arana's Basque nationalist ideology. For example, the Basque Collectivity of Concordia (in Argentina) created in 1982 recalls that during the local celebration of the Five-Hundreth Anniversary of Christopher Columbus's first voyage to the New World, the organizing committee decided that the Basque association should parade under the Spanish flag. However, "The organizers did not take into account the inflamed reaction of the recently created Basque association . . . [Basques] paraded through the streets of Concordia with the 'ikurriña,' pride of an ancestral tradition and the heritage of the Basque blood" (Concordia Basque club's site, www.concordia.com.ar/Vascos).

As a result of the civil war, the Basque peninsular territory, understood as Navarre and Araba, Bizkaia and Gipuzkoa, was politically divided. Bizkaia and Gipuzkoa became the "traitor provinces" because of their support of the Republic and the Basque government, while Araba and Navarre became the allied provinces because of their loyalty to Franco. This division meant, according to Paloma Aguilar Fernández, "the symbolic rupture of a collective identity, assumed to be natural, the Basque Nation" (1998, 151).

This rupture would be symbolically reconstructed by the exiled nationalism in the diaspora in the following decades, still visible in today's Basque institutional diaspora. The Basque diaspora centers would be in the most ethnonationalist sense the "homes" of the "Basque family" for all Basques, regardless of their regional or provincial origin. That meant the pragmatic expansion and implementation of the nationalist *Zazpiak Bat* (Seven [Provinces] are One) project throughout Basque diaspora institutions in America, which, to a certain extent, was already underway in the diaspora prior to the 1930s and 1940s, following an earlier influence of the Basque nationalist ideology (see chapter 5 for a further analysis of the Zazpiak Bat project).

Diasporic Temporalities: A Global Time

In this section, I explore Basque "diasporic temporalities," following Michel S. Laguerre's terminology.[6] According to Laguerre, "diasporic new years, holy days, and holidays incubate the memory of the homeland, heighten the temporal dissimilarity between the mainstream and the ethnic enclave, intensify transnational relations, maximize revenues in the diasporic economy . . . raise the public consciousness about the presence of the group in their midst, induce changes of the diasporic community, and help the group reproduce itself as a transglobal entity" (2003, 5)—that is, as a family across borders (see below; see also Smith 1992).

Some Basque diaspora communities and some groups in the homeland share some highly symbolic temporal commemorations, depending on the type of celebrations. In a sense, these cyclical common celebrations unite Basques from all provinces, including diaspora Basques, under the diaspora's aspirations of becoming a *Zortziak Bat* (Eight provinces as One; see next section)—an organic part of the homeland. These specific temporalities for communal gathering, fraternity, and for renewing pledges of identity, help also diaspora and homeland Basques to imag-

6 Despite the fact that an analysis of the existing literature on temporality in online communities is of great relevance, such an analysis is beyond the scope of this book.

ine themselves as a united entity. The 2003 World Congress's Four-year Plan of Institutional Action 2004–2007 recommended the establishment of a "Day of the Diaspora" to be celebrated in both the *homeland* and the diaspora as a way to achieve an official social recognition in the homeland. As of this writing, the "Day of the Diaspora" has not been established yet (Gobierno Vasco 2004 and 2008).

According to the analysis of the contents displayed on diaspora websites, I have identified different types of temporal commemorations: religious, cultural, political, and hybrid. However, the boundaries between religious, political, or cultural temporalities are not so clear-cut. For example, religious celebrations, such as Saint Michael, the Archangel, and Saint Ignatius of Loyola can be understood as strong Basque nationalist events while nationalist events, such as the Aberri Eguna, are imbued with religious symbolism; and cultural events such as Korrika, the bi-annual pro-Basque language race, are seen as highly political.

Following the Roman Catholic calendar, Basque diaspora communities celebrate different religious festivities, such as Christmas, Easter Week, and Patron Saints days[7]—some of them of Basque origin. The Christmas celebrations include Christmas Eve (December 24), Christmas Day and Olentzero Day (December 25), and the Epiphany or "The Three Wise Men Day" (January 6). For those not familiar with Basque culture, a brief explanation of Olentzero is in order. Olentzero is a popular figure, somehow mythical, who brings presents to Basque children at home as well as in the diaspora. He is a charcoal maker who lives in the forests and only goes to the nearby villages on December 24 to bring presents to the children. The character was almost unknown in many of the Basque urban areas, but for the last few years, Olentzero has been incorporated into today's Basque imagery. Olentzero is used as another identity marker by Basques in both the homeland and in the diaspora. Olentzero has not only found a place on the list of existing holiday figures, like Santa Claus, Papa Noel, or the Three Wise Men—the latter is a main reference for Spanish Catholic society and for many Basques—but he is rapidly replacing them. Figure 4.17 provides some images of Olentzero that are displayed on diaspora sites.

Figure 4.17. Images of Olentzero from Basque diaspora sites.

7 For example, Saint Sebastian (January 20), Saint Prudentius (April 28 Patron Saint of Araba), Saint John the Baptist (which coincides with the summer's solstice, June 24), Saint Fermín (July 7), Saint Ignatius of Loyola (July 31), Our Lady of Begoña (August 15), Our Lady of Arantzazu (September 9), Saint Michael, the Archangel (September 29 Patron Saint of EAJ-PNV), Saint Francis Xavier (December 3), and Saint Thomas (December 21).

Despite the obvious religious content of those festivities, José Ángel Ascunce and Marién Nieva (2004) argue that, for example, Saint Francis Xavier, the Patron Saint of Navarre, and Saint Ignatius of Loyola, the Patron Saint of the provinces of Bizkaia and Gipuzkoa, were not only considered religious symbols but also political symbols. Particularly, the authors argue that the Basque government-in-exile promoted the celebration of those two saints as clear powerful symbols of Basque national unity.

Aberri Eguna means literally the "Patriot Day" or the "Day of the Homeland," and it coincides, intentionally, with the Catholic festivity of Easter Sunday, as a metaphor for the resurrection of the Basque nation. The EAJ-PNV established the Day of the Homeland in 1932, and it became "the single most important symbolic date of Basque resistance to the Franco regime" (Vazquez 1998, 358). It has been, and still is, commemorated in the Basque diaspora—the former home of the Basque government-in-exile and thousands of refugees—for decades (see Álvarez Gila 2013). For instance, on October 1, 1971, a letter sent by the Federation of Basque-Argentineans Entities to the member clubs stated the *obligation* of celebrating the Aberri Eguna as approved by the General Assembly held in Bahía Blanca (*Boletín*-FEVA, December 1971). From 1936 to 1976, the PSOE also commemorated the date, which was legalized in Spain in 1978. Since then, only the Basque nationalist parties, separately, celebrate it.

The Third World Congress's Four-Year Plan of Institutional Action 2004–2007 also proposed the "institutionalization of the Aberri Eguna in all Euskal Herria and in all Euskal Etxeak, that is, in the eight herrialdes (provinces)" (Gobierno Vasco 2004, 258). However, as of February 2009, the Aberri Eguna was not officially institutionalized, because, according to the Directorate for Relations with the Basque Communities, "the Basque society is very plural, and from this pluralism there are sectors that celebrate it as it was officially institutionalized, and there are other sectors that don't. The same thing happens in the Basque centers" (Gobierno Vasco 2008).

Since 2005, the annual Aberri Eguna celebration in Argentina has been jointly celebrated by representatives from the nationalist youth group JO TA KE of Rosario, the extraterritorial assembly of the EAJ-PNV in Argentina, and Eusko Alkartasuna-Argentina. In 2005, those representatives signed a declaration issued by the homeland political organization Udalbiltza-Kursaal calling for the national unity of all Basques to solve the Basque conflict. The Basque associations Asociación Diáspora Vasca from Santa Rosa, Argentina, and the Sociedad Arrano Beltza from Celaya, Mexico, also signed the declaration. (Udalbiltza-Kursaal is the Assembly of Batasuna-elected town councilors from the seven provinces. Originally the assembly created in 1999, known at that time as Udalbiltza, was also composed of elected members from EAJ-PNV and EA. Later on, the assembly broke up into two groups, Udalbiltza of EAJ-PNV and EA, and Udalbiltza-Kursaal.)

In the 2005 Aberri Eguna celebration, only twenty-three diaspora clubs (just a little over 12 percent of total diaspora associations as of December 2005) from seven countries—Argentina, Australia, Chile, Mexico, Spain, the United States, and Venezuela—commemorated the date by celebrating a Catholic homily, hoisting both the *ikurriña* and their host society's flag and organizing different cultural activities, such as handball games, dances, and communal dinners (EuskalKultura, March 26 and March 30, 2005, online). For instance, in the United States, the New York Basque club has celebrated Aberri Eguna for the last decades, regardless of its members' party affiliation. During the 2005 celebration (March 28, 2005), in the annual religious ceremony celebrated almost exclusively in the Basque language, Josu Iriondo, auxiliary bishop of New York (born in the Basque homeland), stated, "Basque is not only who can identify oneself with one's ancestry, but Basque is anyone who can assimilate the spirit that has sprung up from that millennial country . . . I am very happy that, here, in New York we can celebrate the Aberri Eguna with the same spirit that encouraged, for [the] first time, those on the 25 of March, 1932, to meet together in Bilbao to promote culture and religion. Easter Day marks the day of the resurrection of a nation that gets together to rule its own destiny" (the New York club's site, www.eeny.org).

The main common cultural celebrations refer to the Basque language or Euskara. In 1948, Eusko Ikaskuntza, the Society of Basque Studies, instituted Euskararen Eguna, the International Basque Language Day, which is celebrated on December 3, the day of Saint Francis Xavier.[8] Its celebration has continued in the diaspora.[9] The bi-annual and very popular pro-Basque language event called Korrika—a run and walk-a-thon held in March to raise money for Basque language schools—is also celebrated abroad.[10] Korrika was created in 1980 by the Alfabetatze Euskalduntze Koordinakundea (AEK), a popular homeland association aimed at educating adults in the Basque language since the early 1970s (see del Valle, 1994). Other pro-Basque language running events, similar to Korrika, are organized annually in each province by local *ikastolak* or Basque language schools, such as Araba Euskaraz (Araba), Ibilaldia (Bizkaia), Kilometroak (Gipuzkoa), Nafarroa Oinez (Navarre), and Herri Urratz (Iparralde). However, these local or provincial Basque-language events

8 The 1995 First World Congress of Basque Diaspora Communities approved a Four-Year Plan of Institutional Action 1995–1999, which established an International Day of the Basque Language to be celebrated in both the homeland and the diaspora (Gobierno Vasco, 1996). Eusko Ikaskuntza's 2005 Euskararen Eguna declaration stated that (1) Euskara, considered the oldest language in Europe, is part of the international cultural heritage; (2) Euskara, a European language, needs firm support from local, regional, national, and European institutions by enacting legislation that guarantees its development as a contemporary language; and (3) Euskara must be elevated to the rank of official language of the European Union, together with the other languages of member States. The declaration was supported by over six thousand individuals and institutions worldwide, including the Basque diaspora federations FEVA, Federation of Basque-Uruguayan Institutions (FIVU by its Spanish acronym), and NABO. Text messaging through cell phones was designed as part of the promotion campaign of the Euskararen Eguna. The message was "Get hooked on Euskara!" (EuskoSare, December 12, 2005).

9 Thirteen diaspora associations (nearly 7 percent of the total associations as of December 2005) from six countries—Argentina, Chile, Italy, Mexico, the United States, and Uruguay—celebrated the 2005 International Day of the Basque Language edition (EuskoSare, December 12, 2005).

10 Diaspora associations from six countries, including Chile, Spain, and the United Kingdom, celebrated the 2005 Korrika. There is also an Internet version of Korrika, called *ZiberKorrika*, where "runners" can buy online kilometers.

tend not to be celebrated in the diaspora, perhaps due to the fact that they are identified with particular provinces and not with the whole Basque Country, unlike Korrika. Nevertheless, there are some exceptions. For example, Herri Urratz is regularly celebrated at the Basque club in Paris.

Finally, Basque diaspora associations have adopted certain hostland celebrations while adapting them to the Basque culture. For example, the Basque club in Mexico City celebrates a Basque version of Halloween every year on October 31 called *Sorgin eta Mamu Gaua* (The Night of Witches and Ghosts), and the Basque club of Colorado has celebrated an *Akelarre Jaia* or Basque version of Halloween since 2008.

A Family across Borders

Authors such as Walker Connor (1994), Donald L. Horowitz (1985), and Anthony D. Smith (1992) argue that a nation constitutes an "extended family" or "super family" or "great family." This sense of "extended family" also relates to emigrant and diaspora communities, such as the Basque community, as expressed in similar termes on 60 percent of its total websites. As for any family, a "home" becomes essential. As of March 2004, nearly 40 percent of Basque diaspora associations' names exemplified an explicit emotional attachment to the homeland as well as to the other co-diaspora communities and Basques in a sense of constituting an extended family—a home, fraternity, and friendship: for example, Euskal Odola (Basque Blood), Danak Anaiak (All Brothers), Euskal Anaitasuna (Basque Brotherhood), Gure Etxe Maitea (Our Loved Home), Gure Etxea (or Echea) (Our Home; six clubs), Euzko (or Eusko) Etxea (or Echea) (The Basque Home; sixteen clubs), Gure Eusko Tokia (Our Basque Place), Etxe Alai (Happy Home), Eusko Aterpea (The Basque Refuge), Beti Aurrera Aberri Etxea (Always Forward the Homeland Home), Aterpea (The Refuge), Gure Baserria (Our Farmhouse); Lagun Onak (The Good Friends; three clubs), Lagunen Etxea (The Friends' Home), Euskal Lagunak (The Basque Friends; two clubs), and Txoko Lagunartea (The Group of Friends' Place).

Diaspora community-based institutions attempt to re-create a sense of home away from home, of familiarity and solidarity, by promoting communal and fraternal cultural and recreational activities, such as cooking, music, dance, or games. In the clubhouses, members and visitors can communicate in their own primary languages—Basque, French, or Spanish—with total freedom. Diaspora institutions play a role in cultural and identity transmission, socialization, and revitalization of customs in each generation. They are places to share and re-create memories, recount old stories, and keep traditions and temporal commemorations alive.

Numerous examples illustrate the sense of a Basque extended family in biological—"Europe's first family" (at the Zazpiak Bat Basque Society of Vancouver's site, www.bcbasque.com);—linguistic—"pre-Indo-European family" (at the Calgary Basque club's site, www.muturzukin.com/euskalgary.htm); and desterritorial terms—that is, as a transnational uprooted fraternity. For example, the Colorado Basque club (United States, www.coloradoeuskaletxea.com) states that "Euskal Herria, with seven regions in the Pyrenees and an eighth composed by those Basques born or living away, is joined together by a common heritage. They share the feeling of belonging to a great Basque family, which is based on strong roots that desires to continue offering its fruits to the world." Similarly, the Basque club of Santiago de Chile (Chile, www.euzkoetxeachile.cl) "has the objective of creating and maintaining the spirit of union and fraternity between the Basque residents in Chile and their descendants [as well as] to maintain the love for Euskal Herria, its customs and traditions."

In addition, in 30 percent of the cases, Basque diaspora institutions describe their websites as online fraternal communities. According to Daniel Bilbao, founder of the political activist association Asociación Diáspora Vasca (ADV, Argentina, www.diasporavasca.org/), his association is a "virtual community of Basque residents [over 200] from different places across the world [over 20 countries.][11] [However] many of us, who form the community, have met at 'the Basque Weeks' [week-long festivals] in Argentina, in other meetings in Euskal Herria or in Mexico, Chile, Peru . . . Soon, there will be new meetings and other trips that will allow us to transform this virtuality in a beautiful co-fraternity of Basques around the world."

Furthermore, 45 percent of the Basque diaspora sites also refer to their countries of residence as families and their co-citizens as countrymen. For example, the goals of the Basque club of Villa Mercedes (Argentina, www.vascosvillamercedes.sergroup.com.ar) are "to reunite in a cultural, social and recreational center those born in Euskadi from both sides of the Pyrenees, that is: Araba, Bizkaia, Gipuzkoa, Lapurdi, Nafarroa, Nafarroa Beherea, and Zuberoa, and their descendants, in order to strengthen indissoluble links with the great Argentinean family and their national feelings."

In sum, the Basque diaspora acts and defines itself as a "great family." In similar terms, Basque government representatives also understand the diaspora as a family that extends outside the borders of the Basque Country. Those representatives praise diaspora Basques for their loyalty to the homeland, to their origins, and to their identity, while committing the government's resources to support them for such an allegiance. At the inaugural address of the 1982 Basque American Congress, President Carlos Garaikoetxea stated, "Welcome to this motherland Basque brothers of America. As President of Euskadi, I want to express our unbounded recognition to those of you who have known how to keep alive bonds of affection with this country . . . We are all Basque people. Consequently, while there remains only one man or woman who feels roots in this land and desires

---

11 As of July 2006, the countries were: Argentina, Australia, Belgium, Bolivia, Brazil, Castile, Catalonia, Chile, Colombia, Denmark, Ecuador, French State, Germany, Mexico, Peru, Puerto Rico, Spanish State, Sweden, Switzerland, the United Kingdom, the United States, Uruguay, and Venezuela.

to live and feel as Basque, it will be an essential obligation to those of us who represent Euskadi to facilitate the means to make that possible" (*Basque Studies Program Newsletter*, 1982).

"We" and "our" are constant references in political speeches as totalizing figures, which claim to represent *all* Basques, homeland and diaspora, as well as marking the Basque community. Following Garaikoetxea's steps, at the opening ceremony address of the 1995 World Congress of Basque Communities abroad, President José Antonio Ardanza stated,

> I welcome you from the bottom of my heart, welcome to your home, *Euskadi*, and your great family of origin . . . Today, as we face the first World Congress of Basque Communities, we should ask ourselves what has made it possible . . . If we wonder why, we will only be able to find one answer: our firm determination to survive, our unshattering commitment to our origins, our loyalty to our common identity as a people . . . We can say today that, thanks to you, the whole world has become a little more Basque, and we Basques belong more to the whole world. (Gobierno Vasco 1996, 17–19)

During an eight-day trip to Chile, Uruguay, and Argentina, President Juan José Ibarretxe delivered a public conference at the Buenos Aires Basque club Laurak Bat (November 29, 2002) within the context of the deep economic and financial crisis that Argentina had been suffering since 2001.[12] The conference was broadcasted via live satellite to nine Basque clubs in Argentina—Arrecifes, Bahía Blanca, Chacabuco, La Plata, Laprida, Mar del Plata, Necochea, Rosario, and San Nicolás. It was the first time that such technology was used by the Basque diaspora.[13] According to the *Euskal Etxeak* magazine (Issue 57, 2003), hundreds of people watched the very emotionally charged conference, which was "interrupted on several occasions by bursts of applause from the audience." A deep emotional connection between a representative of the homeland and the diaspora was made. President Ibarretxe pledged to the diaspora, "As a President of the Basque government I will never rest while there is a Basque man or Basque woman in the world suffering economic or social hardship. Never . . . . What I want to tell you is that we love you, that we are not going to forget you; you are in our hearts . . . I love you more than ever, that you have us at the other side of the ocean, but very close at the heart" (at the La Plata Basque club's site, www.centrovasco.com).

12 In September 2003, the Basque government established a grant program to help those Basques abroad who are in extreme need—that is, a true transnational welfare program. From 2003 to 2007, an average of one hundred families obtained help annually (Gobierno Vasco 2008). As stated in the previous chapter, this program is open not only to Basques from the BAC but to any Basque regardless of their homeland origin as long as they are members of Basque associations registered with the Basque government. This type of policy is exclusively designed for the Basque diaspora. I am not aware of any other Basque governmental program that directly targets not only its constituency but also the neighboring Navarre and Iparralde populations, because of the Basque ancestry of some of their inhabitants, and because those regions are believed to be part of a greater Basque Country according to the Basque nationalist ideology.

13 There is a precedent on the use of the television to disseminate a message in Argentina. This refers to the conference given by the Basque government delegate to Argentina, Pedro de Basaldua, during the celebration of FEVA's First Basque National Week (Villa María, October 12-29, 1972). The talk was broadcasted by a local television station (*Euzko Deya* October 1972).

Imagining the Basque Diaspora

"Zortzigarren Herrialdea:" The Basque Web 8.0

As a brief introduction to the self-identifications and self-definitions of Basques in the diaspora, I shall outline the different aspects of "other"-imposed definitions versus self-imposed definitions. First, we, academics are writing diasporas into existence in ways that the Basques do not normally refer to themselves in general terms—for example, as a diaspora or a transnational community. On the one hand, the Basque government refers to Basques abroad, from a legal perspective (Law 8/1994), as "Basque Communities or Collectivities Abroad," and, in a more colloquial way, as "Basques around the world" or "Basques worldwide" ("Euskaldunak Munduan" in Basque). On the other hand, Basque media (e.g., EiTB and local press) commonly refers to diaspora Basques as "Basques around the world," and increasingly as "diaspora," but they use "Basque colonies," or "emigrant communities" less and less. The Basque media coverage of the 1995, 1999, 2003, 2007, and 2011 World Congresses of Basque Communities provided a first approach to determine the definitions used to conceptualize Basques living abroad.

At the Third World Congress of Basque Communities (July 2003; Gobierno Vasco 2004, 254), the institutional representatives of the Basque diaspora decided to unanimously define themselves as *Zortzigarren Herrialdea* or "The Eighth Province" as a foundational current narrative of Basque diaspora. At the same time, they encouraged the public, media, and government officials to use this newly coined term to refer to them. However, this has not been the case, and the term *Zortzigarren Herrialdea* has hardly ever been used. Surprisingly, as of August 2005, only 3 percent of the Basque diaspora sites refer to the concept *Zortzigarren Herrialdea.*

In other words, the Basque diaspora is imagined as detachment (collectivities abroad, colonies; i.e., as "them") and dispersion (diaspora as a result of migration; also as "them") as well as attachment (one more province; as "us") in reference to the Basque Country. The homeland is the symbolic central reference for diasporans' identity construction—that is, "the place of fond memories" (Terhune 1964, 258; see also Shani 2002, 17). According to Vartan Matiossian, this illusion of centrality, as in the Armenian diaspora case, "becomes a basis, in the belief that all dispersed parts are bound to become the original whole" (2003, 13). These approaches might bring some insight into the ways that, for example, the Basque government imagines the diaspora.

The definitions of diaspora Basques as "Basque communities abroad," "diaspora," "Basque colonies," and "emigrant communities" imply a detachment and dispersion from the homeland, as a deterritorialized community, an intrinsic condition of any diaspora. It is a symbolic acknowledgment and acceptance of the existence of a diaspora. The degree of their commitment to the homeland and their governmental institutions is still unfolding.

Such terminology is also an acknowledgment and acceptance of the existence of two separate entities—homeland and diaspora—characterized by the reality of belonging to "here" *and* "there"—that is, to their multiple or at least double consciousness and multiple loyalties across their hostlands and homeland. As a Basque emigrant stated, "If in Mexico I sighed for Euskadi, in Euskadi I felt the absence of Mexico. My mother, like me, has been between two shores, dreaming and suffering for the country that was absent. Unfortunately, this is also the life of the exile: to dream the absence" (Ana María Ruiz, about her mother the writer Cecilia G. de Guilarte, quoted in Ascunce and San Miguel 2004, 571).

The current diaspora Basques' theoretical self-identification as "The Eighth Province" implies not only a psychological or emotional attachment and commitment to the homeland, but a desire to belong physically to the homeland as its natural, territorial prolongation. It is a desire to belong as a totality, without distinction between homeland and diaspora, by blurring all physical and emotional barriers that separate one from another.[14] This can only be materialized in cyberspace by means of articulating a strong presence where diaspora and homeland Basques can be reunited in one single social space. Diaspora institutional leaders and individuals from local communities worldwide are helping to design and network a digital Euskal Herria, a metaphorical Basque Web 8.0, where the eight provinces become one (see Alonso and Arzoz 1999b and 2003).

At the same time, the institutional representatives of the Basque diaspora, though asserting their dispersed and deterritorialized condition, began to imagine and perceive themselves as a unitary entity, a geographical entity, eager to seek a presence and a voice in homeland matters. This self-definition also implies a desire to be accepted, recognized, and acknowledged by homeland institutions, the media, and society at large, as an integral part of the homeland, not merely in a symbolic way. The degree of commitment of the homeland to the diaspora is certainly unclear and mostly ambiguous.

Offline and Online Discursive Domains

Toward a Cybernetic Space

According to Mitra (1999, online) discourses are "networks of texts [that] reflect the ideological structure of a particular community or society at a moment in time." Mitra argues that an online text "suggests that what is seen and read on a particular Web page carries a potential for meaning, and in hypertextual combination, these pages constitute a discourse of the web" (ibid., online). In other words, the web as

14 The search for this territorial condition by deterritorialized groups, such as diasporas, does not pertain only to the Basque case. In this sense, Venezuela is known as "the Eighth Canary Island" due to the number of Canary islander migrants who reside in that country, while the Haiti diaspora is referred as "Haiti's Tenth Department," and Buenos Aires as "the Fifth Galician Province," or Catalonia as "the Sixth Galician Province." Also, the Argentineans abroad are difined as the "Twenty-fifth Province" of Argentina.

a set of sites is formed by textual, audio, and graphic contents that constitute a set of interconnected discourses via hyperlinks, which are not homogeneous, linear, or sequential.

The Basque diaspora webscape creates a networked common set of generic discourses across different types of websites—*euskal etxeak,* educational, cultural, or political—and across geographical, political, or linguistic barriers. Consciously or not, the different Basque diaspora institutions create web discourses as a collaborative effort. Those discourses form networks of connections based on shared similarities or commonalities that invite the reader/user to explore the Basque diaspora's cyberspace. In this sense, the Internet facilitates the analysis of diaspora discourses that, despite being constructed online, are intrinsically part of the offline life of diaspora Basques and their institutions. These online discourses need to be taken as a part of real world discourses as they are not detached from real life.

I argue that the diverse communities that constitute the Basque diaspora in the offline world have historically been less capable of producing a common institutional set of discourses, which could stand for themselves in regard to other discourses, such as the ones produced by the homeland. The geographical and temporal distances, and linguistic barriers, among many other factors, have been a detriment, though not a total impediment, to the constitution of Basque diaspora institutional discourses that could be shared by its many communities worldwide.

According to the literature reviewed, the Basque diaspora has been able to constitute all sorts of trade, religious, or fraternal networks, which were established along likely cohesive ethnic/kinship lines—real or imagined—that linked Basque communities and the homeland throughout the Hispanic/Spanish Empire throughout the Old and New Worlds since the 1500s.[15] This suggests that Basques, despite being geographically dispersed, tended to actively promote and manage similar collective actions as a way to enhance their predominant status tied to cultural, ethnic, family, and kinship lines and networks, as well as a way to increase and

15 For example, the confraternity Cofradía de Nuestra Señora de Aranzazu de México (1671) is definitely one of the most important organizations ever constituted by Basques from the four peninsular provinces on both sides of the Atlantic. It remained open until 1860 (Luque Alcaide, 1996, 462–65). The Real Compañía Guipuzcoana de Caracas (1728–1779) was a Basque-controlled trading company with Venezuela. It became a true ethnic monopoly within the late Hispanic/Spanish Empire (Douglass and Bilbao 1975, 88). The Real Sociedad Bascongada de los Amigos del País was established in the Basque homeland in 1765 and was aimed at promoting the improvement of socioeconomic conditions in the Basque provinces: "Its major source of support was clearly the influential and wealthy Basques scattered throughout the empire" [becoming a] "worldwide ethnic organization" (Douglass and Bilbao 1975, 108–110). Other examples of Basque associationism were religious organizations that aimed to secure liturgical services in the Basque language (Pescador 2004, 111–16): Confraternidad de la Nación Vasca, Sevilla (1540); Fraternidad de Nuestra Señora de Aranzazu de la Nación Vasca en Lima, Perú (1612); Confraternidad de la Nación Vasca en Arequipa, Perú (1630); Real Congregación de San Fermín de los Navarros, Madrid (1683–1961); Congregación de Naturales y Originarios de las Provincias de Alava, Guipúzcoa y Vizcaya—later known as Congregación de San Ignacio—Madrid (1713); and the Colegio de San Ignacio de Loyola or Colegio de la Vizcaínas, Mexico, D.F., which was established by the Cofradía de Nuestra Señora de Aranzazu de México in 1767, as an innovative initiative to educate women in New Spain. Originally it remained free of Catholic Church control. It is still open today (see also Escobedo Mansilla, de Zaballa, and Álvarez Gila 1996b; and Escobedo Mansilla et al. eds., 1996a).

maintain their historical-cultural consciousness and solidarity among themselves. Similarly, since the end of the nineteenth century, individual diaspora institutions have been able to produce their own collective narratives (Douglass and Bilbao 1975; Pescador 2004). These arguments demonstrate that the diaspora has produced, and is still producing to a certain extent, interconnected and transnational discourses that could integrate its diverse and heterogeneous communities (see Molina Aparicio and Oiarzabal 2009).

The establishment of diaspora federations in diverse countries—such as Argentina, the United States, Venezuela, Spain, and Uruguay[16]—and the celebration of international diaspora congresses have facilitated the intercommunication among Basque diaspora individuals and associations across borders.[17] Particularly, world congresses have become venues where diaspora institutional leaders meet face-to-face, sometimes for the first time, and are able to articulate institutional declarations and future action plans as well as personal and institutional relationships. For example, on October 20, 2006, NABO hosted a meeting of North American Basque clubs (Ipar Amerikako Biltzarra, Reno, Nevada) from Vancouver, Montreal, and Mexico City in order to explore the willingness of their Canadian and Mexican counterparts in joining NABO. Consequently, in the fall of 2006, NABO acquired a new website domain in order to be more inclusive and acceptable for Basque institutions from Canada and Mexico. The new domain name, *nabasque.org*—short for "North American Basques"—replaced the following domains: *nabo.us, basqueclubs.com,* and *euskara.us*. The Zazpiak Bat-Vancouver Basque club and the Euskaldunak, l'Association des Basques du Québec finally joined NABO in September 2008 and April 2009 respectively. This demonstrates NABO's redefinition of Basque identity by emphasizing its transnational character over a country-based identity.

Similarly, as a result of the Fourth World Congress of Basque Communities, Basque clubs in Europe are attempting to devise a common strategy for their near future. Consequently, the European delegates decided to organize an annual meeting of Basque-European associations. So far, the Basque clubs of Paris, Pau, Mont-

16 Currently, the Basque institutional diaspora federations are: FEVA (established in 1955), NABO (established in 1973), the Federation of Basque Centers of Venezuela (established in 1975), the Federation of Centers Euskal Herria (established in 1985 in Spain), and FIVU (established in 1998).

17 For example: the Basque government-in-exile's 1956 Basque World Congress (Paris, France); the 1960 CEVA Congress (Buenos Aires. See below for more details); the BAC government's 1982 Basque American Congress (Donostia-San Sebastián, attended by representatives from eleven countries from North and South America, and the Philippines); the 1987 International Congress of Basque Centers (Bilbao); and the 1989 World Congress of Basque Centers (Bahía Blanca, Argentina, attended by representatives from eleven countries from the Americas, Australia, and Spain). Another two congresses were celebrated in Argentina: the 1990 Argentinean Congress of Basque Centers (Necochea) was only attended by representatives from Argentina, while the 1997 American Congress of Basque Centers (Buenos Aires) was attended by delegates from FEVA, NABO, the Society of Basque Studies in America (New York), the Basque associations from Santiago de Chile, Caracas, Montevideo (Euskal Erria and Haize Hegoa), and São Paolo (Brazil), as well as by the delegates from twenty-three Basque associations from Argentina. In addition, a Meeting of Basque Centers was also celebrated in Argentina (Buenos Aires, 2004) and was attended by delegates from Argentina, Brazil, and Uruguay. Finally, the Basque government has also organized the 1995, 1999, 2003, 2007, and 2011 World Congresses of Basque Communities. The first three congresses were celebrated in Vitoria-Gasteiz,the 2007 edition in Bilbao, and the 2011 edition in Donostia-San Sebastián. Fifteen countries sent delegates to the 1995 congress, eighteen to the 1999 and to 2007, nineteen to the 2003, and twenty-one to the 2011.

pellier, and Bordeaux (France), Barcelona, Madrid, Murcia, and Valencia (Spain), Rome (Italy), Zurich (Switzerland), and London (United Kingdom) met officially for first time at the Parisian Basque clubhouse on November 30, 2007 and for a second time on September 5–7, 2008 at the Basque clubhouse of Barcelona. The goal of this incipient proto-European federation of Basque clubs is to establish a network to promote cultural and musical activities (EuskalKultura, November 30, 2007, and July 17, 2008).

One of the first contemporary examples of Basque diaspora institutionalized discourses is found in the historical American Confederation of Basque Institutions (CEVA in its Spanish acronym), which expanded throughout the American continent.[18] CEVA produced a pro-nationalist discourse and was vigorously involved in homeland politics during the 1970s—that is, at the end of Franco's dictatorship and during the era of the transition to democracy. For example, CEVA actively campaigned for the amnesty of Basque political prisoners, for workers' rights, for the legalization of the EAJ-PNV and its then trade union Basque Workers Solidarity (ELA in its Basque acronym), and for an autonomous status of the four Basque provinces in Spain, while also sending information about the Basques and their national cause to the Vatican, United Nations, and diverse American governments. Among the goals that CEVA failed to reach was the establishment of a World Confederation of Basque Institutions as it aimed at including the Basque associations from Australia and the Philippines (see de Astigarraga 1986; *Euzko Deya,* September 1 and October 1956).

During the celebration of the 2007 World Congress of Basque Communities, delegates from eleven countries—Argentina (FEVA), Brazil, Canada, Chile, Cuba, El Salvador, Mexico, Peru, the United States (NABO), Uruguay, and Venezuela—held a meeting in order to reactivate CEVA, which had been inoperative since the 1980s. The goal was "to strengthen ties and communication between Basque communities and institutions," according to Carlos Sosa (former President of FEVA, 2002–2006) (Bilbao, July 10, 2007). However, the political content that had characterized CEVA was absent during the discussion. Nearly two years later, the Basque club Denak Bat (Mar del Plata, Argentina) hosted the "First World Encounter of Federations of the Exterior" (January 9–11, 2009), which was attended by FEVA and NABO. The federations decided to constitute a confederation of Basque diaspora associations in the framework of the Basque National Week to be celebrated in Bahía Blanca

18 During the celebration of the 1956 Basque World Congress (Paris, France), delegates of FEVA, the then Federation of Basque Institutions of Chile, the Basque club Euskal Erria from Montevideo (Uruguay), and the Basque club in Caracas (Venezuela) established a pan-American confederation of Basque associations called the American Confederation of Basque Institutions (Confederación de Entidades Vasco Americanas, CEVA) (Gobierno Vasco 1981 437–73). CEVA was constituted following the statutes of FEVA. CEVA organized its first congress in Buenos Aires in 1960. Jesús María de Leizaola, the then-President of the Basque government-in-exile (1960–1979) was the honorary president of the congress. By 1973, CEVA was formed by Basque associations from nine countries—Argentina, Brazil, Canada, Chile, Colombia, Mexico, Uruguay, the United States, and Venezuela (see de Astigarraga 1986).

(Argentina) in October 2009 if their respective delegates approved this initiative.[19] The confederation will take the name of "Euskal Erakundeen Elkartea." The articles of incorporation have not been drafted as of this writing, and the project has been put on hold.

The discourses created by institutional leaders have also focused on the homeland and maintaining Basque identity abroad, while also highlighting their multiple allegiances toward both the homeland and hostlands. For example, the delegates of the 1999 World Congress stated:

> Proud heirs of our roots and our ancestors who were welcomed by the countries that we represent in this Congress and where they so diligently worked for their development, for the welfare of their families and for mutual support between Basque men and women . . . We declare our solemn, unequivocal and permanent commitment to the Basque Country, keeping the Basque Centres alive and uniting the Basque Communities around the identity of this people which is ours and for which we have a profound feeling of fellow citizenship and, therefore, of joint responsibility regarding its national and international future. (Gobierno Vasco 2000, 127)

In the same vein, at the 2003 World Congress the diaspora delegates declared:

> [Our] sense of dual identity, a feeling of belonging to both the Basque Country and the countries we live in . . . We wish to pay tribute to our forebears for the values they instilled in us—democracy, solidarity and a feeling of attachment to the Basque land. All nations with a sense of history feel for past generations. Therefore, we wish to express our determination to continue working on the project we have inherited so as to ensure a successful future for our Basque Centres and to protect and promote Basque culture and relations with the Basque Country. With this perspective, we wish to reassert our commitment to our countries of residence. (Gobierno Vasco 2004, 261)

Despite the historical significance of the institutional declarations of diaspora congresses—including the 2003 controversial declaration—those are to some degree punctual and isolated instances. Their impact on a larger audience (beyond the direct congress attendants) is unclear while the potential readership of the limited edition of the congresses' proceedings seems small.[20] Theoretically, the potential impact of these declarations seems to be minimal if compared to the potential impact of ongoing unlimited online discourse, and the audience of which is also potentially global. However, the online impact is still unknown, and further studies are needed.[21]

---

19 I traveled to Bahía Blanca to attend the meeting as an observer. The Bahía Blanca Basque National Week took place from October 30 to November 1, 2009.

20 For example, the Basque government printed 1,500 copies of the 2003 World Congress's proceedings. In addition, the dissemination of those declarations throughout the Basque diaspora webscape is even less promising. As of August 2005, only four sites from Mexico, the United Kingdom, and the United States, offered information on the 2003 World Congress.

21 To corroborate the potential impact of the Basque diaspora webscape discourses would entail a future survey on the sites' users, which goes beyond the purpose of the current work.

For over a decade, the Basque diaspora has had the capability to formulate and distribute its own discursive production in an *unparalleled* manner. This has been possible due to the increasing and ongoing diaspora institutionalization process, its networking, and the availability of new technological advancements in communication and transport. In this regard, Mitra argues that, "the new digital technologies make it possible for the diasporic immigrants, who often are marginalized, to find a new voice whose articulation helps to produce the new discursive places where the silenced identity narratives can be voiced again . . . The immigrants mobilize the Internet to create new spaces using their own immigrant voices" (2002, online; see also Mitra 2001).

The Basque diaspora manages, unintentionally or unconsciously, to produce a more visible and accessible set of interrelated discourses by sharing an online network of interconnected texts—a common hypertextuality—that re-creates an identity-based webscape, a decentralized horizontal sum of sites. The hyperlinks create both a continuum cyberspace, which does not (cannot) happen in offline life, and a continuum sense of identity regardless of geographical locations, political and territorial structures, and languages spoken, forming a series of interconnected texts that represent diaspora institutions get connected together on the web and create a point of view to be read potentially by a global audience. The web allows the Basque diaspora to "crystallize a shared image" of itself that it distributes to the entire planet (Mitra 1999, online).[22]

Moreover, these web discourses are negotiated in *both* the cyberspace and the physical space, which form a "cybernetic space" (Mitra 2002, online; see also Mitra and Schwartz 2001, online; and Collyer 2003). This concept attempts to move beyond the online-offline dichotomy (Riha and Maj 2009). Technology allows diaspora associations to expand the offline discourses into cyberspace, into a global public space, by re-creating an interstitial space. The offline and online worlds are two interconnected dimensions of one equation—that is, the Basque diaspora constitutes a wider imagined community. The production of a Basque "cybernetic space" integrates both online and offline spaces; for example, discourses similar to those found online are also found in the associations' newsletters, and some of them are also available on the diaspora's sites. In a sense, we move effortlessly across both worlds in our everyday life by constructing a dyadic "liminal space" or cybernetic space (see also Madge and O'Connor 2005; and Marletta 2009). The concept deserves significantly deeper exploration, which requires further analysis that goes beyond the scope of this book.

---

22 Taking into account that the Basques abroad are an extreme minority in quantitative terms (e.g., the 2000 U.S. Census indicates that there are nearly 58,000 self-defined Basques) compared to other diasporas (e.g., the 2000 U.S. Census reports the existence of 42.8 million self-defined German and 30.5 million self-defined Irish), the Internet and the web have potentially increased the awareness of the Basque people and their culture on a global scale instead of alienating them.

Online Discourses

Analysis of all this online networking, via hyperlinks, reveals three geographical discursive domains, by order of priority—homeland (68 percent of total links), diaspora (17 percent of total links), and hostland (10 percent of total links). Similarly, the content analysis of the Basque diaspora websites also reveals the existence of three main discourses: homeland, diaspora, and hostland.

The "homeland" discursive domain refers to the primordial and unconditional attachment of the Basque diaspora to the land of origin as well as the maintenance and reproduction of cultural traits and identity. The diaspora websites re-create a homeland articulated in a united and ancestral territory formed by seven historical provinces on both sides of the western Pyrenees, constituting nationhood. This nationhood is formed by a shared common cultural heritage, history, language, and symbols, such as a flag and an anthem, which strengthen the feeling of belonging (see the following chapter for further analysis).

Despite the Internet's lack of physical presence, several authors (Diamandaki 2003, online; Knoke 1992, 20–21; Mackay and Powell 1997; Mills 2002; and Wilson 1997, 149) argue that it can serve to reinforce place, community, and cultural distinctiveness based on territoriality. For example, according to Mills' (2002) study of the use of the Internet by Tibetans, Kurds, and Zapatistas movements, the Internet "is reifying [their] old-fashioned ethnic/national/communal territorially based identifications" (2002, 69). Similarly, the Basque diaspora online has been able to reify territorially bound communities in a non-territorially-bound space.

The "diaspora" discursive domain refers to the diaspora Basques' own identity, as Basques often exhibit dual or multiple allegiances and identification with both homeland and hostland. This discourse connects to itself, promoting an intra-diaspora bond exemplified by the re-creation of experiences of migration, resettlement in their host countries, institutionalization of their identities, and recounting of their histories. Finally, the "hostland" discursive domain refers to the diaspora Basques' places of settlement (see the following sections).

The three main identity discourses coexist without conflicting with each other in a non-hierarchical manner and are drawn from homeland and hostland migration and settlement experiences. The web discourses assert a sense of being and belonging to specific localities—the place of origin and the places of settlement—while emphasizing the diaspora Basques deterritorialized identity. They re-create and sustain not only past-oriented narratives, which provide a sense of belonging for immigrants and descendants, but also present-oriented narratives, which give a sense of quotidian belonging that articulates diaspora Basques' daily context.

The Basque diaspora web discourses are neither homogeneous, linear, nor sequential, and might alter the perceptions, or self-perceptions, of what it means to be "national" and help to rearticulate preconceived notions on the diaspora, while providing alternative discourses that challenge previously accepted assumptions of homeland and identity. That is, the Basque diaspora discourses allow for heterogeneities, for individuals and groups to speak for themselves outside the main or central diaspora discourses. These alternative discourses, common in diaspora political associations, focus on identity and homeland politics by asserting some criticism of diaspora institutions for their lack of involvement in homeland political matters, as well as criticizing homeland and host governments, for example, for their treatment of ETA political refugees. Diaspora political associations from Argentina challenge intra-diaspora institutional authorities, such as FEVA as well as extra-diaspora authorities, such as the Basque government by constructing alternative and de-centered narratives as they tend to interpret Basque identity, nearly exclusively, in political terms.

In addition, the Basque diaspora constructs in-group and out-group online discourses by differentiating from other groups, while reinforcing the similarities between themselves as they do in the physical world (see Mitra 1997). Far from technological idealism, new technologies have given a forum for groups such as the Basque diaspora to create their own ideological and ideographical discourses. As in the offline world, in cyberspace, the diaspora Basques (individuals and institutions) have also been able to differentiate their identity from other groups, such as Catalans, Galicians, Spaniards, or French, by establishing distinguishable identity markers, such as language, ancestry, and cultural heritage, while strengthening their in-group frontiers—self-awareness of the group's uniqueness and cultural differentness (tangible and non-tangible elements).

In-betweenness: Dual Identities

As mentioned earlier, common to the diasporic nature of some emigrant communities, such as that of the Basques, is the demonstration of dual and even multiple allegiances—that is, a belonging "in-between" national-cultural contexts (Hall 1993, 259–62; Cohen 1996)—as well as the construction of subjective and symbolic cultural group boundaries between an "us" and a "them." In this regard, diasporas establish mechanisms of interaction that flow across geographical and cultural boundaries, constructing interstitial and liminal spaces of identity negotiation, which also move online (see Turner's classical approach to liminality identity, 1969; see also Marletta 2009).

In particular, the emigrants' generation and the first generation born in the host country frequently suffer from a sense of estrangement and a feeling of exclusion in both homeland and hostland—in other words, they undergo a process of "othering" and "foreignization," according to Edite Noivo (2002, 256, 266). Leon Grinberg and Rebecca Grinberg state that emigrants often "return home out of a need to prove to [themselves] that all [they] left behind is still in fact there, that it did not all disappear and turn into a figment of the imagination, that those [they] left behind have forgiven [them] for abandoning them, that they have not forgotten them and love them still" (1989, 181) (see also Núñez Seixas 1998 and 2002).

Eighty percent of Basque diaspora sites present multiple references to diaspora individuals and institutions' strong identification with, and consciousness of belonging to, both the country of origin and the country of residence. However, they do not offer *any* example of estrangement, disjuncture, or lack of belonging in the online world. Consequently, I can argue that, in this sense, the Basque diaspora constructs a dual identity or multiple identities, at once, in positive terms. Corcostegui illustrates this argument as follows: "Dancers from Elko [Nevada] performed Agintariena [a dance where the ikurriña is solemnly saluted and energetically whirled above the heads of the dancers] at their 1998 festival with both the American flag and the ikurriña . . . this patriotic syncretism could also be seen as a reflection of Basque-American identity" (1999, 251, 253; see also Corcostegui 2005).

The 2005 edition of the International Basque Cultural Festival called Jaialdi (July 27–31, 2005; Boise, Idaho, United States) attracted thirty-five thousand visitors including Basques from Argentina, Australia, Canada, Mexico, Puerto Rico, and approximately one thousand people from the Basque Country (*Euskal Etxeak*, 2005). The event was formerly opened by the singing of the U.S. national anthem, "The Star-Spangled Banner." This act provoked mixed reactions within the public: Basque-Americans proudly sang the anthem, while some homeland Basques were shocked or at least were made to feel uneasy by the fact that the opening event of a Basque festival was a powerful American political symbol. Another two songs were also sung—"Agur Jauna" and "God Bless America" and its Basque-language version "Gora Amerika."[23] The organizing committee was made up of different individuals from local Basque associations, and they attempted to please both the American and the Basque communities by choosing songs that reflected, consequently, upon the Basque-Americans' dual identities. Two homeland news correspondents reported on the issue in the following terms:

> At the beginning of the festival, all those attendants stand up and with their hand on their hearts and in solemn attitude sung the U.S. anthem in English and in Basque. Those are the two faces of Boise, a place where the Basque and the American form an inseparable symbiosis." (*Gara*, August 1, 2005)
>
> In some instances, nobody would say that one is outside Euskadi. Some aspects with the genuine American 'flavor' make the visitor realize that she is in the United States' far west; the flag with stars, the wagons of old cowboys, but the decorations such as a small baserri or the American accent of the Bizkaian Basque [dialect from the province of Bizkaia] bring you back to reality. This is the 'far west,' but this west has a Basque heart." (*Deia*, July 31, 2005)

---

23 "Gora Amerika, geure Etxea . . . Biotzetik maite degu/ geure nazio berria" ("Long life to America, our home . . . we love you from our hearts/ our new nation" (Ontario Basque Club's site, www.ontariobasqueclub.dantzariak.net/gora_amerika.htm).

Diaspora sites re-create didactic narratives about the hostland focusing on migration, settlement, and adaptation, or conversely on the resistance to assimilation, the maintenance and promotion of identity, the institutionalization of their communities from boardinghouses and hotels to clubhouses, and the historical ties with their host countries. In some cases, such as in Argentina, Peru, or Uruguay, Basque institutions go back for centuries, emphasizing an assumed continuity and endurance of Basque identity abroad. For example, 63 percent of Basque diaspora sites in the United States, including NABO, implicitly relate to the history of the sheepherding industry as the result of decades of Basque migration in the twentieth century, while the intra-history of the New Mexico Basque association, established in 2004, refers exclusively to the early presence of Basques in the area as a result of sixteenth-century Hispanic colonization.

I have already discussed how Basque diaspora institutional leaders consider the diaspora to be an intrinsic or organic part of the homeland—the so-called *Eighth Province.* In addition, over 17 percent of total diaspora hyperlinks acknowledge the existence of online and offline co-diaspora communities, while re-creating a Basque webscape and ethnoscape. That is, the Basque institutional sites portray intra-diaspora identification with other diasporic communities, which share a common heritage and a place of origin, as well as similar migration and settlement experiences. However, diaspora leaders fail to acknowledge the diaspora as an autonomous entity, which could be expressed as a worldwide diaspora pan-institution similar to the aforementioned CEVA.[24] Therefore, it is not so clear that diaspora institutions online articulate discourses that exhibit consciously a narrative of their own diasporicity—that is, a self-consciousness that encompasses all dispersed Basque communities.

Only two diaspora associations—the London Basque Society (United Kingdom, www.zintzilik.org/london) and the Asociación Diáspora Vasca (ADV, Argentina, www.diasporavasca.org)—strongly reflect their opinions on the diaspora, its current role, and its future. The latter presents a critical perspective on the Basque diaspora and particularly on the Basque institutions in Argentina. It defines the diaspora as extremely folkloric and not politically active enough. It attempts to build an alternative discourse on being Basque, getting away from traditionalist or essentialist discourses displayed intensively in diaspora institutions (see chapter 6).

The London Basque Society holds a different view on the Basque diaspora and attempts to provide a basic internal organization and structure. Consequently, it created two bilingual (Spanish and English) "strategic documents" for the "global Basque diaspora community": the "Basque Diaspora–Media and Public Relations Toolkit" and the "Basque Diaspora–Community Participation and Engagement." The documents reflect a community-based approach that is needed in order to

24 Other diasporas, such as the Indian (the Global Organization of People of Indian Origin) or the Macedonian (United Macedonian Diaspora) have been keen to organize themselves as worldwide entities.

articulate the Basque institutional diaspora. Those documents are two of the first current intra-diaspora policy making tools.[25]

Simultaneously, 60 percent of diaspora sites re-create didactic narratives about the homeland, tailored to new generations of Basques born outside the homeland or to non-Basques, with a clear socialization goal in mind. An example of those instructive narratives is the existence of numerous informal or community-based groups, such as the Basque Educational Organization in San Francisco or the Fundación Vasco-Argentina Juan de Garay in Buenos Aires, and formal educational associations or university-based Basque study programs, such as the Center for Basque Studies in Reno, Nevada.

While migration to the American continent has slowed down considerably, Europe and Asia, to a much lesser extent, have become the new El Dorado for Basque migration—of young liberal professionals, entrepreneurs, and graduate students—as evident in the increasing establishment of Basque associations in diverse European and Asian countries, such as Germany, Italy, Switzerland, the United Kingdom, and China.[26]

For example, the London Basque Society, established in 1997, provides basic information on the United Kingdom for the newly arrived emigrants, something that is rarely offered by other associations in American countries. Consequently, one of its goals is "to provide information seeking to improve the general life conditions of Basque people in London." Therefore, the association created a website, www.zintzilik.org/london—a sort of a "cyber-boardinghouse"[27] for new emigrants—that offers practical information on matters, such as hostland accommodation, employment, health, or social security (Hemen 2003). The site was presented during the 2003 Gaztemundu event—an annual diaspora youth program—as an open source or free software application to be utilized by any diaspora association that wishes to set up its own website (e.g., www.zintzilik.org/paris or www.zintzilik.org/reno). As of this writing, there was no single Basque diaspora association using the software application provided by the London Basque Society. As we will see in the coming chapter, narratives of (self)-discovery of heritage and origin, which promote a re-imagination of a past linked to a common homeland and cultural heritage, are also generally re-created online.

25 The origins of those documents date back to the 2003 World Congress of Basque Communities where the Basque institutional representatives presented a Four-Year Plan for Institutional Action, 2004–2007. The quadrennial plan recommended that each Basque association should "appoint a person to be responsible for communication" (Gobierno Vasco 2004, 255).

26 From 2002 to 2005, over 70 percent of those leaving the BAC went to Europe, over 24 percent to America, 2.5 percent to Asia, 2.3 percent to Africa, and nearly 1 percent to Oceania (Bilbao 2008; Kerexeta 2008). Nearly eight hundred BAC companies have an international presence in dozens of countries. For example, Mondragón Cooperative Corporation, one of the largest Basque companies—made up of 264 companies—has a presence in eighteen countries outside Spain and employs over 13,700 workers abroad (34 percent of its total global workforce) (*Cinco Días*, January 14, 2007; *Deia*, May 29, 2009).

27 The term *cyber-boarding house* refers to the Basque boardinghouses or hotels that were established in the nineteenth and twentieth centuries throughout Argentina and the western United States to accommodate the newly arrived emigrants, constituting "homes away from home" (see Echeverria 1999a, 1999b, and 2000).

Conclusions

I have examined how the Internet and particularly the web help to foster a digital banal nationalism in the Basque diaspora webscape. They allow one to portray and re-imagine, on a global scale, certain Basque national representations about identity, culture, nation, and homeland, while constructing a specific Basque imagined transnational and diasporic community. The texts and graphics displayed on the Basque diaspora sites are similar across the different types of sites and across geopolitical and linguistic spaces. Basque images and symbols, such as *lauburus, ikurriñas, baserris,* or the Gernika Oak Tree, are imbued with history and are part of the collective memory and cultural traditions of specific periods. They convey distinct messages as collective representations of community and identity and are used profusely as representations of Basque identity by both homeland and diaspora Basques, helping to construct a cybernetic space. As *quintessentially* Basque symbols, they are mobilized, alongside temporal commemorations, to establish the connections with the homeland and among themselves.

In particular, Basque homeland nationalist images and symbols have been embedded, for more than a century in some cases, in the landscape of diaspora communities' imagery and ideology. That is to say, they have been reconfigured over time according to different sociohistorical and geographical contexts within and outside the homeland. They are reminders of the existence of a Basque nation.

The Basque diaspora has traditionally produced institutional discourses. However, the potentiality of these discourses in terms of networking, inclusiveness of more diaspora communities, and audience, has exponentially increased over the last decades due to the use of the Internet and the web as platforms of production and distribution. The web allows the diaspora to expand its interrelated discourses into a global arena by re-creating an interstitial or cybernetic space. Furthermore, the technology of hyperlinks connects the online discourses of the diverse Basque diaspora communities, constructing a set of interconnected discourses.

Those discourses refer to the homeland, defined as the ancestral nationhood, the diaspora, depicted as a natural prolongation of the homeland as well as multiple communities that form a family across borders, and the hostlands, depicted as an in-betweenness or liminal cultures that are characterized by multiple allegiances and identities. Diaspora Basques' self-images challenge to some degree the notions of identity and ethnicity in the homeland as the diaspora incorporates discourse migration and resettlement experiences into their own identity. Thus, estrangement becomes an intrinsic characteristic of the relationship between homeland and diaspora.

Imagining the

(05)

Basque Country

Diverse communities, individuals, and institutional representatives from the homeland as well as from the diaspora constitute narratives of Basque nationhood and homeland, each with their own story of what the homeland is. That collage of identities has to come to represent the nation and the homeland. As we will see in the following pages, the Basque diaspora webscape re-creates very particular images of what the Basque nationhood and homeland are. It understands the Basque nation as a people who share common traditions, language, origins, and history; as a nationality—that is, a membership in a specific nation—and as a territory.

In other words, the Basque diaspora online reinterprets the homeland not only as a geographic or territorial space—in terms of latitudes and longitudes—but also as a space formed by well-defined social, religious, and political boundaries. In addition, the ongoing political discourses regarding the representation of the homeland construct have created political identity borders. These political identity borders are based upon the different diaspora institutions' sociohistorical, cultural, and political traditions and backgrounds that build a common discourse about a Basque national homeland.

What are the emergent themes present in the Basque institutional diaspora websites, subsequent discursive elements, and their connections with other discourses? Why does the Basque diaspora articulate those discourses? In what ways do diaspora Basques define and re-imagine the homeland?

Imagining the Basque Country

Reifying the Basque Nation and the Homeland

"Zazpiak Bat": The Seven Provinces

I argue that the Basque diaspora is reifying the Basque nationalist project of building a nation-state based on an imagined ancestral territory formed by seven historical provinces under the nineteenth-century nationalist motto of Zazpiak Bat.[1] Ninety percent of Basque diaspora institutional websites identify with the representation of the homeland as a unified and ancestral seven-province territory, coinciding with the imagined homeland of the Basque nationalist movement—that is, the Basque Country or Euskal Herria. This imagined homeland includes Basques from both sides of the Pyrenees. For example, the following diaspora associations were named Zazpiak Bat: the centennial Centro Vasco Zazpirak Bat (Rosario, Argentina); Centro Vasco del Comahue Zazpirak Bat (Cipolletti, Argentina); Zazpiak Bat Basque Society (Vancouver, Canada); Zazpiak Bat Basque club (Reno, Nevada, United States); and the Basque club's Zazpiak Bat Dance and Klika groups (San Francisco, California, United States).

Eighty percent of the websites also make a physical reference to the Basque Country, suggesting a reproduction of the nation by displaying maps and geographical descriptions of the Basque Country as part of an ideographic digital banal nationalism (figure 5.1). Benedict Anderson defines this practice as "unisonances"—that is, "the echoed physical realization of the imagined community" (1991, 145). Additionally, 75 percent of the websites display the Basque Country's heraldic shield or coat of arms as the iconographic unity of the Basque seven provinces. (The heraldry actually depicts only six of the seven Basque provinces, since Navarre is divided into two provinces by the Franco-Spanish frontier, established by the Treaty of the Pyrenees in 1659, and consequently has only one coat of arms; see figures 5.2 and 5.3).

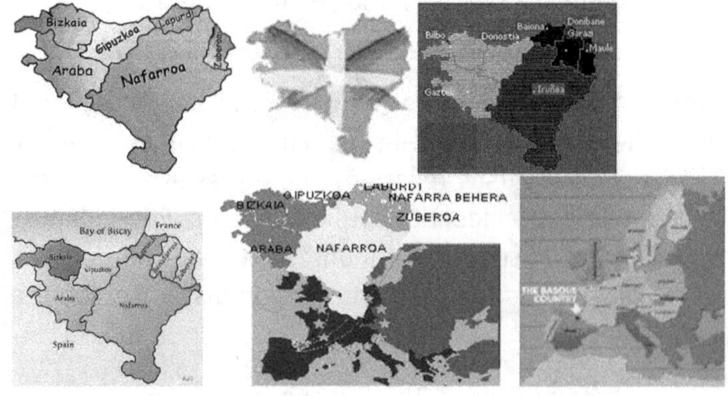

Figure 5.1. Examples of diverse maps of Euskal Herria displayed in diaspora sites.

---

1 The Zazpiak Bat motto was designed by Antoine D'Abaddie and refers to the territorial and political unification of seven provinces—Araba, Bizkaia, Gipuzkoa, Lapurdi (Labourd), Navarre, Lower Navarre (Nafarroa Beherea), and Zuberoa (Soule)—with historical, anthropological, linguistic, and cultural commonalities.

Figure 5.2. Examples of the different versions of the Basque Country coat of arms, designed by Jean Jaugain in 1897, displayed on diaspora sites.

Figure 5.3. Map of Euskal Herria and the coats of arms of the different provinces from the Ontario, Oregon, Basque Club's website (www.ontariobasqueclub.dantzariak.net/).

Only 4 percent of total websites refer to the Basque Country as the political-territorial administration of the BAC, while the two Navarrese websites refer exclusively to Navarre; and the Buenos Aires Basque dancing group Iparralde Dantzariak (Dancers from Iparralde) refers to Iparralde. The BAC official coat of arms refers to three Basque provinces—Araba, Bizkaia, and Gipuzkoa; the fourth space is blank, but its red color symbolizes the Navarrese coat of arms and the wish to incorporate Nafarroa into the BAC. Significantly, the BAC parliament has one hundred seats, but only seventy-five are used. The remaining twenty-five await the Navarrese members.

Some Navarrese emigrants and their descendants belong to Basque diaspora clubs, while others participate in Navarrese institutions abroad that identify with a Navarrese identity over a Basque identity. The institutional presence of Navarreses abroad is not a new phenomenon. For example, the oldest Navarrese diaspora club was founded in 1895 in Buenos Aires. However, its activities have intensified since the creation of the Foral Community of Navarre in 1982. The diaspora politics promoted by the different political administrations of Navarre have stressed a clear-cut sense of Navarrese identity, as opposed to a Basque identity, as a reflection of their anti-Basque nationalist orientation back home; for instance, Basque language is clearly absent in their websites. The Navarrese websites identify exclusively with the Navarrese coat of arms and the Navarrese government.

The Basque diaspora communities have embraced Basques from both sides of the Pyrenees under their institutions as an expression of the promotion of the Zazpiak Bat project abroad. This promotion is not new and goes back to the establishment of the first diaspora associations in the late nineteenth century and the dissemination of the Basque homeland nationalist ideology throughout America. As we saw in chapter 3, the promotion of a nationalist interpretation of identity and culture has been intensified since the establishment of the Basque government of Euskadi.

Modern Basque diaspora organizations were created in Uruguay and Argentina in 1876 in response to the abolition of the homeland *fueros* or provincial consuetudinary laws and the *fueros* supporters' influence in the "Basque-American" communities. The Laurac Bat (Four as One) was established in December 1876 in Montevideo, and then in March 1877, La Sociedad Vasco-Española Laurac Bat (Basque-Spanish Society Four as One), later known as Laurak Bat ("El Hogar de los Vascos"—i.e., The Home of the Basques), was established in Buenos Aires as a pro-*fueros* political organization celebrating annual protests against its abolition (see Irigoyen 1998; Douglass 1999).[2] Both organizations aimed at promoting Basque culture and assisting only Basque-Spanish emigrants. The Laurak Bat motto promoted the unification of the four southern Basque provinces of Spain. This motto became a popular name for the first Basque diaspora associations in the New World, most likely because of the influence of Carlist exiles (see Santiso González 1991).[3] In 1895, the Centre Basque-Français (Basque-French Center) and the Centro Navarro (Navarrese Center), both in Buenos Aires, were also established to attend to the need of their respective fellow "compatriots"—Basque-*French* and *Navarreses*.

The establishment of the Buenos Aires Asociación Cultural y de Beneficencia Euskal Echea (Cultural and Beneficence Association Basque Home 1901/1916) was the first successful diaspora project to integrate all Basques—previously divided in the three aforementioned provincial associations—from both sides of the Pyrenees in one common cultural project, by softening their regional rivalries and characteristics from back home. The Euskal Echea association was used as an asylum for

2 An earlier Basque organization, Sociedad Bascongada de Matanzas (Basque Society of Matanzas), was identified in the locality of Matanzas, Cuba, which dates back to 1868. It is the oldest known Basque diaspora association in the modern period. Another Basque association from Manila, the Philippines, might have also been established in the 1880s.

3 The Sociedad Laurak Bat de Socorros Mutuos (the Society Four as One Mutual Aid, today's Unión Vasca de Socorros Mutuos—Mutual Aid Basque Unity—Bahía Blanca, Argentina, 1899) also promoted a Laurak Bat approach towards its membership.

Basque indigents, the elderly, and orphans. It is still open as an educational institution where the Basque language is currently taught.

Before the end of the nineteenth century, Basque diaspora associations such as the Asociación Vasco-Navarra de Beneficencia (Basque-Navarrese Beneficence Association) from Havana (Cuba 1877) and the Laurac Bat of Montevideo embraced the fuerismo or regionalist ideology based on the abolished provincial laws and its Laurak Bat motto. By the end of the century, they began to promote a more inclusive approach toward Basques from the other side of the Franco-Spanish border. Basque centers, such as the ones from Havana (Cuba) and Montevideo (Uruguay) used a flag called "the Basque-Navarrese" flag, which was designed by Pedro de Soraluce in 1881 as a representation of the Laurak Bat ideology in the homeland. Nevertheless, it found its way into the diaspora. Havana Basque club used the Laurak Bat flag until the 1920s, while the Montevideo Basque club maintained the flag only until 1886.

As a reflection of this new inclusive policy, the Basque club of Montevideo (Uruguay) was renamed as the Euskaldun Guztiak Bat (All Basques as One) a decade after its creation, while the Basque club of Havana (Cuba), replaced the Laurak Bat motto for Euskal-Erria Ari da (the Basque Country on the move) in order to include Basques from Iparralde. The Montevideo Basque club replaced the Laurak Bat flag for the Euskaldun Guztiak Bat (All Basques are One) flag in 1886, which united the Uruguayan, Spanish, and French national flags as a way of including Basques from Spain and France as well as their descendants born in Uruguay. The club used it until its disappearance in 1898. As we have seen, the *ikurriña*—designed by Basque nationalist Luis Arana in 1894—has become the quintessential flag and one of the most powerful symbols for both homeland and diaspora Basques.

Those associations began to construct an early pan-Basque or Zazpiak Bat identity, expressing a new consciousness about being Basque and a new way of imaging themselves as a united people across homeland political divisions. This project would be disseminated to other Basque diaspora associations across the planet.

Currently, the Zazpiak Bat project is exemplified by the inclusive membership approach of diaspora associations and the creation of a cultural project that encompasses most of the peculiar traditions of the seven provinces. The Basque institutional diaspora is promoting the unity of all Basques in one single and common project as Basques, not as Spanish or French-Basques, without explicitly highlighting any province or region in particular, while helping to construct an imagined united homeland based on ancestry (*jus sanguinis*) and birth place (*jus soli*). The diaspora Zazpiak Bat project can be somehow defined as a non-territorial political and cultural experiment on the integration of all Basques regardless of their provincial origin, which coincides with the Basque nationalist aspirations of integrating all Basque territories under one unique political structure.

In an interview, Carlos Sosa, former president of FEVA, argued that, "[In Argentina] the Basque culture is understood as an inclusive concept. That is to say, the

Navarrese, the people from Iparralde and Hegoalde, are integrated in the concept of Euskal Herria. Something that here [in the homeland] because of political problems is not yet resolved" (*El Periódico de Álava,* July 15, 2003).[4]

That is, 90 percent of diaspora associations' memberships include Basques and Basque descendants from any of the seven provinces as well as non-Basques. Since May 2007, the New York Basque club offers also a cybermembership to anyone who lives more than one hundred miles from New York City. This type of membership—the first of its kind in the Basque diaspora webscape—has the same rights, responsibilities, and benefits that an ordinary offline membership would have. However, not all memberships are the same. On the one hand, for example, the New Mexico (United States) Basque club's membership is open to anyone who empathizes with the Basque people and culture—that is, anyone who is Basque by affiliation. On the other hand, the Boise (Idaho, United States) associations'—Oinkari Dantzari Taldea and the Basque Center Euzkaldunak—memberships are restricted exclusively (except for spouses) to those who have at least 25 percent Basque ancestry. Moreover, other Basque associations, such as the Basque club of Santiago de Chile, have established two types of membership: active members—those who have vote and voice, which is reserved to Basques—and collaborators or non-Basques.

Regardless of the short-term impact of educational and socialization activities designed by diaspora associations and federations, such as FEVA and NABO, that embody the Zazpiak Bat "spirit," these organziations are currently designing and executing a Zazpiak Bat policy as part of a diaspora-wide project as they did in the past. For example, dancing groups teach dances from all Basque provinces as a way to integrate different traditions while blurring the particularities between specific provincial or local traditions. At the same time, NABO and FEVA sponsor didactic summer camps or informal schools for Basque children and young adults—such as Udaleku (since 1975) and Gaztealde (since 2007) in the United States and Ume Topaketa (since 1998) in Argentina—to teach about Basque culture through Basque language classes, traditional musical instruments, dances, games, and sports.[5]

These educational gatherings are instrumental for the socialization of Basque children because they promote and construct a generic sense of Basqueness and Basque culture while showing children, parents, and their audience in general different Basque cultural traditions by highlighting their points of Basque territorial commonality as a single entity. Darlene Ammons, former Basque Studies Program's

4 For example, the following names of Basque diaspora associations refer to and exemplify the unity of the Basque people (as of March 2004 from a total of 113 institutions): *Denak Bat* (All are One; five associations take such a name), *Euskaldanak Denak* (or *Danak*) *Bat* (All Basques are One), *Denak Elkarrekin* (All Together), *Eusko Batasuna* (Basque Union), *Euzko* (or *Eusko*) *Alkartasuna* (Basque Union or Solidarity), *Euskal Herria* (or *Erria*) (The Basque Country), *Alkartasuna* (Union, Solidarity or Alliance), and *Euskal Elkartea* (Basque Union, Society).

5 In this sense, the Ontario Basque Club's website (Oregon, United States, www.ontariobasqueclub.dantzariak.net/) offers a section exclusively dedicated to children called Txildren's Txoko (Children's Corner), which displays interactive videos for learning the Basque language and songs, playing games and puzzles, interactive coloring pages, and providing a source of e-mail cards, all of them filled with Basque motifs. This is the only web initiative of its kind in the Basque diaspora online.

assistant coordinator (1978–1981; today's Center for Basque Studies at the University of Nevada, Reno, United States) and Janet Inda, former and first female president of NABO (1979–1980) reflect on the creation of NABO and its Zazpiak Bat mission:

> A group of Basque-Americans met in Reno, Nevada back in March of 1973 with a questionable proposal, especially considering Basque history. This group hoped to forge a federation and create a network with the larger Basque community of the United States. The Basques had never been united, neither in the Old Country nor in the New World. The Basque Country or 'Euskal Herria' had never been 'Zazpiak Bat' . . . representing a unified, self-conscious political community . . . Basques from Bizkaia in the South, for example, had little interaction with Basques in the Northern Province of Zuberoa. This detachment was reflected in the Basque communities of the United States . . . [This group was] attempting to cross the divide—real and imagined—between Basque-Americans . . . Would "French" Basques and "Spanish" Basques join a federation to work together? . . . Seventeen years later, the answer remains a resounding yes! . . . Most Basque-Americans have set aside their Old World differences of 'Spanish' and 'French' to work together. The member clubs of NABO have realized that they all share a common purpose—to promote and preserve their unique cultural heritage—and they know that this can best be accomplished with a strong 'lotura' (bond) to help one another. (Basque Studies Program Newsletter 1981)

Nevertheless, visitors can still witness how diaspora Basques, particularly those born in the homeland, refer to France/French or Spain/Spanish when interacting with each other. For example, Magdalena Mignaburu, director of the Basque-Argentinean Diaspora Association (Avellaneda, Argentina, www.diasporavascarg.com.ar) feels that currently Basque clubs in Argentina demonstrate a lack of political direction while failing to educate their members: "Therefore, you hear members saying 'I'm Spanish or I'm French . . . I'm going to Spain or I was back home, in France.' No, no, and no, I always say; 'this is a Basque club, and we are Basque', otherwise there is no point of being Basque. We will end up being Spanish or French. The clubs need to educate their members. They need to say that there is no such thing as being French-Basque or Spanish-Basque" (Interview, November 3, 2005, Buenos Aires).

In the diaspora, the promotion of some specific regional or provincial identities over others is less than the construction of a homogeneous and united identity in the diaspora. That is, the Basque institutional diaspora endorses a generic sense of Basque identity—as an overarching or umbrella identity concept—that covers a wide range of local, regional, provincial, and national identities, among others, in both the homeland and the hostlands. It is a conscious attempt to dissolve the individual characteristics, generational differences, and inward barriers, all markers of the Basque community, in order to unite all Basques in a more homogeneous manner. In Martin Sökefeld's words, "On a general level, the imaging of a community as unified and more or less homogeneous is a normal or perhaps necessary procedure for any kind of politics of identity because every individual member of a community embodies a multiplicity of diverse identities that may engender conflict and contradiction" (2002, 113).

Commonality, Uniqueness, and Authenticity

The redundancy of ideas and arguments as displayed on 70 percent of the websites and illustrated by the reproduction of similar, if not identical, texts, symbols, photos, and music, tells us about their significance in the reconstruction of diaspora identity discourses around the world. The similarity of contents is reinforced by the fact that diaspora webmasters "borrow" or "exchange" textual, graphic, and audio content from one another or from other sites. For example, the NABO website makes prolific use of content about Basque music, sports, or dance from the Basque government's site.

Additionally, those ideas and arguments are reduced to slogans or catchphrases that are easily transmitted and grasped by online visitors—Basques and non-Basques. These "slogans" work as shorthand, resembling clichés, for different aspects of Basque identity and culture, for example: "the Basque language is unique," "the Basque history is timeless," or "the Basque people are one of the oldest in the world." They make constant references to the assumed authenticity, distinctiveness, and uniqueness of non-tangible elements of Basque identity and culture.

Webmasters not only create original content, but also provide instant access to a variety of materials by the way of hyperlinks, which were previously unavailable or extremely difficult to obtain. For example, 20 percent of sites reproduce the same excerpts on Basque issues from multiple sources.[6] In this regard, access to different quantity and quality of contents has been facilitated in an unparalleled manner by technologies such as the web. The web has become a medium that easily propagates the diaspora vision and understanding of identity, culture, and history. The sites provide abundant straightforward information and detailed resources while facilitating easy access for visitors to learn about their ancestors, heritage, and history in very comprehensible and didactic ways.

The issues of assumed Basque sameness and uniqueness, together with the issue of authenticity—real or imagined—construct three main referential aspects of the Basque diaspora web discourses. As seen previously, between 80 and 90 percent of diaspora sites provide the perception of a united and distinctive homeland and culture. This perception is based on points of commonality—origins, traditions, and particularly, the Basque language—that are central to the diaspora discourse on uniqueness and authenticity. According to 80 percent of diaspora sites, commonality or sameness is a recurrent issue for the Basque diaspora as it emphasizes what are believed to be unique aspects of the Basque identity and culture. The Basque diaspora produces and reproduces discourses that are intercon-

6 For example, Mark Kurlansky's 2001 book *The Basque History of the World;* Larry Trask's web page on Basques and the Basque language (www.cogs.susx.ac.uk/users/larryt/basque.html)); several articles published by local, national, and international newspapers and magazines, such as the *National Geographic;* academic essays by diaspora Basques, such as Cesar Arrondo from Argentina, John Ysursa from the United States, and Amaya Garritz from Mexico; and popular folktales, legends, and literary works.

nected by points of commonality with the diverse nodes—online and offline—that form it. This commonality is expressed, for example, by common goals that help unite individuals across countries and across the webscape, although they might never meet face-to-face.

The claims of commonality, authenticity, antiquity, uniqueness, and distinctiveness act as emotional triggers by directly imploring an audience, Basque or not, for its active participation and commitment toward the Basque culture and language. For example, NABO states on its web page on the Basque language (www.nabasque.org/euskara.htm) that "As one of the world's most distinctive minority languages, Euskara's future will be decided by the current generation of speakers. We need your help to keep our language visible, viable & vital."[7]

As a way of maintaining Basque identity in the diaspora, individuals and institutions re-create certain identity and cultural markers, learned and transmitted from one generation to another, as constituent elements of Basque nationhood. The textual, graphical, and audio contents of their sites re-create a sense of nationhood and homeland by connecting with memories and experiences, either personal ones or those handed down.

Diaspora Basques reproduce a sense of Basque nationhood by attempting to maintain various elements such as language, culture, heritage, and traditions necessary to make sense of their own identity. These elements also help people understand their displacement, resettlement, and new daily life in their host countries. They claim their own nationhood is justified by their shared, common, and "distinctive" ethnicity, culture, language, history, and above all territory—Euskal Herria. As in other diasporas, the Basque diaspora's claim of an ancestral homeland is key to understanding its identity. Basque culture in both homeland and diaspora is defined by visible external expressions of identity and traditions, such as folklore, language, religion, cuisine, sports, and games. Diaspora and homeland re-create the most visible or tangible elements of Basque culture.

Basque diaspora sites, particularly *euskal etxeak* and cultural sites—which make up 75.5 percent of total diaspora sites—reproduce most folkloric aspects of the Basque culture, such as dancing, music, and language, which are regarded as their most unique identity markers. For example, there are fourteen associations' websites (14.3 percent of the total sites) that specifically address Basque traditional dance, music, and language, which tell us about the construction of Basque diaspora identity along the line of a cultural, linguistic, or folkloric dimension.

For example, ten diaspora sites (10.2 percent of the total sites; nine *euskal etxeak* and one educational from Argentina, Canada, Peru, Spain, and the United States) offer forty-eight songs online; 91 percent refer to homeland songs, while 9 percent are hostland songs, and 52 percent of the songs are in Basque. Eighty

7 The page is sponsored by the Basque government's Basque-language department (HABE) to assist U.S. adult learners of the Basque language and as a way to promote the language in America.

percent of the songs are popular, although there are also others that are political in nature, such as the BAC anthem "Eusko Abendaren Ereserkia." In addition, another seven sites (7 percent of the total sites; six *euskal etxeak* and one educational from Argentina, France, Italy, Uruguay, and the United States) reproduce ninety-nine lyrics, all from the homeland and all in Basque. Ninety percent of the songs are popular, such as "Agur Jaunak," "Olentzero," or "Euskal Herriaren Euskaraz," but there are also political lyrics (15 percent) such as the aforementioned BAC anthem, "Batasuna" (Unity), "Eusko Gudariak" (Basque Soldiers; the anthem of the Basque Army during the Spanish Civil War), or "Gernikako Arbola" (The Tree of Gernika), and also songs that address migration, such as "Agur Euskal Erriari" (Good Bye Basque Country), "Nire Etorrera Lur" (My return to my Loved Land), or "Urrun Nabil Euskalerretik" (I am Far Away from the Basque Country).

Music is not only an artistic expression, but also a remarkable vehicle for socialization and for individuals to connect with the community by evoking heartwarming and gratifying memories of past family reunions, and communal celebrations. Songs, particularly in Basque, reinforce the symbolic and emotional connection with the Basque culture and identity and help to reproduce and re-imagine a homeland by establishing emotional links with it.

Surprisingly, the clear advantages that the web provides—multimedia platform, dissemination, and audience—to musical associations, such as the Basque choirs in Argentina and in France are not fully utilized.[8] Although those choirs have recorded their music, no sample of their performances is offered online.

In addition, according to 80 percent of diaspora sites, the Basque diaspora web discourse on the homeland re-creates historicist or pseudohistorical and essentialist accounts of Basque history and culture that tend to idealize Basque traditions and values regardless of the country of residence and type of institutional site. That is, the sites use and maintain stereotypes and origin myths that were created or revived in the nineteenth century by Basque nationalism and the European and local scientific communities.

In other words, the diaspora offers a particular and simplified reading of Basque history by reducing it to stories that reinforce a golden and mysterious past. Clear-cut, well-defined, and stereotypical excerpts are used to illustrate and reinterpret the totality of Basque history. According to those narratives, Basques are seen as a perennial, enduring, authentic, unique, and autochthonous nation. A linear continuity from prehistoric times is thus established. Those stereotypical narratives of Basque identity and culture are exhaustively reproduced by Basque diaspora websites, becoming central to their identity. However, this linearity is displayed in the context of the inherent non-linearity of hypertextual discourse.

---

8 In Argentina, there are Lagun Onak (www.lagunonak.com.ar) and Alkartasuna (www.coralalkartasuna.com.ar), and in France, Anaiki (www.anaiki.com), and Gernika Abesbatza (http://membres.lycos.fr/gernikataldea/).

For example, the Zazpiak Bat Basque Society of Vancouver's site reproduced an article by Thomas J. Abercrombie titled "The Basques: Europe's first family" previously published in *National Geographic* in November 1995. The article serves as an introduction to the Basque people and their culture. It presents a romanticized view of the Basques and their country and re-creates an authentic "unpolluted," idyllic agrarian culture and changeless past:

> From road's end at Arantzazu Monastery it's only a two-hour walk through fragrant forests of beech and pine to the high stony pastures of Urbia. Yet the well-worn track leading to this high mountain valley crosses a dozen millennia . . . Basque shepherds still summer their flocks, surrendering to a seasonal rhythm unbroken since Neolithic times . . . Through the centuries, waves of Romans, Visigoths, Arabs, French, and Spanish overran them. But the Basques endured, often taking their traditions to the hills and forests for safekeeping . . . Basques call their nation Euskal Herria, or "land of the Basque language." And it is their ancient mother tongue that truly unites them. It was spoken here 5,000 years ago. (Vancouver Basque club's site, www.bcbasque.com)

Meanwhile, 11 percent of the websites disseminate other types of narratives that are more balanced and academically sound. These narratives attempt to demythologize the Basques. For example, 5 percent of diaspora sites in the English-speaking world reproduce the late Basque linguist Larry Trask's popular battery of frequently asked questions about the Basque language and the Basque people.[9] The Calgary Basque club site (Canada, www.muturzikin.com/euskalgary.htm) displays in its totality Trask's Basque page. Trask introduced his page in the following way to combat the most idealized and essentialist definition of Basques and their language, where its mysteriousness becomes central:

> But please note: I do not want to hear about the following: Your latest proof that Basque is related to Iberian, Etruscan, Pictish, Sumerian, Minoan, Tibetan, Isthmus, Zapotec, Martian. Your discovery that Basque is the secret key to understanding the Ogam inscriptions, the Phaistos disc, the Easter Island carvings, the Egyptian Book of the Dead, the Qabbala, the prophecies of Nostradamus, your PC manual, the movements of the New York Stock Exchange. Your belief that Basque is the ancestral language of all humankind, a remnant of the speech of lost Atlantis, the language of the vanished civilization of Antarctica, evidence of visitors from Proxima Centauri. I definitely do not want to hear about these scholarly breakthroughs.

Finally, 98 percent of websites constantly reproduce the unclear origins of the Basque people and the "timeless" character of their language, which re-create a "halo" of uniqueness. In this sense, the Basque diaspora searches for an authenticity that implies a durability of the Basque culture and identity seeking a never-ending continuum from the past to the present and on into the future. For example, 5 percent of diaspora sites use Basque Country megaliths or cave paintings (e.g.,

---

9 Robert Lawrence "Larry" Trask (1944–2004) was a professor of linguistics at the University of Sussex (the United Kingdom), author of *The History of Basque* (1997) and of the web page, www.cogs.susx.ac.uk/users/larryt/basque.html, created in 1996 (as of March 2006).

Lascaux or Santimamiñe) to denote not only an everlasting autochthonous culture but also a territorial continuity of the Basques for many millennia (see figure 5.4). FEVA's homepage (www.fevaonline.org.ar) background reproduces cave paintings of mammoths and horses, while other groups, such as the Basque-language association in Rome (Associazione Culturale Euskara's site, www.euskara.it), display photographs of dolmens.

Figure 5.4. The restaurant of the Basque Club Laurak Bat from Buenos Aires reproduces cave paintings on its walls. In the left photograph, there is a seedling of the Tree of Gernika inside a glass case decorated by the Basque coats of arms, and in the background is the reproduction of a prehistoric mural and the ikurriña. The right photograph is a detailed part of the frieze and the ikurriña. Photos by the author.

Having a long and everlasting history projects a sense of certainty about Basque identity and culture into the future—a myth of certainty and survival. Basque diaspora institutions undoubtedly present Euskara as the example of the survival of the Basque people. They understand authenticity as an oath of allegiance to individual or collective memories, embellished over time, full of melancholy and nostalgia. Collective memory is the interaction between the historical memory and the memory experienced by the community. Persistence of the memory is related to the continuity and maintenance of a given social group, to its "collective consciousness." That is to say, memories form experiences of origin and identity.

Consequently, a collective memory plays a significant role in the reproduction of a group throughout time, representing an emotional and intergenerational bond between the present and the past. Although memories are not representations of reality, the members of the group create specific images of a common non-static past that are transmitted to the present. In sum, the past constitutes a social construction; a collective image that is constructed in the present and for the present (see Backhurst 1990). Those images in the collective memory are products of exaggeration and idealization that work as filters, selecting the aspects of the past—that is, shared historical memories or ethno-history according to Smith (1996)—that the group must remember (or at least not forget) in order to keep its identity alive in the present. In the Basque diaspora, individuals and institutions elaborate a collective memory that attempts to "remake" a lost world—a homeland, a culture, a people—that over time grew to differ from the one being constructed in the homeland by including narratives of migration and resettlement in their collective memory.

Far beyond presenting a simplistic interpretation of Basque authenticity as ethnic essentialism by diaspora institutions, I would rather interpret that authenticity as the diaspora's ancestral attraction for culture and identity, which is magnified by "uploading" the discourse to cyberspace. This ancestral attraction and seduction of the origins of the Basques serve a three-fold purpose. The first purpose serves to attract the attention of Basques and non-Basques in relation to the "mysterious" origins of the Basque people. This could be translated into an in-group reinforcement and an out-group empathy and fascination. Second, this fascination with origins also helps to contribute to an increase of individual and collective self-esteem and pride of being Basque, related to the positive values embedded implicitly in such uniqueness. A positive social status is key for the reproduction, maintenance, and transmission of Basque identity and cultural values as well as for attracting new generations of Basques. That is, there is an appreciation and value of culture and traditions that are worth preserving because of their unique and distinctive character. And, finally, this ancestral attraction can reinforce Basque collective identity markers by way of being and showing distinctiveness to other groups based on the premises of its unique language, remote past, unknown origins, and unique cultural traditions (see Oiarzabal and Oiarzabal 2005).

Homeland Politics and the Apolitical and Nonpartisan Diaspora

Katerina Diamandaki argues that the main purpose of expatriate/immigrant diasporic online communities is "to build on the Internet a home away from home . . . These digital diasporas may have no clear-cut political causes and no claims other than to maintain links between members scattered all around the globe and promote their general well-being. The orientation of these digital environments is thus more communitarian and communal than political or strategic" (2003, online). In addition, according to Jolanta A. Drzewiecka's research on the Polish-American diaspora, in general terms, "involuntary migration" seeks to legitimate continued involvement in homeland politics, while "voluntary migration" manifests disengagement with homeland politics (2002, 7).

Diamandaki's arguments portray online diasporas as apolitical communities as the author removes their political motivations from their existence. However, I shall demonstrate that new generations of Basques in the diaspora have increasingly become involved in homeland politics. This is the case of Basque immigration into the western United States as part of the so-called voluntary migration. The analysis of the content of the diaspora online shows that the associations' websites do not exclusively reflect cultural or folkloric issues, though those are overwhelmingly the majority on 80 percent of the sites, but also political issues related almost exclusively to the homeland. Twenty percent of total sites that include not only political sites (7.1 percent of total sites) but also *euskal etxeak*, cultural, and educational sites, address political issues, such as the Basque political conflict, violence, and homeland elections. Also, the cultural dimension promoted for 80 percent of the institutional sites plays a politically edifying role, as expressions and symbols of Basqueness, which might well be read in political terms.

Moreover, we need to take into account the historical and current influence that the Basque government and its main historical political party, the EAJ-PNV, have on the identity, symbols, and political notions of homeland presented by the diaspora. This influence makes it difficult to differentiate between the government's interests in the diaspora and the EAJ-PNV's interests.[10] As seen in chapter 3, for the last thirty years or more, the Basque government has been eager to involve the diaspora in homeland affairs as the "true ambassadors" or international non-state actors of the homeland and the Basque people. Specifically, the Basque government has proposed that the diaspora take an active role in promoting a peaceful, positive, and postmodern identity of the homeland as well as supporting a negotiated end to the Basque political conflict and the right to self-determination of the Basque people.

According to the online discourse created by 80 percent of the sites, the diaspora is reconstructing a homeland nationalist discourse. The diaspora is an emotional or psychological global community linked, to certain degree, to the particular national building project of Basque nationalism since its inception.[11] That is, the diaspora is more related to a national project than a regional or sub-state project within France or Spain. José María Tápiz Fernández (2000) argues that by 1903 the Basque nationalist ideology had already spread throughout the Basque communities in countries such as Argentina and Mexico.[12] However, not until the 1920s did a true process of Basque national politicization of diaspora associations take place in Argentina, Chile, Cuba, Mexico, the Philippines, the United States, and Uruguay.

---

10 The EAJ-PNV, with a total membership of thirty-two thousand people, has seven extraterritorial (outside the Basque homeland) assemblies—Argentina, Chile, Mexico, Spain (Barcelona and Madrid), Uruguay, and Venezuela—with the right to vote in the party's general assembly and to choose four of seventy-one delegates that elect the chairman of the national executive board. Some of the extraterritorial assemblies were established over sixty years ago in the context of the massive exile that resulted from the Spanish Civil War and post-war repression. In addition, in December 2002, Eusko Alkartasuna was set up in Argentina. Eusko Alkartasuna-Argentina created a blog, www.eaargentina.blogspot.com, in March 2004. Also, the Extraterritorial Assembly of the PNV in Argentina established a blog, http://eaj-pnv-argentina.blogspot.com, but much later, in April 2009, within the context of losing the Basque government. Those are the only homeland political parties in the diaspora with an "autonomous" online presence.

11 By the end of the nineteenth century and the beginning of the twentieth century, there were several Basque nationalist periodicals published in America (e.g., *Irrintzi*, *Euzkotarra*, *Aitor*, and *Aurrera*).

12 Basque nationalism was quickly exported to the Basque diasporic communities in America under the motto of *Zazpiak Bat*. The Buenos Aires Basque center, Laurak Bat, witnessed the ideological clashes between pro- and anti-Basque nationalist factions. The anti-Basque nationalists were finally outnumbered not only at the Laurak Bat but in the main diaspora institutions throughout America. The Laurak Bat president paid tribute to the founder of the Basque nationalist movement—Sabino Arana—by attending his funeral ceremony in 1903 (Larronde 1997, 323–24; see also Álvarez Gila 1996).

Since 1910 and particularly during the 1920s, the confrontation between the Spanish and Basque nationalist ideologies was a reality in Basque diaspora institutions in Argentina. For example, in 1921, Basque nationalists gained control of the board of directors of the main Basque emigrant institution, the Laurak Bat of Buenos Aires. In addition, Basque nationalists created their own association, Acción Nacionalista Vasca (Basque Nationalist Action). However, by 1925, Spanish nationalists won the elections in the Laurak Bat and a number of members who were in favor of Basque nationalism left the association. In 1927, Basque nationalists regained control over the institution and refused to raise the Spanish national flag despite of the protest of three hundred pro-Spain members. The statutes were then modified to reflect Basque nationalist sentiments. A similar process took place in the Basque club of Rosario, the Zazpirak Bat, in the early 1920s. Basque nationalists regained control of the institution and proceeded to closed down the political group Eusko Batzokija, which they established in 1913 to oppose the Spanish nationalist forces (Artazu 1923a and 1923b).

Meanwhile, the Basque community in Mexico City witnessed the clashes between Spanish institutions, such as the Casino Español (Spanish Casino), Centro Vasco, and the Basque club of D.F., created in 1907. In November 1911, several members wrote a letter to the Basque club's board of directors arguing the exclusive Basque character of the association as it integrated Basques from the seven provinces. The authors of the letter asked the Board to remain independent from Spanish and French institutions, "although [the Basque center] is formed by French and Spanish subjects, it cannot be defined as French or Spanish, but exclusively Basque." In December 1911, the board of directors defined the club as exclusively Basque.

Two decades later, the Mexico City Basque club was once again affected by homeland politics, particularly in relation to the inclusion of Navarre in a proposal of a Basque statute in 1934. A great percentage of Navarrese members opposed to Basque nationalism began a process to control the club. However, the dissident group, the majority of whose members were of Navarrese and Alavese origin, left to establish El Círculo Vasco Español (The Basque-Spanish Circle) in January 1935. The Spanish Civil War increased the animosity between both associations. The Basque club became the adopted house for many Basque exiles, while El Círculo Vasco Español publicly empathized with Franco (Amaya Garritz, at the Centro Vasco Mexico City site, www.centrovascomexico.com; see also Álvarez Gila 1996 and 2000; and de Pablo, Mees, and Rodríguez Ranz 1999). During the 1930s and onward, diaspora associations and communities were influenced by thousands of Basques who were forced into exile as a result of the Spanish Civil War and World War II. This implied a certain degree of Basque nationalist politicization.

The Basque diaspora presents diverse degrees of politicization or political involvement, mainly related to the homeland, which varies from playing an informative or educational role to a more active and overtly participative role. Some diaspora associations attempt to educate people regarding political issues, while others present a more overt disposition toward homeland politics by stating their political orientations and preferences upfront.

On the one hand, 5 percent of websites are willing to open means of communication by confronting "sticky" issues, such as the complex homeland political situation, which is seen as an extremely polarizing and divisive issue. Confronting such issues could have potential consequences for the associations' cohesiveness. Although this informational and educational goal can be seen as a very hesitant approach to homeland politics, it has the potential for increasing diaspora knowledge of certain homeland political matters. For example, NABO has taken a timid role in informing its club members and by extension anyone who logs onto the website about major political events in the homeland and in the diaspora, such as ETA's 1998 and 2006 ceasefires, the 2002 Idaho Joint Memorial No. 144, or the Ibarretxe Plan. John Ysursa,[13] then coordinator of NABO and editor of its tri-annual newsletter, *Hizketa*, argues:

> ETA action—shall we say—complicated matters for our Basque-American community. Of course the news that "ETA killed today" did little to benefit the Basque image in America. But ETA's action also aggravated our perceived differences . . . Since our Basque community is comprised of Basques from both the North (French) and South (Spanish) sides of the Basque Country, it has not been a small achievement to move beyond this narrow definition to accept others as being Basque. NABO has played significant role in this. Nevertheless, ETA action exacerbated these differences because ETA is a phenomenon of only the southern or Spanish side of the Basque Country. In some circles it thus became easy to brand Basques from Bizkaia, for example, as being the radicals or troublemakers. Furthermore, the interpretation of ETA action poisoned some of our local efforts to build a broader Basque community. One parent for example, refuses to send their kids to NABO's Music Camp [Udaleku] because he believed that it was an ETA training camp! (*Hizketa*, 1998)

On the other hand, 20 percent of diaspora websites from Argentina, Chile, Mexico, the United Kingdom, the United States, Uruguay, and Venezuela (43.7 percent of all diaspora countries) overtly manifest their political affiliation, aspirations, and desires, which in general terms coincide with homeland Basque nationalist goals, such as self-determination, sovereignty, unity of political territory, and/or the resolution of the Basque political conflict by means of political negotiation. The diaspora sites post political material without making any disclaimer statement. Consequently, the majority of the Basque diaspora associations endorse the contents published on their websites.

---

13 Historian and cultural activist John Ysursa became the first professional (paid) position in NABO's history. Ysursa was hired on a part-time basis in October 2005 in the role of facilitator for NABO with financial support of the Basque government. Ysursa offers a weekly electronic mail news service called Astero that has distributed over 700 e-mails as of July 2007. From 2006 to 2013, he has been NABO's webmaster. In 2013, Kathleen Camino, from the Basque club of Reno, Nevada, replaced Ysursa as NABO's facilitator. Lisa Corcostegui, from the Ontario Basque club, assists Camino with the website and Astero. As of June 2013, Astero is sent to approximately 1,000 e-mail accounts.

In addition, those diaspora sites display and disseminate explicit political information that in only 5 percent of the cases is also included in their newsletters. That information relates to instructions about voting in the BAC elections, opinion articles, news, documents, and speeches related almost exclusively to the BAC, the EAJ-PNV, and to a lesser extent to Batasuna.[14] The sites, in a sense, are public forums that facilitate debate by allowing anyone to contribute by stating their opinions and/or by submitting documents or papers related to Basque politics. The political debate thus escapes the physical limitations of the associations themselves and extends far beyond its membership and community.

For example, at the time of my content analysis in August 2005, one of the most prolific contributors to the Basque diaspora in Argentina was historian César Arrondo[15] (vice president of FEVA, 1998–2004). On behalf of FEVA, Arrondo provided the so-called Educational Papers (or Hojas para la Formación) to its member clubs and individuals via e-mail. The Educational Papers referred to the history of the Basque Country, including nationalist figures, such as Sabino Arana (Issue 4), José Antonio de Aguirre (Issue 5), or Telesforo de Monzón (Issue 10), and nationalist organizations, such as ETA (Issue 3), or the EAJ-PNV (Issue 14).

After a dispute between Arrondo and FEVA's leadership over Issue 17 where the author reflected his critical view of the situation of Basque associationism in Argentina, the papers ceased on March 2007. FEVA did not endorse the author's opinions. As a result, the representatives of the Basque club of Laprida, including Arrondo, resigned their position on FEVA's board of directors. (In April 2007, Arrondo began to publish and distribute via e-mail the so-called Basque Essays [Euskal Paperak] on the Basque Country, culture, and migration, "as a way to contribute to the [national] building of the Basque Country" [*Euskal Paperak,* Issue 1, April 2007].)

Among the homeland political documents, the New Political Statute of Free Association or Ibarretxe Plan is the most widely published on diaspora sites. As of August 2005, the document was displayed on 10 percent of the websites. In addition, two San Francisco-based Basque associations—the Basque club of San Francisco (www.basqueclub.com) and the Basque Educational Organization (www.basqueed.

---

14 In relation to the homeland pro-independence movement, the document most widely published on diaspora sites is "Orain Herria, Orain Bakea" (Now the People, Now the Peace), the so-called Anoeta Proposal (November 14, 2004)—a proposal to achieve peace and self-determination. The document is displayed on only 3 percent of the websites.

15 Arrondo is also a founding member of the Centro de Estudios sobre Nacionalismo y Cultura Vasca Arturo Campion (Center for the Study of Basque Nationalism and Culture Arturo Campion), which was established in 2003 at the Basque club Lagunen Etxea in Laprida, Argentina. He was also the general secretary of the homeland Basque nationalist party Eusko Alkartasuna in Argentina (http://eaargentina.blogspot.com). Arrondo published an article titled "The Basque Nation: yesterday and today," which in general terms is a nationalist reading of Basque history. It includes the following events: the origins ("the Basque Nation buried its roots in the prehistory"), general characteristics of the Basque people ("the soul of the Basques" is about "refinement and nobility"), Navarre ("it was an independent kingdom that in one of the phases of its history united the seven historical territories"), and Sabino Arana ("He is the man who sowed the seed; our responsibility is to maintain and multiply it"). The article was posted in 16.6 percent of diaspora sites in Argentina.

org)—reproduced the speech given by Lehendakari Ibarretxe on the Spanish Parliament on February 1, 2005, in defense of the proposal of the New Political Statute. "The Basque Country is not a subordinate part of the Spanish State," Ibarretxe proclaimed. The sites highlighted the sentence in large bold fonts.

Ibarretxe's proposal was rejected by the Spanish members of parliament on February 2, 2005. Ten percent of diaspora associations from Argentina and the United States reacted strongly against such a rejection. For example, Federico Borrás Alcain, president of the Basque-Argentinean Association Urrundik (Asociación Vasco-Argentina Urrundik, Paraná, Argentina) argued that the rejection implied "A clear contempt for the will of the Basque People [one of the oldest people in Europe], legitimately expressed through its Parliament, that has put a proposal for coexistence on the table, and not one of imposition of one country over another. [The refusal] to debate and to agree democratically wastes an historical opportunity to solve a political problem between Euskal Herria and Spain that goes back at least 200 years" (Diáspora Vasco Argentina's site, www.diasporavascarg.com.ar/).

On similar occasions, as seen in chapter 3, the Basque diaspora has also expressed its opinions in relation to homeland political events. For example, the Basque club of Caracas (Venezuela) publicly manifested its adherence to the so-called Lizarra Agreement (September 1998)—the preamble of ETA's fourteen-month cease-fire declared in November 1998—while asking the Venezuelan people to support the peace process:

> The Board of Directors of the Basque Center of Caracas share and support the goals proposed by the Lizarra Declaration, which was the first step in the current process of negotiations that could bring specific aims, much appreciated by Euskadi, such as peace and the right to self-determination of the Basque people . . . As it is known by all Venezuelans for many years, the Basque people are fighting for the acknowledgment of their identity as a nation . . . the final goal of which is the universally accepted right of every people to self-determination. (Caracas Basque club's site, www.kromasys.com/cvc/)

That is, despite the geographical distance, 15 percent of diaspora institutions are willing to commit to the "cause" of the homeland and the Basque people, while connecting with their assumed wishes—e.g., peace and prosperity. For example, the Basque club of Valencia's (Venezuela, www.valenciakoeuskoetxea.com) goals are: "To assert and defend the personality of Euzkadi . . . as Euzkadi is the nation of the Basques; to respect the self-determination of the Basque people; to promote and disseminate Euzkera as the nation's language." Meanwhile the Basque club Zazpirak Bat from Rosario (Argentina) issued a public statement, displayed on its homepage, congratulating Juan José Ibarretxe for being reelected as president of the BAC in 2005:

> Those who are part of the Basque club Zazpirak Bat wish to express our unconditional respect and adhesion to the Basque people's will who through their representatives have decided to renew the confidence in our Lehendakari in order for him to continue the fate of one significant part of Euskal Herria. We support the ongoing process of

> dialogue and negotiation; we make ours the proposed initiatives by the new government in order to achieve peace, the political normalization, and the social, economic, and cultural integration of our loved country. (Zazpirak Bat's site, www.zazpirakbat.com)

I argue that traditional politics in the diaspora seem to be displaced by a reading of those politics in "cultural" terms, which seem to create no major problems with the so-called apolitical and nonpartisan official stand of 80 percent of the diaspora associations. These associations keep away from homeland and hostland "politics" and stay faithful to their sociocultural and recreational goals. If we understand traditional politics as lobbying, campaigning, or fundraising for a specific homeland party, my research does not show that this is currently happening inside diaspora institutions or among their leadership. Many individual Basques and institutions in the diaspora accept the advocacy for the cultural and political unity of all Basques from both sides of the Pyrenees and for the preservation of major cultural traits such as the language. However, homeland politics are found "embedded" in diaspora discourses on identity, culture, and homeland. The diaspora political discourse is exemplified by means of multiple cultural and folkloric activities and symbols. The so-called diaspora's "cultural" ethnonationalist dimension makes assertions that are political in nature. In other words, this dimension disguises to some extent manifestations or expressions of Basque nationalism. That is to say, between 10 percent and 95 percent of diaspora institutions have assumed a Basque nationalist agenda to some extent according to what is displayed on their websites. Consequently, the diaspora understands those expressions as intrinsic to their ethnicity and culture and not as biased partisan or political expressions.

For example, in relation to territorial claims, as seen previously, 90 percent of diaspora institutions promote a project that reifies a Basque ancestral nation conformed by seven provinces or Zazpiak Bat. The diaspora's ancestral homeland is equated with the ancestral homeland imagined and claimed by Basque nationalism. In addition, they explicitly argue that the Basque language is one of the most identifiable identity markers of the Basque people, and consequently, that it should have an official status in the Basque territories in order to protect the Basques' linguistic rights. The Basque language should be the official language of the ancestral homeland. Furthermore, as mentioned earlier, 95 percent of the institutions promote national symbols, such as the *ikurriña,* the BAC anthem, and folklore as part of a digital banal nationalism. Nevertheless, only 10 percent of the institutions with an online presence openly promote the right to self-determination for the Basque people, and the resolution of ETA violence by means of political negotiation, as the conflict is seen not as terrorism but as the consequence of political conflict between the Basque people and the Spanish and French States.

In chapter 3, I left a question unanswered, which was related to the self-proclaimed apolitical and nonpartisan nature of the Basque institutional diaspora. Although far from being representative of any sample population of the diaspora, the following opinions are somehow "dissident voices" in relation to the diaspora's institutional apolitical and nonpartisan attitude. For example, Magdalena Mignaburu argues that the diaspora associations' "apolitical" self-definition makes no sense: "Defining ourselves and our institutions as Basque is already defining ourselves and our institutions in political terms. Being and defining one as Basque is already a political definition. Otherwise, we should call ourselves Spanish or French" (Interview, November 3, 2005, Buenos Aires, Argentina). Similarly, Maite Velasco, member of Emakume Abertzale Batza,[16] a nationalist association housed in the Buenos Aires Laurak Bat clubhouse, argues that "being Basque has always been political, and it is impossible not to be involved in politics since we define ourselves as Basque" (Interview, November 2 and 5, 2005, Buenos Aires, Argentina).

This issue is unequivocally addressed by the Basque Club of Caracas (Venezuela) and by FEVA.The Statute of the Basque club in Caracas defines one of its goals as "To assert and defend the personality as well as the right of self-determination of Euzkadi (the Basque Nation), acting and promoting to that end all kind of historical, cultural and folkloric manifestations, while glorifying the [Basque] nationality" (Chapter one, Article 3 of its Statute, 1942; for further information see San Sebastián and Ajuria 1992). In addition, FEVA's third Article of its Statute (1955) states, "[FEVA] will attempt to unite Basque and Basque-Argentinean associations to better recognize Euskadi or Euskalherria, constituted by Araba, Benabarra, Bizkaia, Gipuzkoa, Lapurdi, Navarra, and Zuberoa. As well as the defense of the perennial rights of the Basque people, that they have as the ultimate goal the accomplishment of greater self-determination, until the achievement of the unity of Euskalherria as an independent state" (Centro Vasco Denak Bat Cañuelas' site, www.geocities.com/canuelasdenakbat/home.html).[17]

Do the Basque Club of Caracas and FEVA consider self-determination, territorial unity, and even independence to be Basque nationalist partisan demands or intrinsic rights of the Basque people, and consequently, nonpartisan? What is self-explanatory is that the above statements cannot be regarded as apolitical by any means, but rather as partisan as it coincides with the fundamental beliefs and goals of Basque nationalism, which argues for the primordial rights of the everlasting Basque nation. (However, it is also true that accepting the status quo is *also* political in nature. And even not having an explicit policy regarding homeland politics is also a policy.) Similar arguments were raised by the Institutional Commission at the National Congress of Basque Centers in Argentina (1995, Necochea), "The Basque Centers in Argentina declare publicly their adhesion to the Basque government as the only Government of the Basques, because it interprets and promotes the validity of Zazpiak Bat, a position that coincides with the Basque-Argentinean institution . . . This congress manifests its support to the Right to self-determination of the Basque people." Paradoxically, the commission stated the nonpartisan charac-

16 Emakume Abertzale Batza was originally the female branch of the EAJ-PNV. According to Velasco, the association is still faithful to its origins, but it lacks new membership.

17 In the same way, Mariluz Artetxe, then-President of FEVA, stated at the 2007 World Congress of Basque Communities, "The Federation of Basque-Argentinean Entities and the Basque Centers support and have supported our ancestors' land by supporting the cause, which is nothing else but democracy, liberty, recognition of the right of self-determination, a human being's most natural right" (in Ayesa and Orbaiceta 2008, 137).

ter of the Basque institutions in Argentina, while proclaiming its nationalist nature: "We propose an authentic institutional nonpartisan position . . . we reaffirm the *abertzale* [Basque nationalist/patriotic] spirit of FEVA and the institutions that form it, recognizing that Euskadi is the *patria* [nation] of the Basques" (at FEVA's site, www.fevaonline.org.ar).

Conclusions

Community leaders of the Basque institutional diaspora provide political guidance for its membership and the Basque population at large by constructing a specific collective memory and an ethnonationalist interpretation of identity, which is constantly reproduced in the diaspora—via the new technologies of information and communication—regardless of linguistic and geographical barriers. The diaspora reconstructs Basque identity, nationhood, and homeland according to a previous interpretation of homeland ethnonationalism.

In other words, the Basque institutional diaspora is promoting and reproducing, consciously or not, a sense of political ethnonationalism. However, it is not doing anything as blatantly or overtly partisan as requesting the vote for certain political options or fundraising for a particular party. Nonetheless, it is political and partisan in the sense that it can be linked to a specific homeland political movement: Basque nationalism and its main referential party—the EAJ-PNV, and to a lesser extent to EA and Batasuna's leftist-nationalism. That is to say, the Basque diaspora has historically internalized the nationalist interpretation of Basque ethnicity.

This ethnonationalism has been found in the diaspora since the early dissemination of the Basque nationalist ideology in the Americas in the nineteenth century. Specifically, this ideology was also inherited from the massive influx of exiles, including the Basque government, due to the Spanish Civil War and the repression that followed, as well as from the contemporary relationship with the BAC government. That is, the current Basque diaspora institutional nationalist discourse goes hand-in-hand with the one currently promoted by the Basque homeland nationalism.

The reproduction of this specific construction of Basque ethnicity is fundamentally based on a traditionalist and primordial interpretation of Basque identity by the nationalist movement. The Basque diaspora clearly reproduces and promotes this traditionalist and primordial interpretation but not so clearly in today's homeland. If for decades, the Basque government-in-exile relied heavily on linguistic, religious, folkloric, and biological criteria in order to define Basqueness, today's Basque government and homeland society tend to depart from this narrow nationalist or essentialist approach to identity and to opt instead for a more inclusive approach based on a subjective identification. The diverse studies conducted for the past decades on the Basque homeland identity indicate that homeland society has moved beyond primordialism, which is based on a common ancestry and language, while emphasizing the subjective and voluntary aspects of Basque identity.

Today's Basque nationalism, particularly the EAJ-PNV, does not overtly promote an identity based on primordialist criteria. Nevertheless, as seen in previous chapters, nationalist leaders and officials of the Basque government still reproduce, at least in a rhetorical or symbolic way, an emotional and primordial dimension of Basque identity and culture, by making constant reference to ancestry, origins, and cultural and linguistic uniqueness.

Additionally, the diaspora adds to this ethnonationalist perspective its own politics of migration, resettlement, and dual or multiple allegiances, which make up an identity that consequently differs from the one promoted in the homeland. That is, the Basque institutional diaspora is re-creating its own sense of identity—multiple, deterritorialized, and diasporic—where nostalgia and idealization cannot be seen as a detriment but as intrinsic and necessary strategic markers.

Several diaspora associations, their vanguard digital intelligentsia, and other individuals are extremely aware of homeland politics. Some address the issue by merely acknowledging it, while others take an active part in politics, playing a political role as human rights support groups, and advocating for the Basque cause in their countries of residence—for example, Argentina, Mexico, the United Kingdom, the United States, Uruguay, or Venezuela. Their activities are directed toward the defense of ETA refugees who have become part of their diaspora communities, while ultimately seeking the creation of an independent state for a seven-province homeland by resolving the conflict by means of political negotiation between the Basque Country and the states of France and Spain.

Online

(06)

Politics

> The day that in Lekeitio, in Zubieta, we'd eat burgers, we'd listen to American rock music, and everybody would dress up in American clothes and stop speaking their language in order to speak English, and everybody would, instead of looking at the mountains, be using the Internet, well, for us, that day will be a such boring world, so boring, that it won't be worthy to live.
>
> — Arnaldo Otegi 2003, 433

Despite Otegi's—the leader of the Basque homeland proindependence-left movement—statement regarding the Internet, his followers are amongst the most active users of digital technologies related to diaspora politics. Diaspora political activism is an example of Benedict Anderson's (1991, 2001) "long-distance nationalism," which is facilitated and enhanced, exponentially, by the Internet and the web.[1] The web allows individuals and associations to communicate, keep in touch, exchange information, organize, and build relationships or networks more easily, quickly, and inexpensively. Significantly, in the Basque diaspora webscape, some of its oldest diaspora websites are political sites as there were in the offline world. This tells us about the potential of the web as a medium for political activism—that is, as a digital platform for public discussion and dissemination of information.[2]

---

1 See also Fuglerud (1999), Schiller (2001), and Skrbiš (1991).

2 Arnaldo Otegi is the leader of the Basque homeland pro-independence-left movement. He was found guilty for attempting to rebuild Batasuna under ETA's direction. Otegi has been in prison since 2009. In June 2013, the

As of August 2005, there were seven diaspora associations with websites (7.1 percent of total sites) from Argentina, Mexico, the United Kingdom, the United States, and Venezuela (31.2 percent of all diaspora countries) that could be categorized as political. As of June 2007, two diaspora sites—Josu Askatu (Argentina, www.josu-askatu.org) and 6 de México (Mexico, www.6demexico.org)—were closed down as their goals had somehow been achieved.[3] Although they are just a fraction of the Basque diaspora webscape, they are examples of restless political consciousness in the diaspora. There are two types of political/humanitarian/advocacy groups. The first group only includes the London-based Basque Children of '37 Association (United Kingdom, www.spanishrefugees-basquechildren.org/), which is the result of the Spanish Civil War, General Franco's postwar dictatorship, and Basque and Republican political exile; while the second type includes ETA prisoners and refugees and the assumed "unlawful" extradition of "diaspora" Basques to Spain as well as to the Basque conflict in relation to human and civil rights violations (e.g., the closure of the only Basque-language newspaper, *Egunkaria*, and the banning of Batasuna in 2003 for their ties to ETA). The associations include the London Basque Campaign (United Kingdom, www.geocities.com/basquecampaign/), 6 de México (6 from Mexico, www.6demexico.org/), Josu Askatu (Argentina, www.josu-askatu.org/), Asociación Venezolana de Amigos de Euskal Herria (Venezuelan Association of Friends of the Basque Country, AVAEH, Venezuela, http://earth.prohosting.com/avaeh/), the International Basque Organization for Human Rights (IBO, United States, www.euskojustice.org/), and Asociación Diáspora Vasca (ADV, Argentina, http://euskalherria.cjb.net).[4]

The diaspora campaign against the closure of *Egunkaria* was not only taken on by political groups but by many cultural and educational community-based groups. For example, the Zurich Basque club's site (Switzerland, www.euskaletxea.ch/) displayed an *Egunkaria*-support banner, which read, "*Egunkaria* forward! Freedom of expression." In the U.S., protests against the closure of *Egunkaria* were organized by Basque groups, such as IBO outside the Spanish Consulate in San Francisco (April 26, 2003), which coincided with the anniversary of the bombing of Gernika, and by the New York Basque club in front of the United Nations headquarters (March 13, 2003). Also, the San Francisco Basque Club sent protest letters to the two Senators

---

Spanish Supreme Counrt ratified his sentence to six years in prison.

3 In January 2007, a new diaspora advocacy group was established in support of Sebastién Bédouret, coordinator of the Paris-based Basque radio station Txalaparta Irratia (France, www.radiopays.org/euskadi/). The Spanish police arrested Bédouret during a public demonstration in Hernani, Basque Country. He was accused of printing and distributing ETA's internal newsletter, *Zutabe*. Bédouret is also a member of the Committee of Solidarity with the Basque Country based in Paris (http://cspb.unblog.fr/). His radio program offers free weekly public service announcements to family, relatives, and friends of ETA members imprisoned in Paris' jails. (As of May 2007, there were 156 ETA members in French jails.) The blog http://libertepoursebas.blogspot.com was immediately set up by the so-called Committee of Solidarity with Sebastién Bédouret after his arrest and informs readers about his situation, while advocating for his freedom. As usual, messages of solidarity from different individuals and associations from all over the globe are posted to the blog. Bédouret was released on bail in March 2007. The blog has not been updated since then.

4 In addition, Lokarria is also a Basque humanitarian association created in 1990 in Paris to support the families of ETA political prisoners; it is housed by the Basque club of Paris. As of February 2010, Lokarria lacked an online representation.

from California, Dianne Feinstein and Barbara Boxer. Emilia Doyaga, founder and president of the New York–based Society of Basque Studies in America, argued that the Spanish government has to accept "the inalienable right of the Basques to self-determination in order to freely decide its own destiny as a nation" (*Deia*, March 15, 2003). Doyaga stated, "We sang Basque songs, read messages, gave interviews, held up signs protesting the Egunkaria event, and even held up a big canvas of Picasso's Guernica" (e-mail communication, March, 21, 2003). After seven years, on April 12, 2010, the Spanish High Court acquitted the five-member management board of *Egunkaria* as public prosecution could not find any evidence of ETA being behind the newspaper.

Coming back to the political groups, the ADV is a self-defined virtual community for diaspora Basques and their descendants, created in 1997 under the motto of "independence, peace, and democracy." ADV claims to have members spread across twenty countries and articulates its mission through a website, a mailing list in five different languages, and two electronic newsletters: *Berriak* focuses on news about the Basque conflict and homeland politics, while *Fitxak*, established in May 2005, focuses on educational information for the diaspora. The ADV's main goals are "To fight for the independence of the Basque Country, defending, and promoting the right to self-determination; to contribute to the creation of a favorable international consensus for the right of self-determination of the Basque people; to unite Basques and their descents dispersed throughout the world around the Basque culture and the essential principles of sovereignty, peace, and democracy."

Moreover, IBO was created by Basques, Basque descendents, and friends of Basques worldwide in 2003 "as a result of another series of attacks against the Basque language as well as attacks on freedom of the press in the Basque Country." IBO's goal is "to educate the public about human and civil rights abuses in the Basque Country," while disseminating "information about the Basque people's struggles and perspective"—in other words, IBO attempts to internationalize the Basque conflict. In April 2003, IBO organized an online petition "to call for immediate negotiations between the governments of Spain, France, the Basque Autonomous Community, the Foral Community of Navarre, and any other relevant organizations dedicated to peace, with the U.S. State Department, or other designated body." As of August 2007, the petition had been signed by 850 individuals and organizations from twenty-three countries (see www.petitiononline.com/basque/petition.html). IBO has not been active since 2005. The website was not to be found as of February 2009.[5]

5 Similarly, as a result of the lack of progress of the 2008 Basque peace process, sympathizers, members, and representatives of Eusko Alkartasuna-Argentina, the extraterritorial assembly of the EAJ-PNV in Argentina and the pro-independence left movement in Argentina, issued the so-called Córdoba Declaration (October 26, 2007) in support of a resolution of the conflict as they believe, the "diaspora is part of the conflict and also part of its solution." Consequently, with the help of the Basque association ADV (Santa Rosa, Argentina), they established a petition online (www.petitiononline.com/herria06/petition.html) to Spanish and French embassies to support the peace process. As of August 2007, 321 individuals from fourteen countries have signed the petition.

All the studied political groups, with the exception of the Basque Children of '37 Association, can be defined as pro-Basque nationalist and even as pro-independence, and close to the dictates of the Basque homeland pro-independence left movement and its coalition party, Batasuna. According to the webmasters of the aforementioned political associations' sites, the origin of some of their associations is found in the failure of diaspora institutions to respond—totally or partly—to the demand for participating in politics or for allowing a space for political discussion within their clubhouses.

In this respect, those groups have set up their own offline and online spaces where they can raise their own voices and consequently construct an alternative and plural discourse (or set of discourses) to counteract the one constructed by the "official" institutional diaspora. Those alternative pro-independence spaces for voiceless diaspora Basques are highly articulated on the web. The "local" conflict of the Basque Country becomes internationalized by means of the Internet, which provides a global framework and stage for localized events. Their sites fill the vacuum left by associations, such as *euskal etxeak,* with regard to promoting hyperpolitics (see McCaughey and Ayers 2003; and Cibergolem 2005). For example, ADV states that "the pro-independence movement has to create its own space in the diaspora so the collectivity won't become a manipulated object of [homeland] partisan politics . . . That all the *gudaris'* [soldiers of the Basque Army during the Spanish Civil War; sometimes the term also refers to ETA members] spilt blood hadn't been wasted. That all the dreams of the grandparents won't be betrayed. In every town, in every Basque center, the sleeping or silenced [national] sentiment must awake!" (*Berriak,* August 10, 2005).[6]

The following event involving the Buenos Aires association Eusko Kultur Etxea or Eusketxe (Basque Cultural House; established in 1988) illustrates the formation of parallel discursive spaces within the Basque diaspora community, in this case in Argentina. Eusketxe is an umbrella organization that encompasses the Basque Publishing House Ekin (established in 1942) and the Basque-language initiative, Euskaltzaleak (established in 1944). Eusketxe has been housed in the Laurak Bat's clubhouse for decades, but it was "evicted" in 2004 because of its political sympathy for the Basque pro-independence leftist movement, thereby clashing with Laurak Bat's board of directors and their Basque moderate nationalist ideology (Maite Velasco, Interview, November 2 and 5, 2005, Buenos Aires).

The event that ignited the "eviction" was the public display of a flag that read "Euskal Presoak Euskal Herrira" (Basque Prisoners to the Basque Country—a slo-

6 For example, the Basque homeland pro-independence movement has already established its own discursive space abroad, which also expands into cyberspace. Several committees have been set up in various European countries in solidarity with the Basque Country—meaning the Basque pro-independence and leftist movement. In Ireland for example we find the Irish Committees in Solidarity with the Basque Country (since February 2006, http://irishbasquecommittees.blogspot.com). In France, there is the Comité de Solidarité avec le Peuple Basque (since September 2006, http://cspb.unblog.fr), and in Portugal, the Associação de Solidaridade con Euskal Herria (since 2005, http://paisbasco.blogspot.com).

gan for ETA members imprisoned in Spanish and French jails to be regrouped in Basque jails) at the front of the Laurak Bat building. "Euskal Presoak Euskal Herrira" has become a popular and political slogan, a demand supported by both the BAC government and parliament. The board believed that people would identify this partisan sympathy with Laurak Bat itself and its official apolitical and nonpartisan policy. Consequently, the board of directors "evicted" the group by increasing the rent to an amount that Eusketxe could not afford, forcing them to leave. Velasco believes that this decision was fundamentally wrong because Eusketxe was the "most active element of Laurak Bat," and instead of uniting Laurak Bat, it was dividing the Basque community in Buenos Aires even further (Interview, November 2 and 5, 2005, Buenos Aires).[7] In 2005, Eusketxe purchased a building to relocate the evicted associations, establishing not only a symbolic and physical separation between two institutions, but also a cultural and political alternative interpretation of Basque culture and identity.

Diaspora associations like Eusketxe have to create their own discursive space when circumstances do not allow it by circumventing the central authority of clubs and federations in order to have a direct voice. In the power struggle between Eusketxe and Laurak Bat, cyberspace is also utilized in order to attract support. While Eusketxe, through Euskaletxeak's site, provided the means for seeking national and international solidarity in a cost effective way, Laurak Bat had to rely on its offline contacts as its website had been "under construction" since 2004. In 2004, Eusketxe established an online petition (www.petitiononline.com/eke1989) demanding the direct intervention of the Basque and Navarrese governments as well as the Department of the Atlantic Pyrenees of which Iparralde is a part. As of August 2007, it has collected over 1,692 signatures from eighteen countries that opposed the eviction. According to María Elena Etcheverry de Irujo, president of Ekin, the Basque government declined to intervene as they considered the "issue" an internal matter of a Basque association (Interview, November 8, 2005, Buenos Aires, Argentina).

These political groups are eager to convey the message that there is another diaspora, less visible and less promoted, that is, a political diaspora "committed to its country" and "to the struggles in Euskal Herria" (*Semanario*, June 2005). Cyberspace has become their new uncharted territory on the outer edges of the Basque diaspora webscape where resistance to their political project has not yet shown itself to be as hostile as in the offline world.

For example, during the celebration of Basque National Week in Córdoba, Argentina, October 2006, sympathizers of ADV and representatives of Udalbiltza-Kursaal held a street demonstration under the slogan of "Another Diaspora Is Pos-

7 On another occasion, some of the Eusketxe members participated in a political protest during the 2004 Basque National Week in La Plata (Argentina), which profoundly bothered the Laurak Bat leadership. "Two of our Basque teachers were expelled from Laurak Bat membership because of their involvement in the protest. They will never be allowed to be inside [the clubhouse] again" (María Elena Etcheverry de Irujo, Interview November 8, 2005, Buenos Aires, Argentina).

sible: Progressive and Committed." The demonstration ended up at the steps of the lodgings of the homeland visiting delegation, which included President Ibarretxe.

As a result of that demonstration, the Extraterritorial Assembly of the EAJ-PNV in Argentina issued a public call directed to the Basque-Argentinean community, exhorting it "to leave aside partisan political activity within [the Basque clubs] . . . [and] "to unify the Basque clubs in Argentina and to reaffirm their fraternal cohabitation just from an *abertzale* [patriotic] perspective" (Junta Extraterritorial de Argentina del PNV, December 2006). The Argentinean EAJ-PNV argued, "We have become aware that Basque political cannibalism has arrived in Argentina, and it is manifested in the Basque [National] Weeks, *on Internet sites*, and finally in the Basque clubs . . . threatening the cohabitation and harmony developed throughout the years thanks to the work of Basque nationalism . . . Now, there have appeared those who proclaim that a new diaspora is possible as if nothing built previously had ever existed or had any value" (ibid., December 2006; emphasis added).

The EAJ-PNV is sending a clear message to the Basque diaspora community in defense of its hegemonic nationalist discourse, which, in turn, evidences the politicization of diaspora identity. While the EAJ-PNV was exhorting the Basque-Argentinean community to avoid partisan politics, ironically, the document was discussed and signed in the library of the Basque club, Denak Bat, of Mar del Plata (Argentina), where the EAJ-PNV representatives met on a regular basis. According to the Denak Bat statutes, political activity is not allowed within the club. Accordingly, that statute was wielded by the Denak Bat's board of directors against the willingness of representatives of Udalbiltza-Kursaal to hold a public meeting in their clubhouse (see Bilbao December 5, 2006).

Similarly, the 2007 Basque National Week (Rosario, Argentina, October 1–7, 2007) was characterized by bitter protests and tensions between the host local club, Zazpirak Bat, and certain elements of its membership and homeland guests. The club's board of directors of the club announced the cancellation of a talk by representative of Batasuna, Josetxo Ibazeta. The talk was scheduled to take place at the Zazpirak Bat's clubhouse at the same time that President Ibarretxe was delivering a speech to nearly one thousand people at the local theater, Fundación. Ibarretxe was on an official trip to Argentina, Chile, and Colombia, and while in Argentina, he attended some of the Basque celebrations in Rosario. Sympathizers of Batasuna, including the Basque-Argentinean group from Rosario, JO TA KE, decided to protest the cancellation of the talk by holding a street demonstration in front of the theater. In addition, the Zazpirak Bat dancers refused to perform the following day. Inside the theater, Ibarretxe presented his new "road map." Against the backdrop of the cancellation of the talk, protesters carried banners reproving the lack of freedom of expression at the Basque clubs and waved Euskal Presoak flags, while, paradoxically, Ibarretxe defended dialogue without exclusions, referring to the banned political coalition, Batasuna. "Illegalize ideas is not the way," he said. "Did you ever see the British government illegalize Sinn Fein or imprison them in order to resolve their problems?" (*EuskalKultura,* October 9, 2007).

JO TA KE and Josetxo Ibazeta accused publicly the Basque government and its General Secretariat for Foreign Action for requesting the Zazpirak Bat's board of directors the cancellation of the talk (*Gara*, October 10, 2007, and October 24, 2007; JO TA KE, November 7, 2007). Secretary of the club, Felipe Eyheraguibel (secretary of FEVA, 2006–2007, and president of FEVA from March 2008 to March 2010) refuted those allegations (*Gara*, October 23, 2007).

Diaspora political groups such as IBO and ADV attempt to mobilize diaspora individuals, institutions, and communities at large because they believe that the Basque national identity is threatened by internal forces, such as conservative diaspora associations, as well as external forces, such as the Spanish government. Therefore, in their opinion, the diaspora needs to be vigorously involved in the homeland reality, understood not only as past, but also as present in order to build a future together. For instance, for the ADV being Basque equates to being politically committed to the Basque "cause" of independence. This commitment and participation go beyond involuntary Basque ancestry or birth and imply the existence of those who are politically active and those who are non-politically active. However, I cannot conclude that there is a hierarchy of political identities between "active Basques" and "non-active Basques." In my opinion, this only suggests different ways to relate to identity markers, which are related to diaspora Basques' diverse sociohistorical backgrounds and political traditions.

Those political groups advocate for diaspora individuals and associations to acknowledge not only the cultural and folkloric dimension of the homeland but also the political dimension. They believe that the apolitical stand of the institutional diaspora, particularly in countries such as Argentina, is just an excuse to disengage with the "other" Basque Country—the most active and committed with the Basque "cause"—that is, the homeland pro-independence movement and its alleged vanguard, ETA. For those political groups, this apolitical status masks its alliance to the EAJ-PNV, which is eager to maintain the bureaucratic and administrative status quo of the Basque Country as an autonomous community within Spain.

For example, at a meeting between FEVA's board of directors and Begoña Errazti, the then president of Eusko Alkartasuna (November 11, 2005),[8] historian Mikel Ezkerro, in charge of FEVA's cultural area, argued,

> The Basque clubs do not want to hear about politics, because they say that they are apolitical associations. That's nonsense. We need to educate our youth and the rest of the members about Basque politics. 'No, no, we don't talk about politics in the Laurak Bat,' [they say]. Let me remind you that until the 1940s, the flag displayed at the Laurak Bat balcony was the Spanish flag . . . they don't want to hear me saying that the original name of the club was "Sociedad Vasco-Española" [Basque-Spanish

8 The meeting took place at the Necochea Basque clubhouse within the framework of Basque National Week (November 9–13, 2005). I attended the meeting as an observer. Mikel Ezkerro is a member of the Centro de Estudios sobre Nacionalismo y Cultura Vasca Arturo Campion (Center for the Study of Basque Nationalism and Culture Arturo Campion, Laprida, Argentina). He has also been the president of Eusko Alkartasuna in Argentina.

Society] . . . Then, since the 1940s, the flag displayed at the Laurak Bat has been the ikurriña. Isn't this politics?[9]

(The criticism of the apolitical character of the Basque diaspora and the lack of "national consciousness" is not new. For example, during the Spanish dictatorship of General Miguel Primo de Rivera (1923–1930), several leaders of a pro-independence and non-confessional split of the EAJ-PNV, later known as Acción Nacionalista Vasca (Basque Nationalist Action), had to go into exile. Some of its leaders arrived in the U.S., and they began publishing the newspaper *Aberri* (September 1925–1928). Its first editorial, titled "To the Basques in the U.S.," stated, "It is heart breaking, in a great degree, to see the moral inertia in which the Basque colony in the U.S. is found. Every single country in the world fights in order to maintain or to obtain freedom, in the meantime the Basques residing in America sleep quietly without seeing the worldwide movement, without hearing the scream of distress of thousands of Basques, women and children, oppressed under the military yoke" (*Aberri*, September 1925). The Basque government-in exile in the United States, in the 1940s, was also astonished that the western U.S. Basque communities lacked any national consciousness (see San Sebastián 1991).

One constant demand of the diaspora political associations is the need to inform and educate the diaspora. ADV believes that "increased knowledge [of the homeland political situation] will imply commitment and solidarity with the Basque Country" (*Fitxak,* May 15, 2005). Specifically, ADV's site offers over 440 documents, mainly political news, and opinion articles about the Basque Country and its political conflict. ADV invites the visitor "to see Euskal Herria as a live country, not as a melancholic or folkloric postcard" by highlighting other aspects of Basque culture that are not purely ethnic or folkloric. ADV states, "even today in many Basque centers it is possible to hear people to say 'Spain' referring to the Basque Country, because there are those who understand the Basque land as a 'region' of the Spanish State. The Basques are not 'a people who sing and dance to the sound of a flute in the Pyrenees' as we were described by a geographer, but a nation without a state that fights for its independence from two states that deny its identity and its rights" (*Fitxak,* May 22, 2005, and June 12, 2005).[10]

Consequently, ADV and Udalbiltza-Kursaal signed an agreement in October 2005 in order to provide "accurate" information about the Basque political, cultural, social, and economic reality, in order to convert the Basque diaspora clubs as the "embassies" of the Basque Country in the world, as well as to internation-

9 Similarly, the then-editor of NABO's newsletter, John Ysursa, argued, "We can—and should—continue with our efforts here to promote our heritage, but we cannot pretend that something is not happening in the Basque homeland [in reference to the Basque conflict and ETA's violence] because this is usually the only news that most all non-Basques ever receive" (*Hizketa*, 2001).

10 In an effort to propagate the "true" conflict in the Basque Country, several individuals and associations have set up websites for news across Europe, such as *Berriak-News* (Germany, www.berriak-news.de), *Euskadi Information* (Switzerland, www.euskadinfo.net), and *Euskal Info* (United Kingdom, www.euskalinfo.net).

alize the Basque conflict (*EuskalKultura,* October 1, 2005).[11] That is, for the ADV, the "reality" of the Basque Country is not completed if the Basque conflict and its consequences are not taken into account, that is, if the diaspora ignores this other Basque "reality." ADV blames not only the diaspora for its disengagement with homeland politics, but also the Basque government, which, according to ADV, hides and/or disguises the "true" Basque Country as the main diaspora policymaker in the homeland. In the words of Bilbao, ADV's founder, "Members of the Basque Autonomous Community Government arrived at the diaspora to talk only about a fantastic Disneyland where there are no tortured people, nor dead prisoners' relatives on the road, nor an average of 100 workers dead every year in working accidents, nor . . . " (*Berriak,* August 2, 2005). That is to say, diaspora political associations and the Basque government compete with each other in their attempt to convey to Basques abroad the "true" image of Euskal Herria.

Diaspora Politics and the Hostlands

How does diaspora political activity affect an organization's relationship with its country of residence? What are the Basque diaspora attitudes portrayed on the Basque institutional diaspora websites toward the hostland—opposition, neutrality, or support? And why does the Basque diaspora exhibit such attitudes?[12]

In most cases, political groups work as advocacy groups for "political exiles"—those subjected to forced or involuntary migration, whose extradition has been requested by Spain for alleged ties with ETA. In this situation, their hostland governments become active agents in the extradition process, and consequently those governments are targets of criticism by diaspora individuals and associations. Such criticisms provoke a certain degree of friction and even conflict between hostlands and the diaspora, as well as between the hostland governments and Spain. ADV argues,

> More than two thousand Basque women and men [have been] forced to leave their land behind, simply because they dared to defend the right of Euskal Herria—the land of the Basques—to decide its own future, and to achieve its freedom. This is in fact one more chapter of a long political conflict that neither France nor Spain have been able to resolve, or better said, one they expected they could solve by repressive measures, tortures, bans, and crimes against Basque nationalism. We take the chance to tell, from the diaspora, that they are wrong; the resolution will take place within a framework of dialogue and with the utmost respect for the rights of Euskal Herria as a nation.

---

11 Udalbiltza-Kursaal argues that "Establishing and reinforcing the links within that community [the Basque diaspora] is one of the aims of Udalbiltza. Because the 'eighth province' also has a right to speak and to be heard and to take part in the process of building the Basque Country, which is their country too" (Udalbiltza-Kursaal's site, www.udalbiltza.net/en/basque_diaspora).

12 See the following literature on the political role of diasporas: Eccarius-Kelly (2002); Ellis and Khan (1998); and Fair (2005).

At the time of analyzing the diaspora webscape, there were some ongoing cases of extradition of "political refugees" for alleged ETA membership and collaboration. In the following pages, I shall address some of those cases in the countries of Mexico, Uruguay, Argentina, the United Kingdom, and Venezuela. Common to all of those cases is the creation of diaspora associations, and online platforms, that act as advocacy groups of individuals who have been arrested and who await extradition to Spain.[13] These associations become mediators, on behalf of the detainees and Basque communities at large, between the governments, while bypassing other institutional authorities, such as FEVA in the case of Argentina, and which has intentionally excluded itself from any involvement.

In Mexico, six Basque refugees—five Basque citizens and a Basque who became a nationalized Mexican citizen—were detained in July 2003 and were finally extradited to Spain as of May 19, 2006. The association 6 de México (the six from Mexico) was established in order to raise awareness about the case and vindicate the rights of the detainees. The association's website, www.6demexico.org, which is no longer available, was hosted by ADV. On the 6 de México's site, there was a Flash presentation: the Mexican and the Basque flags appeared first, then the photograph of the six people and a message in Spanish and Basque that read "La Solidaridad es la Ternura de los Pueblos; Elkartasuna, Herrien Arteko Xamurtasuna" (Solidarity is the Tenderness of Nations). The six Basques are Asier Arronategui—Mexican—Jon Artola, Axun Gorrotxategi, Joseba Urkijo, Félix García, and Ernesto Alberdi (see figure 6.1). The site organized an online petition to the Mexican government in order to free the "six Basque nationalists [pro-independence people] imprisoned in Mexico" and to deny the Spanish extradition request.

13 Almost every time that a person has been arrested abroad under the accusation of ETA membership, an advocacy or solidarity committee has been set up. In many instances, those organized groups have established an online presence to rally their cause. For example, in the Netherlands, in 1999 a solidarity committee for Esteban Murillo—arrested for alleged ETA membership—was set up by the so-called Basque Information Center (www.baskinfo.org), which was established in 1997 in order to transmit to the public the real conflict in the Basque Country. Murillo was extradited to Spain in July 2000, but he was declared innocent. He had previously lived in Chile and Mexico, where he had obtained a political refugee status. In addition, the solidarity association Gruppe Irrintzi (www.nadir.org/nadir/initiativ/irrintzi) was established in relation to Gabriele Kanze, a German citizen accused of cooperating with ETA. She was arrested in Germany in 2002, extradited to Spain, and then released in 2004 after dropping the charges. Other recent cases include the following. Gorka Perea Salazar and Eduardo Plágaro Pérez de Arrilucea were condemned by the Spanish Court System to several years for sabotage acts, but escaped to Montreal, Quebec, seeking refugee status. In 2001, Spain requested the extraditions of both Basque citizens, which was granted in June 2005. (This was the first time that Canada granted any extradition to Spain.) A support group for the two Basque "political prisoners," called Euskal Preso Politokoen Sostengu Taldea, was set up. On March 10, 2005, 250 people participated in a demonstration in Montreal in support of refugee status for Perea and Plágaro (*EuskalKultura*, March 10, 2005). More recently, Basque citizens Bittor Tejedor Bilbao and Iván Apaolaza were arrested respectively in Vancouver on June 1, 2007, and in Quebec on June 20, 2007, for alleged ETA membership. Tejedor and Apaolaza were extradited to Spain in June 2008 and October 2008 respectively. Tejedor was absolved for lack of evidence in April 2009. Similarly, in 1993, 1996, and 2004, the Spanish government requested the extradition of Basque citizens Luis Moreno and Rakel García residing in Belgium for alleged ETA membership. The Belgian government denied the extradition demands on all occasions.

Figure 6.1. The banner from the 6 de México site states "Freedom for the Six Basques!" Image source: 6 de México's site.

As of April 2006, over 1,600 individuals and organizations from thirty-six countries— including Basque and non-Basque individuals as well as internationalist, leftist, nationalist, and pro-independence organizations—signed the petition.[14] This created an international solidarity network in support of the Basques that clearly exceeded the Basque diaspora. In addition, other diaspora associations, such as the IBO from the United States and the Basque club in Mexico City also joined the human rights campaign. The board of directors of the Basque club in Mexico City issued a press release stating, "We would like to reaffirm clearly our human solidarity with those people [six Basques] because they are Basque, and they belong to our community, which is not going to abandon them to their own fate . . . independently of what they have done in the past."

As is evident in the rest of the cases that we are going to address in this section, some diaspora community-based groups portray the diaspora as a redemption space where Basques can start a new life leaving their past behind insofar as the past does not interfere with the present. If this occurs, the community is confronted with the dilemma of whether or not to advocate for the individual. In the following examples, the community always campaigns in favor of the individual's rights by wielding the discrimination card of being persecuted for the simple reason that they are Basques.

According to the ADV, the detentions of the 6 de México were "illegal" without "any solid evidence being presented by Spain." The ADV presented the case not as an attack against specific Basque individuals, but against the entire Basque nationalist movement, while strongly criticizing the Mexican government for bending its own judicial system to satisfy the Spanish government's demands. The ADV warned the Mexican government about the dangers of extraditing the six Basques to Spain "based on the reports of torture in Spain by Amnesty International and the dossier on the same issue by the United Nations."

In this sense, Mexican opposition parties, jurists, and non-governmental organizations expressed their concerns for the injustice carried out against the six Basques: "During the length of the process, numerous irregularities have been identified. Such irregularities blemish the image of the Mexican government, a government that has been unable to uphold the human rights and civil liberties

14 For example, the National Liberation Movement of Quebec, the Arizona Socialist Party (United States), the Consejo Indígena Popular de Oaxaca "Ricardo Flores Magón" (Popular Indigenous Council of Oaxaca "Ricardo Flores Magón," Mexico), and the Irish Republican Socialist Movement (Northern Ireland).

of the six prisoners that have been jailed." For example, Cauhtémoc Cárdenas, the Mexican political leader of the Partido de la Revolución Democrática, or Democratic Revolutionary Party in English, visited the "six Basques" in prison a day after a judicial sentencing favoring the extradition of the Basques was made public. Cárdenas stated, "I come here to state with my presence my rejection of the judicial process that has been full of irregularities" (*EuskalKultura,* April, 20, 2006). On July 28, 2005, the Basque government's Human Rights Commission issued a petition to the Mexican government for the "strictest fulfillment of the legality and the judicial guarantees" in relation to the six Basque citizens (at the online Basque community of Mexico City, www.vascosmexico.com).[15] It is not known whether the Mexican government has taken any initiative to clear its name against the 6 de México association's accusations of corruption.

In Uruguay, the case of Josu Lariz Iriondo provoked a similar reaction to the one in Mexico. In 1988, Lariz Iriondo arrived in Uruguay, and in 1992 he was detained because of an extradition request issued by Spain.[16] But in July 1993, Uruguay denied the extradition. In 2002, he was once again arrested but the extradition process was again stopped. At the time, the then–Spanish Minister of Interior Ángel Acebes considered Lariz Iriondo "the maximum ETA leader in Uruguay [and] one of the most wanted ETA members in Latin America" (*El País,* July 31, 2002). Consequently, former president of Uruguay Jorge Battle signed a decree to expel Lariz Iriondo from Uruguay. He was taken to Buenos Aires, where he was imprisoned to await extradition to Spain. Lariz Iriondo was released in 2005, and he is back in Uruguay after the then-president of Uruguay Tabaré Vazquez revoked the decree of expulsion.

The ADV hosted another website, www.josu-askatu.org, which is no longer available, and also set up an online petition, which was signed by over five hundred individuals and associations from twenty countries as of July 2005. In a public letter to the president of Argentina, the ADV stated, "It is a true shame that Argentina serves as a prison for political refugees. Even worse, because he is Basque. Ten percent of the surnames in our country have Basque origin. This collectivity has more than a well-deserved respect. Argentina cannot be associated with the politics of the Spanish right-wing, which is allied with President [George W.] Bush and his inauspicious actions against poor and undefended nations like Iraq."

15 In May 2007, "vascosmexico.com" was registered as a non-profit organization in the offline world. This is an unusual case. Normally, diaspora associations expand themselves into the online world, and not vice versa. As of October 2007, the association, "vascosmexico.com," has 1,255 registered users.

16 There are similar antecedents to the case of Lariz Iriondo in Uruguay. In 1992, twenty-eight Basques with false documentation were arrested. In 1994, another three Basque citizens—José María Goitia Unzurrunzaga, Luis María Lizarralde Izaguirre, and Miguel Ibáñez Oteiza—with political refugee status granted by the Uruguayan government were also detained in order to be extradited to Spain for involvement with ETA. Different Uruguayan organizations—such as the National Liberation Movement, Tupamaros—took the streets of Montevideo on August 24, 1994, to defend the detainees' right of asylum. As a result of police oppression, two people were killed. The Uruguayan Chamber of Deputies issued a statement titled, "Being Basque is not a Crime," which favored asylum for the Basques. It was signed by half of the chamber across all parties (*El País*, April 4, 1994). The three Basques were finally extradited. See Parissi (2006).

That is to say, the ADV utilized the positive status and the relative quantity of diaspora Basques in Argentina in order to articulate its defense against the extradition process of the Basque detainee. This argument has constantly been used in other countries where the Basque population has a positive and high socioeconomic status. At the same time, the ADV argued that the new global order established by the international coalition front that emerged after September 11, the "so-called coalition of the willing," meaning the United States, Spain, and the United Kingdom, "on the war against terrorism" could not become an excuse to limit human and civil rights.[17]

(At that time, the Spanish government's ruling party, the PP, insisted on identifying ETA with Al-Qaeda in an effort to rally international support against ETA. For example, then–Spanish Ambassador to the United States Javier Rupérez (see *The Idaho Statesman*, March 19, 2003), and Minister of Foreign Affairs Ana Palacio gave a speech that argued that ETA and Al-Qaeda were the same. In addition, Palacio stated, "the problem of the Basques is nothing less than the problem of freedom. Half of the population lives under the threat of terror from the other half" (*National Review*, January 28, 2004; see also *Deia*, February 13, 2004). Palacio implied that half of the Basque population—that is, the Basque nationalist community—was made up of terrorists.[18]

Basque diaspora individuals and associations, such as the Basque-Venezuelan AVAEH, ADV, six Basque diaspora community-based associations, and Eusko Alkartasuna, all from Argentina, mobilized against the extradition while seeking political refugee asylum for the Basque citizen, Lariz.[19] For example, the association Zazpirak Bat stated, "Only the full exercise of the basic rights that the Basque people should enjoy will be the solution of the Basque political conflict . . . We assert our willingness to support the national building of Euskal Herria . . . Consequently, as Basques and Argentineans, descendants of Basques, we express our solidarity with the Basque citizen Josu Lariz Iriondo, with his family and friends."

Between February and March 2006, I communicated with five of the aforementioned associations in order to find out whether their statutes addressed any reference to their apolitical status. The representative of the Basque club Ibai Guren, María Noel Balla, stated that her institution is "apolitical" while the clubs Eusko Aterpea and General Villegas'ko Euskaldunak stated that their statutes do not reflect clearly its apolitical or political nature. However, the board of directors of

---

17 In March 2003, American President George W. Bush, British Prime Minister Tony Blair, and Spanish Prime Minister José María Aznar issued the so-called Azores Summit Resolution, which leaded to war against Iraq without the approval of the United Nations Security Council and the European Union.

18 David Bieter, the Basque American mayor of Boise, has argued about the difficulty to communicate "the real image of the Basques [good and peaceful people] if the Government of Spain says that they are like Al-Qaeda" (*Deia*, February 12, 2004). Bieter also recalled a visit of Rupérez to Boise on November 3, 2001, when the former Ambassador compared the Basques to Bin Laden, while denying the existence of any political conflict in the Basque Country (*Gara*, March 6 and 8, 2002).

19 Those six associations were Euskaltzaleak (Buenos Aires), Eusketxe (Buenos Aires), Eusko Aterpea (General Rodríguez, province of Buenos Aires), General Villegas'ko Euskaldunak (General Villegas, province of Buenos Aires), Ibai Guren (Paraná), and Zazpirak Bat (Rosario).

those three associations issued political declarations rejecting the extradition process while demanding that the Argentinean government grant political asylum to Lariz. Furthermore, the representative of General Villegas'ko Euskaldunak stated that her association does not do partisan politics while arguing that

> An institution [i.e., FEVA] that says that 'it's representing all of us' is always looking for any excuse for not working with some people or institutions that are outside the influence of the Basque government . . . For example, the people of Udalbiltza [Kursaal] came to Argentina to offer the processing of EHNA [or Declaration of Basque Nationality] to the euskal etxeak. FEVA didn't like it. [However, what about] the presentation of the so-called New Political Statute (Ibarretxe Plan), with the arrival of representatives of the Basque government, including the Lehendakari, and the profuse dissemination of propaganda? Aren't those political acts?[20]

Despite General Villegas'ko Euskaldunak's self-defined nonpartisan status, Ibai Guren's board of directors signed an agreement in November 2005 with Udalbiltza-Kursaal to allow EHNA issuing on an institutional level in Argentina.[21] EHNA is a declaration of Basque nationality that states that the seven provinces form a sovereign nation that has the right to decide its own future, and that the Basque language is its national language.[22]

One could argue that the EHNA principles have been adopted by the Basque institutional diaspora a long time ago, and it is not surprising that some Basque associations are promoting the document among their members. At a meeting between FEVA and Udalbiltza-Kursaal (November 11, 2005), representatives from the homeland organization presented the EHNA document, while requesting FEVA to sign a joint declaration in its favor, by endorsing the right of self-determination of the Basque people.[23] The declaration was never signed by FEVA. Carlos Sosa, the then-president of FEVA, highlighted the *apolitical* status of FEVA as the main reason for refusing to sign any document: "As Carlos Sosa, I am in favor of the self-determination of the Basque people and the resolution of the Basque conflict by means of political negotiation. We wish the independence of the Basque Country.

---

20 The EHNA is not only a personal identification document, but an individual voluntary declaration of Basque nationality that states that the Basque Country is a nation made up of the following provinces: Araba, Bizkaia, Gipuzkoa, Lower Navarre, Navarre, Lapurdi, and Zuberoa; that Euskara is the language of the Basque Country and that it deserves respect and must have official status throughout the Basque Country; and that the Basque Country is a sovereign, independent, and free nation and has the right to democratically decide its future.

21 As of November 2006, fifteen Basque diaspora institutions and individuals were issuing EHNA in Argentina. Since April 2006, EHNA is also issued in the Basque club of Barcelona.

22 In order to obtain the EHNA document, homeland Basques need to demonstrate that they are registered with a local town hall from any of the seven provinces. In the diaspora, a Basque needs to prove her Basque ancestry. That is, Udalbiltza-Kursaal presents a double standard in relation to the definition of being Basque. On the one hand, in the Basque Country, the EHNA document can be acquired by anyone who lives in the jurisdiction of the local town hall—local residency proof, *jus domicile*—without presenting any proof of Basque ancestry and/or proof of being born in the Basque Country—that is, a territorial or circumstantial identity. On the other hand, Basques in the diaspora need to prove their Basque ancestry—in other words, *jus sanguine* or primordial identity.

23 The meeting took place at Necochea's Basque clubhouse within the celebration of the Basque National Week. FEVA gave me permission to attend the meeting as an observer. Representatives of Udalbiltza-Kursaal did also travel to the United States to meet NABO's board of directors in 2005.

However, as FEVA, I cannot sign anything, because we cannot be involved in politics as we represent many political sensibilities within our federation."

However, as we have seen in similar circumstances, FEVA had never had any problem issuing political declarations, such as the declaration in favor of the Ibarretxe Plan. So, I am inclined to believe that the decision is not related to the political character of the document, but about siding with an association allegedly tied to ETA, which could provoke some potential animosity with the Basque government and with their own member-clubs. In this regard, the Basque government delegation in Argentina issued a public statement (January 3, 2006) warning Basque individuals and associations in Argentina about the "unofficial status" of the EHNA document and its mere "emotional value."[24] The ADV came to the defense of the EHNA arguing that Euskal Herria is not official, but the Basques defend it and sustain its rights, and that for many diaspora Basques the connection with the Basque Country is merely based on emotional ties.

In the United Kingdom, Iñigo Makazaga was imprisoned in London in 2001 and was extradited to Spain in February 2006. A solidarity group called "Basque Campaign" was set up in 2001 to support Makazaga. Its website, www.geocities.com/basquecampaign, like the rest of the sites that we have seen so far, works as a catalyst for support. The group states, "Iñigo is just one of thousands of Basques, who due to their political actions, have had to seek refuge in different parts of the world, as a consequence of the repression and conflict in the Basque Country . . . He would be at risk of ill treatment if extradited to Spain . . . We think it constitutes a bad precedent for the U.K. Terrorism cannot be used as an excuse to cut our rights and liberties."

Similarly to the Argentina-based ADV, the Basque Campaign's goals extend beyond the timely fight against the extradition of Makazaga, to an attempt to obtain the recognition of the so-called "Basque problem" as a political clash among the Basque Country, Spain, and France, following Batasuna's proposal for conflict resolution, as well as showing, and practicing "active solidarity with any genuine struggle for freedom and justice all around the world."

Venezuela has been a country where Basques have traditionally enjoyed the right of asylum. In 1989, under an agreement between Venezuela and Spain, six Basque citizens allegedly linked to ETA were deported from Algeria to Venezuela where they obtained a political refugee status.[25] In 1996, the PP-ruled Spanish government sought the extradition of the six to Spain. However, the request was denied by the Venezuelan judicial system due to their refugee status. In April 2002,

---

24 As of December 2007, the Basque government has official delegations or proto-embassies in Brussels (Belgium), Buenos Aires (Argentina), Caracas (Venezuela), Mexico, D.F. (Mexico), Madrid (Spain), New York (United States of America), Paris (France), and Santiago de Chile (Chile). Those delegations, including the one in Madrid, are established under the general secretariat for foreign action.

25 These citizens were Eugenio Barrutiabengoa, Miguel Ángel Aldana, José Lorenzo Ayestarán, José Martín San Sebastián, Jesús Ricardo Arteaga, and Luis María Olalde. Ayestarán was arrested in France on February 27, 2010, in company of the alleged ETA leader Ibon Gogeaskoetxea.

under a new agreement between the late Hugo Chávez, president of Venezuela, and José María Aznar, orders of detention against the six Basques were issued. The Spanish government declared that forty other ETA members were living in Venezuela, and consequently, between 2002 and 2003, three Basques, legal residents in Venezuela, with political refugee status, were extradited.[26] However, none of them were part of the previously mentioned group of six Basques. Meanwhile, the Venezuela Supreme Tribunal of Justice denied the extradition of one of the six Basques, Luis María Olalde.

Those deportations provoked a reaction within the Basque and non-Basque community. Venezuelan human rights associations, such as the Committee of Family Members of Victims of the Events of February and March 1989 (COFAVIC), stated their opposition to any type of extradition of political refugees with legal residence in Venezuela. Plataforma BAI (Platform Yes) formed by an undisclosed number of Basque residents in Venezuela in favor of the right of self-determination of the Basque Country, and AVAEH, formed mainly by members of the Basque club of Caracas, which predates the specific extradition cases, opposed the extradition of any Basque resident. AVAEH's website helped to articulate the campaign against the extradition of Basques. The Federation of Basque Centers in Venezuela also stated their concerns about the situation of some members of "their community." That is, there was an institutional defense of all Basques, since it was felt that the community as a whole was under attack. The federation argued, "We express our rejection to the government authorities involved in the illegal detention and deportation of Juan Victor Galarza, legal resident in Venezuela . . . For no other reason than being Basque we have been discriminated against and oppressed" (at AVAEH's website, http://earth.prohosting.com/avaeh/).

A representative of the Venezuelan government "denied that the State was promoting a policy against the Basque community residing in the country." The representatives of Plataforma BAI, Luis Alberto Trincado and Mikel de las Heras, argued that, "If the six refugees who have been here for many years were to be deported, an enormous, painful, and deep wound would be inflicted on the Basque community in Venezuela [estimated between 250,000 and 500,000 people] . . . We all have a relative who has been persecuted since the exodus of the Spanish Civil War and we and Venezuela never failed them . . . On September 11 not only the World Trade Center towers fell, but also the certainty that Venezuela was a welcome house for [Basque] political asylum" (ibid.).

The advocacy groups argued their cases by utilizing the positive status of the Basque community in Venezuela while establishing continuity between the Spanish Civil War refugees and the current wave of ETA refugees. They do not differentiate between those who fought against Franco and those who are fighting against today's democratic Spain. That is, the legitimacy of fighting against fascism is

26 Juan Víctor Galarza, Sebastián Echaniz, and José Ramón Foruría.

transferred to the current fight against democracy.[27] For example, César Arrondo, then–vice president of FEVA, argued:

> Today, 65 years later, the President of the Spanish government, Mr. José María Aznar has sent a law on political parties to the Congress, which . . . is anti-constitutional and also anti-democratic. The only goal . . . is to declare illegal the Basque political party Batasuna. However, this law has another goal that is to legalize a tool that makes possible to threaten any nationalist manifestation in the State whenever Madrid feel like it . . . We only need to take into account that today, in April 2002: the bombs are still falling over Gernika. (Centro Vasco del Chaco's site, www.ecomchaco.com.ar/centrovasco/default.htm)

Once again, Basque advocacy or humanitarian groups argued that the post–September 11 international order has imposed a new agenda on many countries such as Venezuela, an agenda that followed the principles of the "war on terror" touted by the United States and its allies. It can be said that the use of the recurrent "post–September 11" argument by Basque diaspora advocacy groups strategically attempted to further their international scope by attracting other groups to their cause, groups that may be unhappy with this new post–September 11 global order. This "war on terror," consequently, did not leave much room for Venezuela to be seen as a haven for alleged terrorists. That is, Venezuela could no longer view Basques as political refugees but instead had to view them as terrorists.

Finally, in the United Kingdom, the Basque Children of '37 Association is not related to the current Basque political conflict, but rather to the Spanish Civil War exiles. The association, created in November 2002, is made up of Spanish Republicans and Basque "children" and their descendants residing in the United Kingdom (see Sabín-Fernández 2011). It is estimated that four thousand Basque children sought refuge in the United Kingdom at one point, while a total of twenty-five thousand Basque children left the Basque Country in 1937 for countries such as France, Belgium, the United Kingdom, the former Union of Soviet Socialist Republics, as well as Switzerland, Mexico, and Denmark (Legarreta 1984). By the end of 1939, after two years in the United Kingdom, most of the refugees had gone back to the Basque Country.

This association's site presents more narratives related to Basque internal history in a given hostland. The association's discourses of "injured memories" of oppression (Drzewiecka 2002, 7) refer not only to Franco's dictatorship, but also to the United Kingdom as well as to Gernika. The discourses are an open wound that has not healed yet, as closure has not been reached, specifically because of the

---

27 In 1964, exiled leaders of the EAJ-PNV established the Gudari Eguna (The Day of the Basque Soldier), and since then it has been celebrated to commemorate all fallen gudaris (Vazquez 1998, 363). The birth of ETA and the execution of its first activists—Juan Paredes Manot, aka Txiki, and Anjel Otaegi—on September 27, 1975, marked a new day of remembrance also called Gudari Eguna. The latest reference I have in relation to the celebration of the Gudari Eguna in the diaspora dates back to 1998, when the Basque club in Caracas might have celebrated the September Gudari Eguna. This point has been difficult to corroborate.

British Government's lack of recognition of Spanish refugees' contribution to the British war effort during World War II.

The association's main goal is "to keep alive for their descendants the memory of the experiences that the 'niños' [children] lived through when they came to Great Britain as refugees in 1937." The association firmly criticized the British press's treatment of the Basque children at that time: "The Basque children were targeted by the right-wing press, most who covertly supported Franco and its fascist allies. The press reported a great number of 'crimes,' such as car stealing, which, in turn, contributed to a down turn in donations to the BCC [British Children's Committee] and colonies." It also criticized the British government's neutrality toward the Spanish Civil War and the lack of recognition of Spanish Republicans who fought voluntarily for Britain in World War II since 1940, after losing their own war in Spain:

> Several fought in Norway, Crete and other countries . . . These proud and courageous men have never been recognized by the British military, British legion and government authorities . . . They were all told by the British that they had to say that they were from South America and not Spanish . . . The reason given to us by a living member of the Spanish Company is that the British military and government did not want to offend General Franco . . . They were not allowed to march on [the 1986] Remembrance Sunday. Not to be together with other soldiers . . . They were alone that Sunday; alone . . . It seems that the British Government cared more about not offending Franco and less about defending the people of Spain.[28]

Conclusions

Basque political, humanitarian, and advocacy groups in the diaspora mobilize politically in a variety of ways. In some cases, those groups have been able to lobby in order to rally enough support from their host societies. They portray Basque refugees as helpless victims trapped in complex realities of tragedy, loss, and uncertainty. That is, exile is not understood in romantic or heroic terms, but rather in terms of radical uprootedness and disconnectedness. In some instances, the active defense of Basque refugees' rights provokes a direct conflict between diaspora groups and their hostlands because the activists attempt to exert political influence on their host governments. For example, the Argentine and Uruguayan governments have stopped extradition processes in spite of Spain's political pressure, while other countries, such as Mexico and Venezuela, have succumbed to international law despite internal opposition.

Moreover, these diaspora groups also exhibit a great deal of criticism toward the Basque government. They conceive of Basque identity from an almost exclusively political perspective, disregarding to some extent the folkloric or ethnic aspect, which is the one that the Basque institutional diaspora and the Basque government mainly promote. In a sense, by synchronizing politically with the home-

28 See, for example, Moradiellos (2005).

land and its political demands, the diaspora political associations gain legitimacy as "true" or "authentic" Basques who care about the homeland and its future in the eyes of homeland Basques, who can no longer regard diasporic Basques as folkloric, politically passive, or estranged from homeland reality.

At the same time, the existence of a few political groups confirms that the majority of the Basque diaspora is to a certain degree politically disenfranchised with the homeland. The diasporic discourse takes on the intellectual mission of awakening the assumed dormant national consciences of diaspora Basques by alerting them that the future of Basque identity is endangered due to Spanish and French oppression and the BAC government's idle politics.

A common characteristic of all diaspora political groups is their hyperpolitics. The political potentiality of the Internet goes beyond the fact that facilitates the communication and information flow. It also increases the groups' campaigns and/or goals and chances to become successful (for example, through new means of influence). The groups' effective instrumentalization of the Internet and the web bring awareness of localized events such as the Basque conflict to a global audience in order to promote social and political mobilization and support. Consequently, this attracts the support of thousands of individuals and associations from all over the planet that share similar human rights, civil rights, and political goals. The groups are able to establish networks of solidarity beyond their immediate area of action and their constituencies. This network is particularly intense among the Basque diaspora political groups studied here. The Basque diaspora online poltical activism allows for horizontal communication in a space that encourages socialization, participation, debate and action (e.g., influencing public opinion), and complements traditional action tools in the physical realm.

The degree of connectivity—via hyperlinks—between diaspora political sites favors cooperation between diaspora associations—online and offline—and signifies a consciousness of themselves, while reinforcing each other's ideas and actions. These associations use the web to further their pro-independence goals and to transmit ideas and ideology while bypassing censorship and mainstream mass media. The Internet facilitates and empowers the diaspora, radiating its strength from an individual to a more organized level to encourage more active involvement in homeland and international politics. The pragmatic instrumentalization of the web is exemplified by the fact that pages are taken down as soon as their goals and campaigns have come to an end, affecting the act of remembering those past events and the diaspora's collective memory. However, the imperfectness of that forgetting crystallizes around personal and institutional archiving of those webs.

Beyond

(07)

Cyber-Imagination

This book has captured both dimensions, online and offline, of a historical diaspora such as of the Basque, defined here as a global imagined community, which is, indeed, still unfolding. It has opened a paronamic window to a migrant world that has profusely changed due to technological development and the varying goals of diaspora institutions, within a three-decade time frame. Looking back to the then incipient presence of Basque migrant associations on the web, some of the described characteristics of such a presence do not sound surprising nowadays, even though the technology and its usage was uncommon back then. If in the 1990s, there were only a few diaspora associations online in four countries, as of June 2007, over 62 percent of Basque diaspora institutions in nineteen countries throughout the continents of America, Asia, Europe, and Oceania have established a presence in cyberspace by creating official websites that represented their institutions online, including *euskal etxeak,* educational, cultural, business, and political sites. Within this ever-changing webscape ecosystem, one of the newest sites was established by the Basque Club of Rhode Island, United States, in 2011 (http://ribasque.weebly.com/), against the backdrop of the swell of social network sites, profusely "colonized" by Basques associations worldwide.

The figure of the webmaster—under the supervision of the board of directors, membership, and website committees of the various institutions—is central to the creation of the Basque webscape and maintenance of the institutional sites, helping to construct an active digital diaspora as part of a Basque cyberspace. The webmaster, as part of what I have described as Basque digital intelligentsia, is predominantly young; male; university educated; informally or formally educated in information technology, computer, or Internet studies; of Basque descent; is a volunteer; and is a member of a Basque diaspora association. The webmasters are in charge of the design, maintenance, upgrading, and authoring of the website content, but the associations' administration, membership, and individuals from the community also play a role in content creation. Almost all webmasters believed that the associations' administration and membership viewed the websites as positive and significant, while some webmasters believed that the survival of the site was essential to their association's future.

Nearly all webmasters had specific goals when they established the associations' sites. The establishment of the sites was the result of careful planning. The main goals were several. First, to provide informational narratives of (self-)discovery and (self-)education that reinforce positive social status of being Basque. Second, to position diaspora Basques in relation to homeland Basques, allowing those in the diaspora to have a voice and a presence in cyberspace as a global public space. Third, to establish effective channels of communication among the different parts of the diaspora, and between Basques and non-Basques. And fourth, to have an online presence allowing the diaspora to create a cyberexpansion of itself in the online world. The majority of the webmasters believed that they were successfully reaching their goals. They also adopted new goals in relation to their institutions' agendas, including new purposes, activities, and services provided online. However, some webmasters argued that they were not reaching their goals because of the lack of financial and human resources, time, and technological knowledge. In this regard, nearly half of the sites were mainly funded by their associations and by the webmasters themselves.

The main languages used by the webmasters were English, Spanish, Basque, and French. The main reasons for the webmasters' selection of languages were the use of the hostlands' official language(s); the languages spoken by the webmasters; and the languages spoken in the homeland. Although the Basque language is highly regarded by diaspora institutions as one of the most powerful Basque identity markers, its actual use on websites is residual, limited to a few sentences, words, and introductory epigraphs.

The main intended audience and/or potential users of the websites were, by order of preference, the diaspora association's membership, the local Basque association, Basques in the country of residence, homeland Basques, diaspora Basques, and non-Basques. The activities provided by the sites were intrinsically related to the aforementioned goals and intended users specifically to offer information about the association, to promote it, to attract new members, and to inform about Basque history, culture, or language. This is reinforced by the fact that the majority of the webmasters would like to offer more content on Basque-related issues, particularly the ones pertaining to the homeland.

Finally, the majority of webmasters argued that the Internet makes possible two main activities. First, it helps to maintain Basque identity in the diaspora because it informs and educates the diaspora about being Basque. That is, there is a tendency toward synchronous knowledge in order to reduce the gap between diaspora and homeland. And secondly, the Internet increases the communication, connection, and interaction amongst diaspora communities, and between those communities and the homeland. The webmasters emphasized the possibility for community creation by empowering diaspora consciousness.

The analysis of the Basque diaspora webscape's hyperlink network offered insight into the social networking, and geographical, linguistic, and thematic directionality of the Basque diaspora online, demonstrating its sense of commitment to the homeland, hostland, and diaspora. As of August 2005, the majority of the Basque diaspora websites were linked to the Basque homeland, understood as the Basque Autonomous Community, Navarre, and Iparralde. The second-highest number of links was directed toward the Basque diaspora itself, called intra-diaspora connectivity, leaving only a small percentage of links directed at the hostland. Geographically, the Basque diaspora online was connected to North American Basque sites, South American Basque sites, and European Basque sites. Linguistically, the digital diaspora was connected to English-speaking countries and Spanish-speaking countries. Although geographical and political barriers are meaningless in cyberspace, linguistically the Basque diaspora online is divided into two main blocks as happens in the offline world: English- and Spanish-speaking countries.

The use of audio-visual and graphic content attempt to express and promote a digital banal nationalism while conveying messages of collective representation in relation to both homeland and hostland—in other words, a diaspora "in-between" national spaces. It is here, in this "in-betweenness," where the Basque institutional diaspora produces and distributes its own sense of Basque culture, while articulating identity discourses for a potential global audience by means of digital technology. At the same time, some minority elements of the Basque diaspora profusely utilize the Internet in order to gain support for their political causes, particularly in relation to alleged ETA members residing abroad resulting in hyperpolitics understood as long distance nationalism and activism.

In general terms, the Basque institutional diaspora online is promoting not only a notion of Basque identity related to an essentialist definition of Basqueness (e.g., anyone who is of Basque ancestry), but also a notion of nationhood and Basque homeland based on Basque nationalist principles that portray the homeland as a unified political and territorial nation delineated by seven historical provinces.

The Basque institutional diaspora self-defines and self-represents as an organic and integral part of the Basque homeland—that is, the eighth province or Zortzigarren Herrialdea—as well as a transnational family across borders. However, it is not so clear that diaspora online discourses consciously exhibit an explicit narrative of their own diasporicity—a consciousness about itself—or as an autonomous entity.

In addition, the Basque diaspora online has reproduced three main discourses that preexisted the Internet. The homeland discourse is articulated through narratives of nationhood. The diaspora discourse is articulated by narratives of dual or even multiple identities as well as political and national allegiances. The hostland discourse is articulated by narratives of migration, settlement, identity maintenance, and institutionalization. The Internet and the web allow the diaspora to expand its aforementioned discourses into the global arena by creating a liminal, interstitial, or cybernetic space.

Ninety percent of Basque diaspora institutional websites from sixteen countries identify with the representation of the homeland as a unified and ancestral territory, coinciding with the imagined homeland of the Basque nationalist movement. According to the Basque diaspora, the Basque Country consists of seven provinces with historical, anthropological, and cultural commonalities. Consequently, the Basque diaspora online fosters a digital nationalist Zazpiak Bat project, reflecting the Basque diaspora's offline world nationalist interpretation of Basque ethnicity, which has enhanced a unified national territorial project since the nineteenth century. Moreover, the examination of the Basque government's current ethnonationalist discourse on the diaspora has facilitated the assessment of its influence on the Basque institutional diaspora's current discourses.

Consequently, we see that the diaspora reconstructs a primordial or essentialist Basque identity, nationhood, and homeland following a previous reinterpretation of homeland ethnonationalism, mainly tied to the Basque Nationalist Party. In addition, the concepts of commonality, uniqueness, and authenticity become central to the diaspora's discursive production in relation to the reconstruction of the Basque nation and homeland. Similarly, the Basque government's discourses also re-create a perennial, timeless, and authentic nation. Within this context, Gernika becomes a highly symbolic identity discourse for the diaspora.

The Basque government's ethnonationalist discourses are useful vehicles for reconnecting with the diaspora, at least on an emotional level, as well as for maintaining national consciousness amongst diaspora Basques and institutional intelligentsia. However, the government attempts to close the existing disjuncture between homeland and diaspora as the result of spatial and temporal dislocation, by utilizing, for example, the Basque public satellite television as well as terrestrial television and radio, which are currently broadcasted via the Internet. The Basque diaspora challenges notions of identity and ethnicity in the homeland as it promotes an essentialist discourse. This primordialist discourse is based on reminiscences of the homeland and notions of identity that were inherited from their forefathers and subject to specific generations, localities, and time, as well as previous nationalist interpretations of identity and culture.

Meanwhile, the diaspora also incorporates migration and resettlement experiences into its discourse, experiences that translate into dual or multiple identities. Nevertheless, this essentialist discourse does not impede the diaspora from holding different national loyalties. That is, the Basque institutional diaspora re-creates its own sense of identity—multiple, deterritorialized, and diasporic—where nostalgia and idealization are not detrimental, but rather intrinsic and, to some degree, necessary strategic markers. As seen, the Basque diaspora essentialist discourse has some strategic value of in-group positionality in reference to their hostlands, as well as a way to articulate a community that might overcome assumed individuality and chaos by infusing order, certainty, and familiarity.

In this regard, the Basque government attempts to bring the diaspora up to date, in synchrony with the twenty-first century "real" homeland, which has to some extent departed from ethnification and primordialism. For the last decades, the Basque society has been promoting a more inclusive approach to Basqueness, which emphasizes the subjective aspect of being Basque in opposition to objective criteria, such as ancestry or birth. We come to terms with the fact that the identity created in the Basque Country is not purer or more perfect than the one in the diaspora, and that the identity generated in the diaspora is not just a reflection of the one created in the homeland, but rather different interpretations of a common generic identity. In this context, synchronous communication regains an increasing relevance.

The stand of the Basque institutional diaspora is assumed to be apolitical and nonpartisan. Conclusively, the evidence contradicts such an assumption. The data corroborates that the Basque diaspora is to some degree a political actor by re-creating a Basque nationalist interpretation of Basque identity and culture, and consequently acting according to nationalist principles. As we have seen, the Basque diaspora mobilizes politically in different ways. The Basque institutional diaspora is promoting and reproducing, consciously or not, a sense of political ethnonationalism linked to specific Basque homeland nationalist parties, such as the Basque Nationalist Party and, to a lesser extent, to Batasuna. What is more, for decades the Basque government has bestowed the diaspora with the role of becoming an active political agent, if only symbolically, not only in the promotion of a peaceful Basque Country, but also in the defense of Basque self-determination.

In addition, a minority of diaspora associations across six countries are actively involved in homeland politics, particularly in the defense of alleged ETA refugees abroad, while seeking the independence of the Basque homeland. These groups enter in direct conflict with their hostlands as they attempt to resist any extradition demand made by the Spanish government. However, there was no evidence that the host governments reacted negatively against those groups, or by extension against the Basque communities or their institutions. The diaspora political associations' instrumentalization of the Internet and the web is a prime example of how diaspora groups can benefit from the potential of such technologies for empowering, networking, lobbying, and raising awareness of localized issues among a global audience. Those groups have not only re-created an online alternative space, but have also created their own discourses, which depart from the institutional diaspora's mainstream spaces and set of ethnocultural or folkloric discourses. It is not a coincidence that the first-ever institutional diaspora websites were political.

Into the Future

The ephemeral nature of the web suggests the need for longitudinal studies to track changes over time. Those are related to the Basque diaspora webscape itself—that is, webmasters and the usage of the Basque language—hyperlink network analysis, and the websites' users. Also, future longitudinal research on the Basque digital diaspora would be more than welcome in order to assess the changes, if any, of its political discourses and ways of reconstructing Basque ethnicity and nationalism online.

The particular application of a longitudinal study would be useful in order to study the evolution of the Basque diaspora websites' goals in relation to the input of new webmasters and different overseeing committees and boards of directors. Similarly, a study on the evolution of the usage of the Basque language in the online Basque diaspora would measure the presence of one of the most distinguished identity markers of the Basques. Would the Internet encourage the usage of minority languages, such as Basque, or quite the opposite? How may the existing diasporic linguistic barriers deter the interconnectedness of different diaspora communities online and offline?

Research on the hyperlink network would offer new insight into the networking and directionality of the Basque diaspora online. Elements to be taken into account are the study of internal links or "deep" links, which refer to relevant pages or sections within the websites themselves, and the reciprocity of links between the three main geographical and discursive domains: homeland, hostland, and diaspora. The reasons why webmasters, boards of directors, and committees choose to hyperlink with certain sites will begin to help us understand why Basque diaspora websites interconnect the way they do.

User-based research on the Basque diaspora webscape will complement the content-based research on offline world effects of diaspora websites, expanding, for example, on questions of who uses them, for which purpose, and what difference they make. This line of analysis could establish the correlation between the creation of websites by Basque diaspora institutions, and their potential impact on maintaining Basque identity in the diaspora. At the same time, there is still much to be understood on the issue of online groups and mailing lists, a traditional subject of web studies.

In addition to longitudinal studies, a comparative examination between the Basque diaspora online and other digital diasporas (e.g., the Galician or Catalan) would provide enormous beneficial insight into the ways that they articulate their presence online. In this sense, it would also be useful to explore homeland websites—governmental, non-governmental, educational, and media sites—that might help to introduce the Basque diaspora to the homeland. Such research could measure the significance of the Basque diaspora at home and how homeland Basques imagine and represent the Basques abroad as a way to introduce it to homeland Basques.

Moreover, future analysis on the institutional relationships between the Basque government and the organized and nonorganized diaspora would deepen our understanding of the impact of governmental policies, funding, political discourses, and their evolution, in relation to the Basque diaspora. It would also be beneficial to analyze the discursive production, and the impact of the Basque government's diaspora-oriented media, such as the intra-diaspora magazine *Euskal Etxeak*, and other types of Basque public television and radio programs. At the same time, a significant area for future research could be the political role of Basque diaspora institutions and their use of new technologies, such as the web, with respect to the following issues: the role of ethnicity amongst diasporans' political activism in relation to the homeland and hostlands; the international political mobilization of ethnonational groups, such as the Basques; the transnational networking of diaspora political associations within the Basque diaspora and with other ethnic and migrant groups; and the meaning of ethnonationalism for diverse Basque diaspora institutions across different countries, and the expressions of such ethnonationalism.

Toward Social Networking

According to the 2001 U.S. census, nearly fifty-eight thousand people self-defined as Basque. However, as of August 2007, only approximately six thousand were members of Basque institutions in the United States. Similarly, in Argentina, several diaspora institutions, such as the Buenos Aires–based Juan de Garay Foundation, argue that over 10 percent of the population is of Basque ancestry, but only approximately eighteen thousand are members of Basque associations as of August 2007. In 1996, the Basque government (Gobierno Vasco 1996, 47) estimated that there were 4.5 million people of Basque ancestry abroad, while indicating that the number of members of Basque diaspora associations worldwide was nearly eighteen thousand (Gobierno Vasco 2000). If those estimates are correct, only 0.4 percent of Basques abroad are members of diaspora institutions.

Furthermore, according to a statistical report carried out also by the Basque government (Gobierno Vasco 2000, 27–32), the Basque diaspora institutions' membership was aging: 64 percent were over 46 years old, while the emigrant generation was slowly disappearing—in other words, 83 percent of the members were already born outside the homeland. Furthermore, the Basque institutional diaspora was failing to reach new members and particularly the youth.[1] Consequently, the Basque institutional diaspora's future looks bleak, opening a debate about the relationship and further involvement with the Basque homeland institutions, headed

1 According to information provided to the Basque government by eighty nine (or 55 percent) of the existing Basque clubs registered with the Basque government in 2006, 59 percent of their members were over forty-six years old, and only 13 percent were between eighteen and twenty-nine years old (Kerexeta 2008). Similarly, as of 2007 according to a study on 54 percent of the members of FEVA, 64 percent were over forty-six years old, 14 percent were between sixteen and thirty years old, and only 2 percent were born in the Basque Country (Ayesa and Orbaiceta 2008).

by the government, as well as the role that the government may play regarding its financial and moral support.

Nevertheless, between October 2005 and August 2007, thirty-four new websites were created by diaspora associations, and four additional platforms were created by associations with an established online presence. Evidence shows an increasing tendency to articulate an online presence. That said, the Basque diaspora online has not reached its full potential yet, as also happens in the offline world. As of June 2007, nearly 38 percent of diaspora associations had no presence on the web. The growth of the Basque diaspora in cyberspace, particularly in countries such as Argentina and Uruguay, is still significant. For the most part, there is no reason for not being connected.

The creation of websites or other online platforms of communication and interaction such as mailing lists and blogs should be viewed by diaspora institutions as neither trendy nor superfluous. The Basque diaspora presence on the web should be encouraged by the community and institutional leaders as well as by homeland institutional representatives. Moreover, it should be backed up by strategic long-term plans, which should address the financial and human dimension while measuring not only the input, but also the outcome of the commitment for such a presence.

Beyond the criticism that the fashionable "Web 2.0" concept provokes in the academic community, there is a new feeling about the web, which entails the practical use of web platforms, such as weblogs.[2] Although many of the web 2.0 applications are over a decade old, it seems that in fact they are new, at least in the way that now they are being used in order to share, collaborate, and self-publish.

Since the initial research took place in 2005, new diaspora associations have opted for having a presence in cyberspace; other associations renewed their sites and domains; others constituted themselves into weblogs, facilitated by the release of new software architecture coined as "Web 2.0." This second face or generation of software facilitates the exchange of data and possibly the existence of social networking or collaborative websites, such as weblogs; textual blogs, photoblogs, audio blogs, such as MySpace, Facebook; microblogs, such as Twitter; or podcasting, such as YouTube; and wikis, such as Wikipedia.

Increasingly, however, Basque diaspora associations are beginning to move away from static and encyclopedic sites, which currently dominate their webscape, to more dynamic and collaborative ones, such as blogs and social networks sites including Facebook. Basque diaspora websites are beginning to move from forming communities of interest and (self-) representation to forming communities of relationships by interacting with people who share similar interests. The focus has shifted from displaying information to producing information by way of sharing in a

2 The so-called Web 2.0, based on XML (eXtensible Markup Language), defines in retrospect the previous known web as Web 1.0, which is based mainly on HTML.

constructive manner. Internet means not only that users can influence each other's lives in any part of the globe, but also that they can learn from each other as well as collaborate with each other.

The user would most likely become central to the reconfiguration of the Basque diaspora webscape, displacing to a certain extent the central figure of the webmaster as the main author of the websites and other online platforms. The Basque diaspora associations' initial establishment of blogs can be not only a response to the availability of those technologies, but also a response to the lack of interactivity present in their current websites. It is a new way to attract members by offering a space where they express their points of view and build some sense of community—that is, a place where they can express their individuality by connecting to a collective identity (see Oiarzabal 2010 and 2012a).

However, I do not believe, and the evidence does not support, the notion that the Internet and the web—in the form of sites or blogs or whatever comes next—are the magic elixir for resolving the most crucial difficulties that the Basque diaspora is currently experiencing. Nevertheless, the intrinsic characteristics of the Internet and the web—global scope, speed, inexpensive cost, connectivity, and interactivity—are *stimuli* for diasporas to use those information and communication technologies. They enhance the ability for diasporas to be more connected and more present while educating and informing a potential global audience not only about their associations but about their own ways of reinterpreting Basque identity and culture. These technologies might complement and amplify many of the activities already carried out by the offline associations, such as Basque language e-learning; Basque heritage and genealogy; and information about the homeland—that is, direct access to media news.

In this sense, the Internet and the web are attractive tools, particularly for young members of the community, as well as outreach tools for gaining, at least, the interest of new potential members, inside and outside the immediacy of their institutions and communities—that is, for maintaining and increasing social capital. These technologies provide a valuable infrastructure for diaspora institutions to network within themselves as well as with the homeland, which might translate into offline, cross-border, and transnational cooperation.

The Internet and the web allow for the horizontal and decentralized interconnection of Basque diaspora communities or nodes of a Basque global network—in other words, an identity-based cybercommunity limited neither by time nor by space. These computer-based technologies allow the Basque diaspora to expand their discourse from a local-bounded community to a global audience. Through the Internet and the web, the diaspora is able to re-create, express, and spread their culture to the world, while claiming and promoting their identity. The web is a form of media for cultural preservation and transmission for the twenty-first century just as the diaspora's institutional newspapers, newsletters, or radio programs were in the nineteenth and twentieth centuries. The diaspora should realize and embrace the potential of the Internet and the web as new models for cultural transmission. The Internet is an excellent tool for communication and interaction as well as for networking and socializing.

In addition, the existing *two-way* estrangement between the diaspora and the homeland could be substantially reduced by consuming information distributed by means of the Internet. Meanwhile, the homeland could also benefit from the Basque diaspora presence in cyberspace by consuming their discursive production on identity, migration, and settlement histories. This disjuncture can be overcome by both sides. The diaspora online has already begun to build bridges toward the homeland, as exemplified by the number of hyperlinks created with it. However, future research on the Basque homeland online (media, governmental, private, and personal) is needed in order to evaluate the significance of the diaspora for the homeland and its level of connectivity as well as the discourses created in relation to the diaspora.

We are witnessing the beginning of a Basque global cybercommunity that should encompass not only the homeland, but also the diaspora. The Basque diaspora presence in cyberspace has contributed to the distribution of its own discursive production, which adds a new dimension to the existing Basque cyberculture—mainly a homeland production. The Basque diaspora discourses are widely available in an unprecedented manner by the use of a distributive channel, such as the web. The Basque diaspora, consciously or not, is contributing to the creation of Basque cyberculture—a horizontal discursive and nonhierarchical culture. It is also up to both diaspora associations and homeland public institutions to preserve such a cyberculture for the benefit of both communities (see Oiarzabal 2011).

To conclude and to begin, the present work has opened a window to new dimensions of the Basque diaspora in cyberspace. It has given us the opportunity to rethink Basque identity, culture, nation, and homeland and their intersections with technology from different points of view, allowing us to look beyond ourselves as an imagined community rooted in a geographical territory. We are beginning to comprehend the software and hardware that makes up the Basque diaspora webscape and even more the Basque Web 8.0. The first step to understanding the complex reality of the projection of the Basque diaspora into cyberspace has already taken place. What would it lay beyond this new cyber-imagined Basque diaspora? The book also aims at opening new venues for future multi- and interdisciplinary analysis as well as comparative and longitudinal works that could clearly be of interest to researchers, scholars, and students of migration, diaspora, and new technologies. I am confident that many promising studies on the interaction between the Basque diaspora and information and communication technologies might follow this initial step.

Epilogue

As of this writing, I returned to my hometown after sixteen years abroad. At the University of Deusto in Bilbao, I conducted further research on the Basque institutional diaspora presence on the web in order to study the evolving use of different digital platforms by the diaspora and their potential impact on maintaining Basque identity abroad (see Oiarzabal 2010, 2011, and 2012a). By focusing on the Basque diaspora case, I draw attention to the implications that information and communication technologies might have on international migrant diasporas (see also Alonso and Oiarzabal 2010; and Oiarzabal and Reips 2012a).

As stated earlier, since 2005, there has been a clear evolution of the usage of online platforms by Basque diaspora institutions. Between 2005 and 2007, the Basque digital landscape or webscape was dominated by websites, while the 2007–2009 period is characterized by the increasing establishment of social network sites (first blogs—mainly hosted in Fotolog and Blogger—and then MySpace and Facebook) to the detriment of websites. The Basque digital diaspora is constructing new digital landscapes—*blogosphere* and *networkscape*—but without abandoning its initial webscape. It is promoting a hybrid and networked space by combining different online and offline platforms in order to advance their institutions as well as their sociocultural, recreational, folkloric, linguistic, and political agendas.

As of March 2009, the diaspora had formed 211 associations throughout twenty-four countries, of which 135 (or nearly 64 percent) had a presence in cyberspace in twenty countries (or over 83 percent of the total).

In addition, I have completed research on the users of Basque diaspora associations' groups on Facebook as the largest social network site on the web, with particular emphasis on how migrant associations and their members perform to accomplish their activities and goals (see Oiarzabal 2012a). For instance, the results of the study showed that social network sites such as Facebook seem to be a positive factor in the reality of how Basque diaspora associations and members perform. Most users strongly state that Facebook has had a varying degree of influence or impact on their ability and the ability of diaspora groups to keep in contact, be informed and reaffirm and maintain their identity, with a strong emphasis on learning about their shared culture. As of June 2013, 143 Basque diaspora groups from nineteen countries had created a profile on Facebook alone.

Particularly, within the historical context of ETA's declaration of the definitive end of its fifty long years of "armed activity," issued on October 20, 2011, the diaspora-homeland sociopolitical relationships need to be explored in depth. We would need to take into consideration the aforementioned hyperpolitics, the Socialist government's initiatives, policies, and programs toward the diaspora, the comeback of the Basque Nationalist Party into government in 2012, and the evolution of the diaspora and its growing involvement with emerging media and digital technologies in a time of an international socioeconomic and financial crisis.

In August of 2012, President Patxi López called for early elections after the Popular Party ended the agreement with the PSE in May. In an eleven-page statement, López dedicated three lines to its foreign policy without mentioning the Basque diaspora and their institutional networks. "We have radically reformed the government's foreign action," he said, "in order to serve our companies and our economy, and not to serve a particular ideology" (Presidencia 2012). The elections took place on October 21, 2012. EAJ-PNV won the elections and formed government, though in simple majority, allowing EAJ-PNV members of parliament to elect Iñigo Urkullu as president of the Basque government. Regarding the government's foreign affairs goals, Urkullu stated that one of the goals is "to strengthen our ties with the Basque community around the world . . . The Basque diaspora is part of this nation [the Basque Country]. The Basque diaspora is one of the main players in making Euskadi so well-known all over the world . . . That diaspora has worked to make that known all over the world for years, and we definitely have to carry on protecting that treasure by working together" (Bieter 2013).

Between 2009 and 2013, there has been an increase of 35 percent (from over 53,000 to nearly 72,000) of Basques registering with a Spanish consulate. Not surprisingly, this has resulted into the formation of new diaspora associations such as the Basque club in Stockholm, Sweden (Euskaldunak Suedian Zazpiak

Bat). With 140 members, it was established in January 2013, following the creation of a group on Facebook a few years earlier.

By focusing on the specific case of the Basque diaspora, we have learned about the historical significance of technologies on its development and networking across the globe. The implications and the potential of emerging technologies for dispersed populations are still unleashing.

Appendix

Table A.1. Basque Institutional Diaspora as of December 2005 and June 2007

BASQUE INSTITUTIONAL DIASPORA (Own Database)	**December 2005** **Total Associations: 189 (100%)** **Total Countries: 22 (100%)**	**June 2007** **Total Associations: 198 (100%)** **Total Countries: 24 (100%)**
Associations:		
Online	**98 (51.85%)**	**123 (62.12%)**
• Online Registered	63 (33.3%)	86 (43.43%)
• Online Unregistered	35 (18.51%)	37 (18.27%)
• Offline Registered	**91 (48.14%)**	**75 (37.87%)**
Additional Online Platforms:	**0**	**4**
Total Online Platforms:	**98**	**127**
Associations:		
Online	**16 (72.72%)**	**19 (79.1%)**
• Online Registered	14 (63.63%)	16 (66.66%)
• Online Unregistered	2 (9.09%)[1]	3 (12.5%)[3]
• Offline Registered	**6 (27.27%)[2]**	**5 (20.83%)[4]**
Total Online Countries:	**16**	**19**

Source: Based on my research and on the Basque Autonomous Community government's database as of December 2005, June 2007, and March 2009.

1 Two associations from Germany and Switzerland with a presence on the Web were not registered with the Basque government.

2 Basque diaspora associations from Brazil, Colombia, Dominican Republic, El Salvador, Paraguay, and Puerto Rico, registered with the Basque government, did not have an institutional presence online.

3 Three associations from China, Germany, and Switzerland with a presence on the Web were not registered with the Basque government.

4 Basque diaspora associations from Cuba, Dominican Republic, El Salvador, Paraguay, and Puerto Rico, registered with the Basque government, did not have an institutional presence online.

Table A.2. Basque Diaspora Webscape as of October 2005

BASQUE DIASPORA WEBSCAPE (Own Database)	Europe (total No. of countries: 7) (total No. of websites: 21)	Latin America (total No. of countries: 5) (total No. of websites: 39)	North America (total No. of countries: 3) (total No. of websites: 36)	Oceania (total No. of countries: 1) (total No. of websites: 2)	Total Countries: 16 Total Websites: 98 (100%)
Basque Clubs—Euskal Etxeak	13	27	20	2	**62 (63.26%)**
Basque Clubs—Euskal Etxeak Federations	0	0	1	0	**1**
Other Diaspora Institutions:	Subtotal 8	Subtotal 12	Subtotal 15	Subtotal 0	**Subtotal 35 (35.71%)**
• Cultural	4	4	4	0	**12**
• Educational	2	4	6	0	**12**
• Political	2	3	2	0	**7**
• Portals	0	0	3	0	**3**
• Business	0	1	0	0	**1**
Additional Online Platforms	0	0	0	0	**0**
Total Online Platforms	**21**	**39**	**36**	**2**	**Total 98**

Source: Based on my research and on the Basque government's database as of December 2005.

214

Table A.3. Basque Diaspora Webscape as of June 2007

BASQUE DIASPORA WEBSCAPE (Own Database)	Asia (total No. of countries: 1) (total No. of websites: 1)	Europe (total No. of countries: 7) (total No. of websites: 23)	Latin America (total No. of countries: 7) (total No. of websites: 57)	North America (total No. of countries: 3) (total No. of websites: 40)	Oceania (total No. of countries: 1) (total No. of websites: 2)	Total Countries: 19 Total Websites: 123 (100%)
Basque Clubs—Euskal Etxeak	1	14	33	24	2	**74 (60.16%)**
Basque Clubs—Euskal Etxeak Federations	0	0	1	1	0	**2**
Other Diaspora Institutions:	Subtotal 0	Subtotal 9	Subtotal 23	Subtotal 15	Subtotal 0	**Subtotal 47 (38.21%)**
• Cultural	0	6	13	4	0	**17**
• Educational	0	1	6	7	0	**15**
• Political	0	2	2	1	0	**5**
• Portals	0	0	0	3	0	**3**
• Business	0	0	2	0	0	**2**
Additional Online Platforms	0	[1]	0	[3]	0	**[4]**
Total Online Platforms	**1**	**24**	**57**	**43**	**2**	**Total 127**

Source: Based on my research and on the Basque government's database as of June 2007.

Table A.4. Basque Diaspora Webscape as of October 2005, Full List

EUROPE [21]	
Andorra [1]	
Basque Clubs (1) **Euskal Etxeak ONLINE**	**Website address (URL)**
Euskal Etxea D'andorra, Andorra La Vella	http://es.geocities.com/euskaletxea_andorra
France [7]	
Basque Clubs (4) **Euskal Etxeak ONLINE**	**Website address (URL)**
Eskualdunen Biltzarra, Bordeaux	www.euskaletxea.org
Association des Basques de Montpellier et Languedoc, Montpellier	www.eskualdunak.com (old) http://eskualdunak.midiblogs.com (old) www.eskualdunak.jimbo.com (new)
Pariseko Eskual Etxea	www.eskualetxea.com
Lagunt eta Maita – Paueko Euskaldunen Batasuna, Pau	http://basquesdepau.chez.tiscali.fr (old) http://lesbasquesdepau.free.fr/spip (new)
Other Institutions: [3] • **Cultural (2)**	**Website address (URL)**
Anaiki Gizon Abesbatza, Paris	www.anaiki.com
Gernika Taldea, Paris	http://membres.lycos.fr/gernikataldea
Other Institutions • **Educational (1)**	**Website address (URL)**
Sustraiak-Erroak Elkartea, Paris	www.eskualetxea.com/sustraiak/fr/Intro.html
Germany [1]	
Basque Clubs (1) **Euskal Etxeak ONLINE**	**Website address (URL)**
Gernika Euskal Alemaniar Kultur Elkartea, Berlin	www.geocities.com/gernika_kultur
Italy [1]	
Basque Clubs (1) **Euskal Etxeak ONLINE**	**Website address (URL)**
Associazione Culturale Euskara, Rome	www.euskara.it
Spain [4]	
Basque Clubs (4) **Euskal Etxeak ONLINE**	**Website address (URL)**
Euskal-Etxea Hogar Vasco, Madrid	www.euskaletxea-madrid.com
Centro Vasco Gure Txoko, Valladolid	www.geocities.com/guretxoko
Centre Cultural Euskal Etxea, Barcelona	http://euskaletxeak.org
Euskal Etxea, Sevilla	http://groups.msn.com/EuskalEtxeaSE/home.htm (gone)
Switzerland [1]	
Basque Clubs (1) **Euskal Etxeak ONLINE**	**Website address (URL)**
Euskal Etxea Elkartea - Baskischer Kulturverein, Zurich	www.euskaletxea.ch
United Kingdom [6]	
Basque Clubs (1) **Euskal Etxeak ONLINE**	**Website address (URL)**

London Basque Society - Euskal Elkartea	www.zintzilik.org/london
Other Institutions: [5] • **Cultural (2)**	**Website address (URL)**
Basque Dancing Society at New Castle University	www.societies.ncl.ac.uk/basque.dancing
Cambridge University Basque Society, Cambridge	www.geocities.com/cu_bs
Other Institutions • **Educational (1)**	**Website address (URL)**
The Institute of Basque Studies, London	http://ibs.lgu.ac.uk (gone)
Other Institutions • **Political (2)**	**Website address (URL)**
Basque Campaign, London	www.geocities.com/basquecampaign
Basque Children of '37 Association: UK, London	www.spanishrefugees-basquechildren.org
LATIN AMERICA [37+2] **Argentina [28+2]**	
Basque Clubs (18+2) **Euskal Etxeak ONLINE**	**Website address (URL)**
Laurak Bat, Buenos Aires	www.laurakbat.com.ar
Asociación Vasca Denak Bat, Cañuelas	www.geocities.com/canuelasdenakbat
Centro Vasco Argentino Zingirako Euskaldunak, Chascomús	www.chascomus.com.ar/ArteyCultura/Baile/CentroVasco/index.html (old) www.chascomus.com.ar/centrovasco/ (new)
Centro Vasco Villegas'ko Euskaldunak, Villegas	www.vascos.villegas.net.ar (gone)
Centro Vasco Toki Eder, José Paz	www.telefonica.net/web/ibarezkerra/ikasweb/tokieder (old) www.josepaz.com.ar/cym/centro_vasco.html (new)
Centro Vasco Euzko Etxea, La Plata	www.centrovasco.com
Centro Vasco Gure Txokoa, Rauch	http://ardanberaenrauch.cjb.net
Centro Vasco Itxaropena, Saladillo	www.saladillo.gov.ar/centrovasco.htm
Centro Vasco Hiru Erreka, Tres Arroyos	www.3net.com.ar/instituciones/hiruerreka (old) www.hiruerreka.com.ar (new)
Centro Vasco Danak Bat, Bolívar	www.danakbat.com.ar
Centro Vasco del Chaco Kotoiaren Lurra	www.ecomchaco.com.ar/centrovasco/default.htm
Centro Vasco Denak Bat, Mendoza	www.denakbat.com.ar (gone)
Colectividad Vasca, Concordia	www.concordia.com.ar/Vascos
Sociedad Vasca, Villa Mercedes	www.vascosvillamercedes.sergroup.com.ar (old) http://vascosvillamercedes.com.ar/ (new)
Centro Vasco, San Nicolás	www.euzkalnik.com.ar
Eusko Etxea, Necochea	www.euzkoetxea.com.ar
Centro Vasco Ibai Guren, Paraná	http://vascos.8m.net/ibaiguren.htm
Centro Vasco Zazpirak-Bat, Rosario	www.zazpirakbat.com
Centro NAVARRO, Buenos Aires	www.centronavarro.org
Centro NAVARRO, Rosario	www.centronavarro.com
Other Institutions: [9] • **Cultural (4)**	**Website address (URL)**
Asociación Coral Lagun Onak, Buenos Aires	www.lagunonak.com.ar
Coral Vasco Argentino Alkartasuna, Buenos Aires	www.coralalkartasuna.com.ar

Grupo de Bailes Vascos Cordobatarrak, Córdoba	http://groups.msn.com/Cordobatarrak/inicio.msnw
Iparralde Dantzari Taldea, Buenos Aires	www.iparraldedantzaritaldea.8m.com
Other Institutions • **Educational (4)**	**Website address (URL)**
Diáspora Vasco Argentina, Buenos Aires	www.diasporavascarg.com.ar
Euskaltzaleak, Buenos Aires	www.euskaltzaleak.tk (old) www.euskaltzaleak.org.ar (new)
Euskal Echea Asociación Cultural y de Beneficencia, Bueno Aires	www.euskalechea.esc.edu.ar
Fundación Vasco Argentina Juan de Garay, Buenos Aires	www.juandegaray.org.ar
Other Institutions • **Political (2)**	**Website address (URL)**
Josu Lariz Askatu	www.josu-askatu.org (gone)
Asociación Diáspora Vasca – Euskal Diaspora Nazioarteko Elkartea, Santa Rosa	http://euskalherria.cjb.net www.diasporavasca.org
Chile [3]	
Basque Clubs (2) **Euskal Etxeak ONLINE**	**Website address (URL)**
Eusko Etxea Casa Vasca, Valparaíso	www.euskoetxea.cl
Euzko Etxea-Centro Vasco, Santiago de Chile	www.euzkoetxeachile.cl
Other Institutions: [1] • **Business (1)**	**Website address (URL)**
Asociación de Empresarios de Origen Vasco, Santiago de Chile	www.empresariosvascos.cl
Peru [1]	
Basque Clubs (1) **Euskal Etxeak ONLINE**	**Website address (URL)**
Euskal Etxea de Perú, Lima	http://perso.wanadoo.fr/amitiesbasco-peruviennes/pagina6.htm (old) www.euskaletxeaperu.org (new)
Uruguay [2]	
Basque Clubs (2) **Euskal Etxeak ONLINE**	**Website address (URL)**
Centro Vasco Euskal Erria, Montevideo	www.euskalerria.org.uy (gone)
Saltoko Euskaldunen Taldea, El Salto	www.vascosensalto.org
Venezuela [3]	
Basque Clubs (2) **Euskal Etxeak ONLINE**	**Website address (URL)**
Centro Vasco de Caracas, Caracas [Blog]	www.kromasys.com/cvc (old) www.euskoetxeacaracas.blogspot.com (new)
Centro Vasco de Valencia, Carabobo	www.valenciakoeuskoetxea.com
Other Institutions: [1] • **Political (1)**	**Website address (URL)**
Asociación Venezolana de Amigos de Euskal Herria, Caracas	http://earth.prohosting.com/avaeh
North America [36] **Canada [3]**	

Basque Clubs (3) **Euskal Etxeak ONLINE**	**Website address (URL)**
Zazpiak Bat Basque Society, Vancouver	www.bcbasque.com
Calgary Euskal Etxea	http://membres.lycos.fr/euskalgary/home.htm (old) www.muturzikin.com/euskalgary.htm (new)
Euskaldunak, l'Association des Basques du Québec	www.euskaldunakquebec.com
Mexico [3]	
Basque Clubs (1) **Euskal Etxeak ONLINE**	**Website address (URL)**
Centro Vasco de México, Mexico D.F.	www.centrovascomexico.com
Other Institutions [2]: • **Political (1)**	**Website address (URL)**
Seis de México	www.6demexico.org (gone)
Other Institutions • **Portal (1)**	**Website address (URL)**
Vascos de México, Mexico D.F.	www.vascosmexico.com
USA [30]	
Basque Clubs (16+1 Federation) **Euskal Etxeak ONLINE**	**Website address (URL)**
NABO - North American Basque Organization *(Federation)*	www.basqueclubs.com (old) www.nabasque.org (new)
Euzko-Etxea of New York, New York	www.eeny.org (old) www.newyorkbasqueclub.com (new)
Euzkaldunak Basque Club, Boise, Idaho	www.basquecenter.com
Txoko Ona Basque Club, Homedale, Idaho	www.txokoona.org
Zazpiak Bat Basque Club, Reno, Nevada	www.powernet.net/~renobasqueclub (old) www.renobasqueclub.org (new)
Euskaldunak Club, Elko, Nevada	www.elkobasque.com
Lagun Onak Las Vegas Basque Club, Las Vegas, Nevada	http://communitylink.reviewjournal.com/servlet/lvrj_ProcServ/dbpage=page&mode=display&gid=01310001051029199863261457
Basque Club of California, San Francisco, California	www.basqueclub.com
Basque Cultural Center, San Francisco, California	www.basqueculturalcenter.com
Kern County Basque Club, Bakersfield, California	www.kcbasqueclub.com
Ontario Basque Club, Oregon	www.ontariobasqueclub.dantzariak.net
Basque Club of Utah, Salt Lake City, Utah	http://members.aol.com/utahbasq
Alkartasuna Southwestern Wyoming Basque Club, Rock Springs, Wyoming	www.rsalkartasuna.com (old) www.alkartasuna.us/ (new)
Seattle Euskal Etxea, Washington	www.seattleeuskal.org
Colorado Euskal Etxea, Denver	www.coloradoeuskaletxea.com
Arizonako Euskal Etxea	http://members.cox.net/pescoz/arizonako
New Mexico Euskal Etxea	www.buber.net/NMEE
Other Institutions: [12] • **Cultural (4)**	**Website address (URL)**
Oinkari Basque Dancers, Boise, Idaho	www.oinkari.org
Gauden Bat, Chino, California	www.gaudenbat.com (gone)
Jaialdi, Boise, Idaho	www.jaialdi.com
Zenbat Gara Euskal Dantzari Taldea, Reno, Nevada	www.dantzariak.net

Other Institutions • **Educational (6)**	**Website address (URL)**
Center for Basque Studies, Reno, Nevada	http://basque.unr.edu
Basque Museum & Cultural Center, Boise, Idaho	www.basquemuseum.com
Society of Basque Studies in America, New York	www.basque.ws
Basque Educational Organization, San Francisco, California	www.basqueed.org
Cenarrusa Center for Basque Studies, Boise, Idaho	www.cenarrusa.org
Euskara.US-NABO	www.euskara.us (old) (gone) www.nabasque.org (new)
Other Institutions • **Political (1)**	**Website address (URL)**
International Basque Organization For Human Rights, Corte Madera, California	www.euskojustice.org
Other Institutions • **Portals (2)**	**Website address (URL)**
San Francisco Basque Groups, San Francisco, California	www.sfbasque.org
Boise Basque Groups, Boise, Idaho	www.boisebasques.com
OCEANIA [2] **Australia (2)**	
Basque Clubs (2) **Euskal Etxeak ONLINE**	**Website address (URL)**
The Basque Club of North Queensland, Townsville, Queensland	www.basqueclubnq.tripod.com/id4.html (old) http://basqueclubnq.com/index.html (new)
Gure Txoko Basque Club, Sydney	http://members.optushome.com.au/txoko/default-en.htm (old) http://www.guretxoko.com.au (new)

Table A.5. Basque Diaspora Webscape as of June 2007, Full List

ASIA [1] **China [1]**	
Basque Clubs (1) **Euskal Etxeak ONLINE**	**Website address (URL)**
Shangaiko Euskaletxea, Shangai	www.chinaeuskaletxea.com
EUROPE [4] **France [1]**	
Other Institutions: [1] • **Cultural (1)**	**Website address (URL)**
Zazpiak Bat, St. Pierre et Miquelon, Newfoundland	www.cheznoo.net/zazpiak-bat
Spain [3]	
Basque Clubs (2) **Euskal Etxeak ONLINE**	**Website address (URL)**
Euskal Etxea Artea, Mallorca	www.euskaletxeakmallorca.com
Euskal Etxea de Murcia, Murcia	www.euskaletxea-murcia.com
Other Institutions: [1] • **Cultural (1)**	**Website address (URL)**
Asociación Cultural Laminiturri, Logroño	www.laminiturri.org
Additional Online Platforms: • **Euskal Etxeak**	**Website address (URL)**
Centre Cultural Euskal Etxea, Barcelona [Blog]	http://blog.euskaletxeak.org
LATIN AMERICA [22] **Argentina [18]**	
Basque Clubs (7 +1 Federation) **Euskal Etxeak ONLINE**	**Website address (URL)**
FEVA- Federation of Basque-Argentinean Entities *(Federation)*	www.fevaonline.org.ar
Centro Vasco-Argentino Gure Txokoa, Córdoba	www.centrovascocordoba.com.ar
Centro Vasco Lagun Onak, Pergamino	www.santxo.com.ar/lagunonak (old) www.centrovasco.pergamino.com (new)
Asociación Vasco-Argentina Urrundik, Paraná	www.urrundik.com.ar
Centro Rincón Vasco Euzko Txokoa, General Acha	www.generalacha.com/centrovasco.htm
Centro Vasco Denak Bat, Mar del Plata	http://www.denakbat.org.ar/
Centro Vasco Gure Txokoa, Suipacha [Blog]	http://vascosdesuipacha.blogspot.com
Centro Vasco Beti Aurrera, Chivilcoy [Blog]	http://www.centrovascochivilcoy.blogspot.com/
Other Institutions: [10] • **Cultural (9)**	**Website address (URL)**
"Denak Bat" (Centro Vasco Euzko Etxea), La Plata [Blog]	http://fotolog.terra.cl/centrovasco (old) http://www.fotolog.com/denakbat (new)
"Ugarritzak" (Euskaldunak Denak Bat), Arrecifes [Blog]	http://fotolog.terra.com/dantzaris (old) http://www.fotolog.com/edb_ugarritzak (new)
"Eusko Hazi" (Centro Vasco Zingirako Euskaldunak), Chascomús [Blog]	http://fotolog.terra.cl/cvchascomus (old) http://www.fotolog.com/eusko_hazi (new)
"Gazte Alai" (Eusko Etxea), Necochea [Blog]	http://www.fotolog.com/gazte_alai
"Urrundik" (Asociación Vasco-Argentina Urrundik), Paraná [Blog]	http://www.fotolog.com/urrundik

"Beti Alai" (Centro Vasco Denak Bat), Mar del Plata [Blog]	http://www.fotolog.com/beti_alai
"Denori Alai" (Asociación Vasca Denak Bat), Cañuelas [Blog]	http://www.fotolog.com/denori_alai
"Badia Txuria Dantzariak" (Centro Vasco), Bahía Blanca [Blog]	http://www.fotolog.com/badia_txuria
"Emakume Abertzale Batza Dantzariak" (Emakume Abertzale Batza), Buenos Aires [Blog]	http://www.fotolog.com/dantzaris_baires
Other Institutions: • **Educational (1)**	**Website address (URL)**
Centro de Estudios de la Cultura y el Nacionalismo Vasco Arturo Campion, Laprida	http://arturocampion.com.ar
Brazil [1]	
Basque Clubs (1) **Euskal Etxeak ONLINE**	**Website address (URL)**
Euskal Etxea Brasil, Sao Paolo	http://euskaletxeabrasil.locaweb.com.br
Colombia [3]	
Basque Clubs (1) **Euskal Etxeak ONLINE**	**Website address (URL)**
Centro Vasco Colombia, Bogotá	www.euskaletxeacolombia.com
Other Institutions: [2] • **Business (1)**	**Website address (URL)**
Fundación Euskolombia, Bogotá	http://digitalstreamstudio.com/euskolombia
Other Institutions: • **Educational (1)**	**Website address (URL)**
Centro de Estudios Vascos en Antioquia (Universidad de Antioquia; also known as Centro de Estudios Vascos de Medellín, Antioquia), Medellín	www.vascocentro.6x.to
North America [7] **USA [7]**	
Basque Clubs (4) **Euskal Etxeak ONLINE**	**Website address (URL)**
Big Horn Basque Club, Buffalo	www.bighornweb.com/nabo2006/index.htm
Chino Basque Club, Chino, California	www.chinobasqueclub.us
Southern California Basque Club, Chino, California	www.socalbasqueclub.us
Washington, D.C. Euskal Etxea, Washington, D.C.	www.wdcbasqueclub.org
Other Institutions: [3] • **Cultural (1)**	**Website address (URL)**
Bihotzetik Basque Choir, Boise, Idaho	www.bihotzetikbasquechoir.net
Other Institutions: • **Educational (2)**	**Website address (URL)**
Basque Studies Program, Boise, Idaho	http://basquestudies.boisestate.edu
Boiseko Ikastola, Boise, Idaho	www.boisekoikastola.org
Additional Online Platforms: • **Euskal Etxeak**	**Website address (URL)**
Zazpiak Bat Basque Club, Reno, Nevada [Net Site]	http://myspace.com/renobasqueclub
"Members" Colorado Euskal Etxea, Denver [Blog]	http://coloradoeuskaletxea.blogspot.com (old) http://ceemember.blogspot.com (current)
"Topagunea" Colorado Euskal Etxea, Denver [Blog]	http://topagunea.blogspot.com

Table A.6. Statements that obtained the Highest Level of Agreement (those closer to 1) amongst the Basque Diaspora Institutional Leaders as of July 2003

Highest Level of Agreement (Own Database) STATEMENTS	MEDIA Σ
20. The attendance of my Club at the Basque World Congress does help its future.	**1.4**
9. Basques in your country should have an active participation in the Basque Country's culture.	**1.69**
16. My Club currently maintains a positive relation with the Basque Government.	**1.78**
25. For the Basque Government the Basques abroad[5] are a tool to promote Basque culture abroad.	**1.78**
4. Basques abroad and born in the Basque Country should have direct political representation in the Basque Autonomous Community (BAC) Parliament.	**2.11**
6. Basques in your country should have an active participation in relation to the resolution of violence in the Basque Country.	**2.15**
8. Basques in your country should have an active participation in the Basque Country's economy.	**2.19**
28. The Basque Government establishes financial and economical support according to technical criteria.	**2.26**
31. The Basque Government's benefits should also be extended to Basques from outside the BAC, i.e., Navarre, and Iparralde, who return home.	**2.28**
5. Descendents of Basques abroad should have direct political representation in the BAC Parliament.	**2.46**
1. The majority of the population in the Basque Country is knowledgeable of Basques abroad.[5]	**2.58**
17. My Club believes that the Basque Government's policy towards my Club should be more efficient.	**2.74**
26. The Basque Government is more likely to support financially those Basques who enhance Basque nationalist cultural projects.	**2.77**
19. The existence of my Club does not depend totally on the Basque Government's financial help.	**2.91**
29. The Basque Government's current funding toward the Basques abroad is not satisfactory.	**2.91**
	TOTAL MEDIA 3.04

5 Note: The expression "Basques abroad" refers to the Basque people who live outside the Basque Country. It was used for this specific questionnaire to avoid the use of the word "diaspora," as it could be misunderstood.

Table A.7. Statements that obtained the Lowest Level of Agreement (those closer to 5) amongst the Basque Diaspora Institutional Leaders as of July 2003

Lowest Level of Agreement (Own Database) STATEMENTS	MEDIA Σ
23. The Spanish Government is responsible for financing Basque cultural activities abroad.	4.44
11. The passing of the Law 8/94 was not necessary.	4.28
2. Basques abroad are not "as Basque" as those born and living in the Basque Country.	4.23
22. The Basque Government is not doing an efficient job on dealing with Basques abroad.	3.97
24. For the Basque Government the Basques abroad are a tool to obtain political parties' benefits.	3.88
21. The allocated budget to organize the Basque World Congress should be redirect to other needs of Basques abroad.	3.82
3. Basques abroad (no matter the generation) should not enjoy the same rights and obligations as Basques in the Basque Country as Basques who live there.	3.77
30. For the Basque Government the Basques abroad are a tool to obtain economic objectives.	3.71
10. Basques in your country should not have an active participation in the international relations or foreign diplomacy of the Basque Government.	3.69
15. If not from the financial support of the Basque Government, my Club would have not been created.	3.69
27. For the Basque Government the Basques abroad are a tool to obtain political goals.	3.64
32. The future of Basque cultural identity does not depend on the Basque Government political and economical support.	3.56
12. My Club would disappear if the Basque Government's programs stop.	3.46
14. My Club has not maintained a positive historical relation (prior 1982) with the Basque Government.	3.37
7. Basques in your country should not have an active participation in the Basque Government.	3.18
13. The Law 8/94 is sufficient to maintain the current status of Basque culture abroad.	3.14
	TOTAL MEDIA 3.04

Table A.8. Level of Agreement by Basque Diaspora Institutional Leaders' Country of Origin as of July 2003

Media by Country (Own Database)	COUNTRIES	MEDIA Σ
	Chile	3.48
	United Kingdom	3.34
	Argentina	3.29
	Australia	3.19
	Peru	3.19
	United States	3.15
	Uruguay	3.08
	Spain	3.06
	Venezuela	3.05
	Mexico	3.01
	Brazil	2.97
	Puerto Rico	2.96
	El Salvador	2.94
	Colombia	2.85
	Andorra	2.77
	Canada	2.67
	Dominican Republic	2.66
		TOTAL MEDIA 3.04

Bibliography

Books and Articles

Abercrombie, Thomas J. (2005). "Europe's First Family: The Basques." *National Geographic*, Vol. 188, No. 5: 74-97.

Adams, Paul C. and Rina Ghose. (2003). "India.com: The Construction of a Space between." *Progress in Human Geography*, Vol. 27, No. 4: 414–37.

Aguilar Fernández, Paloma. (1998). "La Guerra Civil Española en el Discurso Nacionalista Vasco. Memorias Peculiares, Lecciones Diferentes," in Javier Ugarte (ed.) *La Transición en el País Vasco y España*. Bilbao: Servicio Editorial de la Universidad del País Vasco.

Ainslie, Ricardo. (1998). "Cultural Mourning, Immigration, and Engagement: Vignettes from the Mexican Experience," in Marcelo Suarez-Orozco (ed.) *Crossings: Mexican Immigration in Interdisciplinary Perspectives*. Cambridge: Harvard University Press.

Aksoy, Asu and Kevin Robins. (2002). "Banal Transnationalism: The Difference that Television Makes. Transnational Communities Programme." Working Paper. http://www.transcomm.ox.ac.uk/working_papers.htm

Alba, Richard D. (1985). *Italian-Americans*. Englewood Cliffs: Prentice Hall.

Aldecoa, Francisco and Michael Keating. (1999). *Paradiplomacy in Action: The Foreign Relations of Subnational Governments*. London: Frank Cass.

Alonso, Andoni. (1998). "The Peasant and the Computer: The Technological Transformation of the Basque Country." *Technology in Society*, Vol. 20: 287–96.

Alonso, Andoni and Iñaki Arzoz. (1999a). "Basque Identity on the Internet," in William A. Douglass, Carmelo Urza, Linda White, and Joseba Zulaika (eds.) *Basque Cultural Studies*. Reno, Nevada: Basque Studies Program, University of Nevada, Reno.

——. (1999b). *Euskal Herri Digitala 1.0*. Donostia: Gaiak.

——. (2003). *Basque Cyberculture: From Digital Euskadi to CyberEuskalherria*. Reno, Nevada: Center for Basque Studies, University of Nevada, Reno.

Alonso, Andoni and Pedro J. Oiarzabal. (eds. 2010). *Diasporas in the New Media Age: Identity, Politics and Community*. Reno, Nevada: University Nevada Press.

Álvarez Gila, Óscar. (1996). "Vascos y Vascongados": Luchas Ideológicas entre Carlistas y Nacionalistas en los Centros Vascos del Río de la Plata (1900–1930)," in Escobedo Mansilla, Ronald, Ana de Zaballa Beascoechea, and Óscar Álvarez Gila (eds.) *Emigración y Redes Sociales de los Vascos en América*. Vitoria-Gasteiz: Servicio Editorial de la Universidad del País Vasco.

——. (2000). "Los Inicios del Nacionalismo Vasco en América: El Centro Zazpirak Bat de Rosario (Argentina)." *Boletín Sancho el Sabio*, Vol. 12: 153–76.

——. (2005). "Euskal Herrias Americanas: Los vascos y las Emigraciones Ultramarinas (1825–1950)," in Joseba Agirreazkuenaga (dir.) *La Crisis de la Civilización de los Vascos del Antiguo Régimen y Estrategias de Revolución Liberal e Industrial: 1789–1876*. Historia de Euskal Herria. Historia General de los Vascos, Vol. IV. Donostia-San Sebastián: Editorial Lur.

Álvarez Gila, Óscar and José María Tápiz Fernández. (1996). "Prensa Nacionalista Vasca y Emigración a América (1900-1936)." *Anuario de Estudios Americanos*, Vol. 8, No. 1: 233–60.

Ambrosio, Thomas. (2002). *Ethnic Identity Group and United States Foreign Policy*. Westport, Connecticut: Praeger.

Amezaga, Josu. (2004). *Satelite Bidezko Nortasunak: Latinoamerikan Canal Vasco Ikusten*. Donostia: Utriusque Vasconiae.

Anderson, Benedict. (1991). *Imagined Communities: Reflections on the Origin and Spread of Nationalism*. London: Verso.

Anderson, Jon W. "Cybernauts of the Arab Diaspora: Electronic Mediation in Transnational Cultural Identities." Couch-Stone Symposium "Postmodern culture, global capitalism and democratic action." University of Maryland. April 10–12, 1997. www.bsos.umd.edu/css97/papers/anderson.html

Appadurai, Arjun. (1991). "Global Ethnoscapes: Notes and Queries for a Transnational Anthropology," in Richard Fox (ed.) *Recapturing Anthropology. Working in the Present*. Santa Fe, New Mexico: School of American Press.

——. (1996). *Modernity at Large. Cultural Dimensions of Globalization*. Minneapolis: University of Minnesota Press.

Arthur, Paul. (1991). "Diaspora Intervention in International Affairs: Irish America as a Case Study." *Diaspora*, Vol. 1, No. 2 (Fall): 143–62.

Arzoz, Iñaki. (2002). "Divulgando la Cibercultura Vasca. Una Apuesta Social." *Revista Internacional de Estudios Vascos*, Vol. 47, No. 2: 417–27.

Ascunce, José Ángel and María Luisa San Miguel. (Coord. 2004). *Los Hijos del Exilio Vasco: Arraigo o Desarraigo*. Donostia: Editorial Saturraran, S. L.

Ascunce, José Ángel and Marién Nieva. (2004). *Mítica y Cultura del Exilio Vasco: Ignacio de Loyola y Francisco Javier*. Bilbao: Universidad de Deusto.

Ayesa, Mariano and José Orbaiceta. (2008). "Euskal Etxeak of Argentina (FEVA): Diagnosis and Projection of the Future," in Gobierno Vasco (2008) *Zubigintzan, 4th World Congress of Basque Communities 2007. Bilbao, July 2007*. Vitoria-Gasteiz: Servicio Editorial de Publicaciones del Gobierno Vasco.

Backhurst, David. (1990). "Social Memory in Soviet Thought," in David Middleton and Derek Edwards (eds.) *Collective Remembering*. London: Sage Publications.

Balibar, Etienne. (1991). "The Nation Form: History and Ideology." *Review*, No. 13: 329–46.

Bateman, Robyn Driskell and Larry Lyon. (2002). "Are Virtual Communities True Communities? Examining the Environments and Elements of Community." *City and Community*, Vol. 1, No. 4 (December): 373–90.

Baxok, Erramun, Pantxoa Etxegoin, Terexa Lekunberri, Iñaki Martinez de Luna, Larraitz Mendizabal, Igor Ahedo, Xabier Itzaina, and Roldán Jimeno. (2006). *Identidad y Cultura Vascas a Comienzos del Siglo XXI*. Donostia: Eusko Ikaskuntza.

Benedikt, Michael. (ed. 1991). *Cyberspace: First Steps*. Cambridge, Massachusetts: MIT Press.

Berners-Lee, Tim. (1999). *Weaving the Web*. San Francisco, California: Harper Collins.

Bilbao, Miren. (2008). "Gaztemundu Program: Participants' Opinions," in Gobierno Vasco (2008) *Zubigintzan, 4th World Congress of Basque Communities 2007. Bilbao, July 2007*. Vitoria-Gasteiz: Servicio Editorial de Publicaciones del Gobierno Vasco.

Bieter, Mark. (2013). "A Conversation with the Basque President." http://bieterblog.com/2013/05/07/a-conversation-with-the-basque-president.aspx

Billig, Michael. (1995). *Banal Nationalism*. London: Sage Publications.

——. (2003). "Banal Nationalism," in Roxy Harris and Ben Rampton (eds.) *The Language, Ethnicity and Race Reader*. London: Routledge.

Blainey, Geoffrey. (1966). *Tyranny of Distances: How Distance shaped Australia's History*. Melbourne: Sun Books.

Boase, Jeffrey, John B. Horrigan, Barry Wellman, and Lee Rainie. (2006). "The Strength of Internet Ties: The Internet and Email Aid Users in Maintaining their Social Networks and provide Pathways to help when People Face Big Decisions." *Pew Internet & American Life Project*, (January 2006, online). www.pewinternet.org/pdfs/PIP_Internet_ties.pdf

Brah, Avtar. (1996). *Cartographies of Diasporas.* London, New York: Routledge.

Brinkerhoff, Jennifer M. (2006). "Digital Diasporas and Conflict Prevention: The Case of Somalinet.com." *Review of International Studies*, Vol. 32 (January): 25–47.

——. (2004). "Digital Diasporas and International Development: Afghan-Americans and the Reconstruction of Afghanistan." *Public Administration and Development*, Vol. 24, No. 5: 397–413.

Bromberg, Heather. (1996). "Are MUDs Communities? Identity, Belonging and Consciousness in Virtual Worlds," in Rob Shields. (ed.). *Cultures of Internet.* London: Sage Publications.

Brunn, Stanley. (1996). "The Internalization of Diasporas in a Shrinking World," in Georges Prévélakis (Ed.). *The Networks of Diasporas.* Cyprus, Nicosia: Kyken.

Butler, Kim D. (2001). "Defining Diaspora, Refining Discourse." *Diaspora*, Vol. 10, No. 2 (Fall): 189–219.

Cairncross, Frances C. (1997). *The Death of Distance: How the Communication is Changing Our Lives.* Boston: Harvard Business School Press.

Calhoun, Craig. (ed. 1994). *Social Theory and the Politics of Identity.* Oxford: Blackwell.

Carlson, Richard C. and Bruce Goldman. (1991). *2020 Visions: Long View of a Changing World.* Stanford, California: Stanford University Press.

Castells, Manuel. (1996). *The Rise of the Network Society.* Malden, Massachusetts: Blackwell Publishers.

——. (2001). *The Internet Galaxy: Reflections on the Internet, Business, and Society.* New York: Oxford University Press.

Cava Mesa, María Jesús. (1996). *Memoria Colectiva del Bombardeo de Gernika.* Gernika-Lumo: Gernika Gogoratuz.

Center for Digital Future. (September 2004). *The Digital Future Report: Surveying the Digital Future. Year Four. Ten Years, Ten Trends.* Los Angeles, California: University of Southern California, Annenberg School. Center for Digital Future.

Chasteen, John Charles and Sara Castro-Klarén. (eds. 2004). *Beyond Imagined Communities: Reading and Writing the Nation in Nineteenth-century Latin America.* Baltimore: Johns Hopkins University Press.

Cibergolem (Andoni Alonso and Iñaki Arzoz, 2005). *La Quinta Columna: Antitratado Comunal de Hiperpolítica.* Barcelona: Gedisa.

Cohen, Erik H. (2004). "Components and symbols of ethnic identity: a case study in informal education and identity formation in diaspora." *Applied Psychology: an International Review*, Vol. 53, No. 1: 87–112.

Cohen, Robin. (1994). *Frontiers of Identity: The British and the Rest*. London: Longman.

——. (1996). "Diasporas and the Nation-state: From Victims to Challengers." *International Affairs,* Vol. 72: 507–20.

——. (1997a). "Diaspora, the Nation-state, and Globalization," in Wang Gungwu (ed.) *Global History and Migrations*. Boulder, Colorado: Westview Press.

——. (1997b). *Global Diasporas: An Introduction*. Seattle: University of Washington Press.

Collyer, M. (2003). "Are there National Borders in Cyberspace?" *Geography*, Vol. 88, No. 4: 348–57.

Connor, Walker. (1994). *Ethnonationalism. The Quest for Understanding*. Princeton, New Jersey: Princeton University Press.

Constas, Dimitri and Athanassias Platias. (eds. 1993). *Diasporas in World Politics: The Greeks in Comparative Perspective*. London: Macmillan.

Corcostegui, Lisa M. (1999). "Moving Emblems: Basque Dance and Symbolic Ethnicity," in William A. Douglass, Carmelo Urza, Linda White, and Joseba Zulaika (eds.) *The Basque Diaspora/La Diáspora Vasca*. Basque Studies Program Occasional Papers No. 7. Reno, Nevada: Basque Studies Program, University of Nevada, Reno.

Couldry, Nick. (2004). "The Digital Divide," in David Gauntlett and Ross Horsley (eds.) *Web.Studies*. 2nd ed. Edward Arnold (Publishers) Limited.

Curry, Michael R. (2004). "Cyberspace and Cyberplaces: Rethinking the Identity of Individual and Place." *Communication Technology Policy Section* (eCTP). www.komdat.sbg.ac.at/ectp/curry_p.htm

Dahan, Michael and Gabriel Sheffer. (2001). "Ethnic Groups and Distance Shrinking Communication Technologies." *Nationalism and Ethnic Politics,* Vol. 7, No. 1 (Spring): 85–107.

Dashtipour, Parisa. (2009). "Contested Identities: Using Lacanian Psychoanalysis to Explore and Develop Social Identity Theory." *Annual Review of Critical Psychology*, No. 7: 320–37.

Davis, David. and Will H. Moore. (1997). "Ethnicity Matters: Transnational Ethnic Alliances and Foreign Policy Behavior." *International Studies Quarterly*, Vol. 41, No. 1: 171–85.

Davis, Thomas C. (1999). "Revisiting Group Attachment: Ethnic and National Identity." *Political Psychology*, Vol. 20, No. 1: 25–47.

de Aguirre y Lecube, José Antonio. (1944). *Cinco Conferencias pronunciadas en un Viaje por América*. Buenos Aires: Ekin.

——. (1981). *Obras Completas de José Antonio de Aguirre y Lecube*. Vols. I and II. Donostia: Sendoa.

de Astigarraga, Andoni. (1986). *Abertzales en la Argentina*. Bilbao: Alberdi Argitaldaria.

de Pablo, Santiago, Ludger Mees, and José Antonio Rodríguez Ranz. (1999). *El Péndulo Patriótico: Historia del Partido Nacionalista Vasco. Vol I: 1895–1836*. Barcelona: Editorial Crítica.

del Valle, Teresa. (1994). *Korrika: Basque Ritual for Ethnic Identity*. Reno, Nevada: University of Nevada Press.

Dentice-Clark, Lucia. (2001). "My Home Town is a URL in Cyberspace: The Internet, Italian Ethnic Identities and the European Union." *Cultural Survival Quarterly*, Vol. 24 (January).

Dery, Mark. (1996). *Escape Velocity: Cyberculture at the End of the Century*. London: Hodder and Stoughton.

Diamandaki, Katerina. (2003). "Virtual Ethnicity and Digital Diasporas: Identity Construction in Cyberspace." *Global Media Journal*, Vol. 1, No. 2 (Spring, online). http://lass.calumet.purdue.edu/cca/gmj/SubmittedDocuments/archivedpapers/Spring2003/diamondaki.htm

Díaz Noci, Javier. (2001). "Historia del Periodismo en Lengua Vasca de los Estados Unidos: Dos Semanarios de Los Ángeles en el Siglo XIX." *Revista Zer*, Vol. 10 (May): 309–29.

Douglass, William A. (1999). "Creating the New Basque Diaspora," in William A. Douglass et al (eds.) *Basque Politics and Nationalism on the Eve of the Millennium*. Reno, Nevada: Basque Studies Program, University of Nevada, Reno.

——. (2000). "Interstitial Culture, Virtual Ethnicity and Hyphenated Basque Identity in the New Millennium." *Nevada Historical Society Quarterly*, Vol. 43, No. 2 (Summer): 155–65.

Douglass, William A. and Jon Bilbao. (1975). *Amerikanuak: Basques in the New World*. Reno, Nevada: University of Nevada Press.

Douglass, William A., M. Lyman Stanford, and Joseba Zulaika. (1994). *Migración, Etnicidad y Etnonacionalismo*. Bilbao: Universidad del País Vasco.

Douglass, William A., Carmelo Urza, Linda White, and Joseba Zulaika. (eds. 1999a). *Basque Politics and Nationalism on the Eve of the Millennium*. Reno, Nevada: Basque Studies Program, University of Nevada, Reno.

——. (eds. 1999b). *The Basque Diaspora/La Diáspora Vasca*. Reno, Nevada: Basque Studies Program, University of Nevada Press.

Drzewiecka, Jolanta A. (2002). "Reinventing and Contesting Identities in Constitutive Discourses: Between Diaspora and Its Others." *Communication Quarterly*, Vol. 50, No. 1 (Winter): 1–23.

DuBois, W. E. Burghardt. (c.1903, 1961). *The Souls of Black Folk*. Greenwich: Fawcett.

Eccarius-Kelly, Vera. "Political Movements and Leverage Points: Kurdish Activism in the European Diaspora." *Journal of Muslim Minority Affairs*, Vol. 22, No. 1 (2002): 91–119

Echeverría, Javier. (1992). *Telépolis*. Valencia: Pretextos.

Echeverría, Javier, Andoni Alonso, and Pedro J. Oiarzabal (eds. 2010). *Knowledge Communities*. Conference Series. Vol. 4. Reno: Center for Basque Studies, University of Nevada, Reno.

Echeverria, Jerónima. (1999a). *Home Away from Home: A History of the Basque Boardinghouses*. Reno, Nevada: University of Nevada Press.

——. (1999b). "The Basque Hotelera: Implications for Broader Study," in William A. Douglass, Carmelo Urza, Linda White, and Joseba Zulaika. (eds.) *The Basque Diaspora/La Diáspora Vasca*. Reno, Nevada: University of Nevada Press.

——. (2000). "Expansion and Eclipse of the Basque Boardinghouse in the American West." *Nevada Historical Society Quarterly*, Vol. 43, No. 2, (Summer): 127–39.

Ellis, Patricia, and Zafar Khan. (1998). "Diasporic Mobilization and the Kashmir Issue in British Politics." *Journal of Ethnic and Migration Studies*, Vol. 24, No. 3: 471–89

Escobedo Mansilla, Ronald, Ana de Zaballa Beascoechea, and Óscar Álvarez Gila. (eds. 1996). *Emigración y Redes Sociales de los Vascos de América*. Vitoria-Gasteiz: Servicio Editorial de la Universidad del País Vasco.

Escobedo Mansilla, Ronald, Ana de Zaballa Beascoechea, and Óscar Álvarez Gila. (1996). *Comerciantes, Mineros y Nautas: Los Vascos en la Economía Americana*. Vitoria-Gasteiz: Servicio Editorial de la Universidad del País Vasco.

Etzioni, Amitri and Oren Etzioni. (1997). "Communities: Virtual vs. Real." *Science*, Editorial Vol. 277, No. 5324 (July 18): 295.

——. (1999). "Face-to-face and Computer-mediated communities, a Comparative Analysis." *Information Society*, Vol. 15, No. 4 (October–December): 241–49.

Fair, Christine. (2005). "Diaspora Involvement in Insurgencies: Insights from the Khalistan and Tamil Eelam Movements." *Nationalism and Ethnic Politics*, Vol. 11, No. 1 (2005): 125–57.

Feenberg, Andrew and Maria Bakardjieva. (2004). "Virtual Community: No 'Killer Implication'." *New Media and Society*, Vol. 6, No. 1: 37–43.

Fernández, Luis. (1998). *Etxepare Porno*: San Sebastián: Alberdania.

Foster, Derek. (1997). "Community and Identity in the Electronic Village," in David Porter (ed.) *Internet culture*. London: Routledge.

Fox, Nick and Chris Roberts. (1999). "GPs in Cyberspace: The Sociology of a 'Virtual Community'." *Sociological Review*, Vol. 47, No. 4 (November): 643–72.

Fox, Steve. (2004). "The New Imagined Community: Identifying and Exploring a Bidirectional Continuum Integrating Virtual and Physical Communities through the Community Embodiment Model (CEM)." *Journal of Communication Inquiry*, Vol. 18, No. 1 (January): 47–62.

Fuglerud, Oivind. (1999). *Life on the Outside: The Tamil Diaspora and Long-distance Nationalism.* London: Pluto Press

Galaskiewicz, Joseph, and Stanley. Wasserman. (1993). "Social Network Analysis: Concepts, Methodology, and Directions for the 1990s." *Sociological Methods & Research,* Vol. 22, No. 1: 3–22.

Galston, William A. (2000). "Does the Internet Strengthen Community?" *National Civic Review*, Vol. 89, No. 3 (Fall): 193–202.

Gans, Herbert J. (1979). "Symbolic Ethnicity: The Future of Ethnic Groups and Cultures in America." *Ethnic and Racial Studies*, Vol. 2 (January): 1–20.

——. (1994). "Symbolic Ethnicity and Symbolic Religiosity: Towards a Comparison of Ethnic and Religious Acculturation." *Ethnic and Racial Studies*, Vol. 17 (October): 577–92.

Garton, Laura, Caroline Haythornthwaite, and Barry Wellman. (1997). "Studying Online Social Networks." *Journal of Computer-Mediated Communication,* Vol. 3, No. 1 (online). http://jcmc.indiana.edu/vol3/issue1/garton.html

Geisler, Michael E. (ed. 2005). *National Symbols, Fractured Identities: Contesting the National Narrative.* Middlebury Bicentennial Series in International Studies. Lebanon, New Hampshire: University Press of New England.

Gellner, Ernst. (1983). *Nations and Nationalism.* Ithaca, New York: Cornell University Press.

Gerrand, Peter. (2006). "Cultural Diversity in Cyberspace: The Catalan Campaign to win the New .cat Top Level Domain." *First Monday,* Vol. 11, No. 1 (January). http://firstmonday.org/issues/issue11_1/gerrand/index.html

Giddens, Anthony. (1990). *The Consequences of Modernity.* Cambridge: Polity Press.

Glick Schiller, Nina, L. Basch, and C. Blanc Szanton. (1992a). "Transnationalism: A New Analysis Framework for Understanding Migration." *Annals of the New York Academy of Sciences*, 645: 1–24.

——. (1992b). *The Transnationalization of Migration: Perspectives on Ethnicity and Race.* New York: Gordon & Breach.

——. (1995). "From Migrant to Transmigrant: Theorizing Transnational Migration." *Anthropological Quarterly*, Vol. 68. No. 1: 48–63.

Glick Schiller, Nina. (1999). "Transmigrants and Nation-states: Something Old and Something New in the US Experience Immigrant Experience," in Charles Hirschman, Philip Kasinitz, and Josh DeWind (eds.) *The Handbook of International Migration: The American Experience.* New York: Russell Sage.

Gobierno Vasco. (1981). *Euskal Batzar Orokorra – Congreso Mundial Vasco*. Vitoria-Gasteiz: Presidencia y Servicio Central de Publicaciones del Gobierno Vasco.

——. (ed. 1983). *El Lehendakari en América, Viaje del Presidente de Gobierno Vasco D. Carlos Garaikoetxea a Panamá, Caracas y Bogota. 17 al 25 de Mayo 1983*. Vitoria-Gasteiz: Presidencia y Servicio Central de Publicaciones del Gobierno Vasco.

——. (ed. 1986). *Mezuak-discursos. José Antonio Ardanza*. Vitoria-Gasteiz: Presidencia y Servicio Central de Publicaciones del Gobierno Vasco.

——. (ed. 1993). *Conferencias Pronunciadas por el Lehendakari José Antonio Ardanza: Pacificación y Democracia; Euskadi en el Estado de las Autonomías*. Vitoria-Gasteiz: Presidencia y Servicio Central de Publicaciones del Gobierno Vasco.

——. (1994). *Law of Relations with Basque Communities Outside the Autonomous Community of the Basque Country*. Vitoria-Gasteiz: Servicio Editorial de Publicaciones del Gobierno Vasco.

——. (1996). *Euskaldunak Munduan, Building the Future*. Vitoria-Gasteiz: Servicio Editorial de Publicaciones del Gobierno Vasco.

——. (2000). *World Congress on Basque Communities, 1999. Vitoria-Gasteiz, October 26–29*. Vitoria-Gasteiz: Servicio Central de Publicaciones del Gobierno Vasco.

——. (2003a). *Retratos de Juventud* No. 5 (February). Gabinete de Prospección Sociológica del Gobierno Vasco. Vitoria-Gasteiz: Presidencia y Gabinete de Prospección Sociológica.

——. (2003b). *Sociometro Vasco* No. 21 (February). Gabinete de Prospección Sociológica del Gobierno Vasco. Vitoria-Gasteiz: Presidencia y Gabinete de Prospección Sociológica.

——. (2003c). *Sociometro Vasco* No. 23 (December). Gabinete de Prospección Sociológica del Gobierno Vasco. Vitoria-Gasteiz: Presidencia y Gabinete de Prospección Sociológica.

——. (2004) *Aurrera Goaz. III World Congress of Basque Communities*. Vitoria-Gasteiz: Servicio Editorial de Publicaciones del Gobierno Vasco.

——. (2005a). *Sociometro Vasco* No. 25 (December). Gabinete de Prospección Sociológica del Gobierno Vasco. Vitoria-Gasteiz: Servicio Editorial de Publicaciones del Gobierno Vasco.

——. (2005b). *Opiniones de la Ciudadanía de la CAPV sobre la Consecución de la Paz en el País Vasco*. (December). Gabinete de Prospección Sociológica del Gobierno Vasco. Vitoria-Gasteiz: Servicio Editorial de Publicaciones del Gobierno Vasco.

——. (2007). *A Political Initiative aimed at Resolving the Basque Conflict*. Vitoria-Gasteiz: Servicio Editorial de Publicaciones del Gobierno Vasco.

——. (2008). *Zubigintzan, 4th World Congress of Basque Communities 2007. Bilbao, July 2007.* Vitoria-Gasteiz: Servicio Editorial de Publicaciones del Gobierno Vasco.

——. (2012). *Guztion Artean, V Congreso Mundial de Colectividades Vascas en el Exterior 2011. Donostia-San Sebastián, 2-4 de Noviembre de 2011.* Vitoria-Gasteiz: Servicio Editorial de Publicaciones del Gobierno Vasco.

Gobierno Vasco, Gobierno de Navarra, and Institut Culturel Basque. (1997a). *Sociolinguistic Study of the Basque Country 1996 –The Continuity of Basque II.* Vitoria-Gasteiz: Servicio Central de Publicaciones del Gobierno Vasco, Departamento de Cultura, Viceconsejería de Política Lingüística.

——. (1997b). *Encuesta Sociolingüística de Euskal Herria 1996: La continuidad del Euskera II.* Vitoria-Gasteiz: Servicio Central de Publicaciones del Gobierno Vasco, Departamento de Cultura, Viceconsejería de Política Lingüística.

Grinberg, Leon and Rebecca Grinberg. (1989). *Psychoanalytic Perspectives on Migration and Exile.* New Haven and London: Yale University Press.

Gulli, Antonio and Alessio Signorini. (2005). "The Indexable Web is more than 11.5 Billion Pages." (May, online). www.cs.uiowa.edu/~asignori/web-size/

Hakken, David. (1999). *Cyborgs@cyberspace: An Ethnographer looks to the Future.* London: Routledge.

Hall, Stuart. (1993). "Culture, Community, Nation." *Cultural Studies*, Vol. 7, No. 3 (October): 349–63.

Harvey, David. (1989). *The Condition of Postmodernity.* Oxford: Blackwell;

Haythornthwaite, Caroline. (2001). "Introduction: the Internet in Everyday Life." *American Behavioral Scientist*, Vol. 45, No. 3: 363–82.

Heidegger, Martin. (1971). *"The Thing." Poetry, Language, Thought.* New York: Harper and Row.

Henzinger, Monika R. (2001). "Hyperlink Analysis for the Web." *IEEE Internet Computing,* Vol. 5, No. 1: 45–50.

Hobsbawn, Eric. (1990). *Nations and Nationalism since 1780: Programme, Myth and Reality.* Cambridge: Cambridge University Press.

Horowitz, Donald L. (1985). *Ethnic Groups in Conflict.* Berkeley, California: University of California Press.

House Joint Memorial No. 144, 2002. Legislature of the State of Idaho, in the Second Regular Session, Fifth-sixth Legislature.

Ignacio, Emily Noelle. (2002). "Filipino ka ba? Internet Discussions in the Filipino Community," in Linda Trinh Võ and Rick Bonus (eds.) *Contemporary Asian American Communities.* Philadelphia: Temple University Press.

Instituto Nacional de Estadística (INE) (2002–2012). "Estadística de Variaciones Residenciales. Bajas por Variación Residencial de Españoles con Destino al Extranjero Clasificadas por Provincia de Procedencia (Agrupadas por Comunidades), Lugar de Nacimiento y Sexo." Madrid: Instituto Nacional de Estadística.

Irigoyen Artetxe, Alberto. (1998). *Laurac Bat de Montevideo: Primera Euskal Etxea del Mundo (1876–1898)*. Vitoria-Gasteiz: Servicio Central de Publicaciones del Gobierno Vasco.

Karim, H. Karim. (ed. 2003). *The Media of Diaspora: Mapping the Globe*. London: Routledge.

Kerexeta, Kontxi. (2008). "Basque Centers and Members," in Gobierno Vasco (ed.) *Zubigintzan, 4th World Congress of Basque Communities 2007. Bilbao, July 2007*. Vitoria-Gasteiz: Servicio Editorial de Publicaciones del Gobierno Vasco.

Kivisto, Peter and Ben Nefzger. (1993). "Symbolic Ethnicity and American Jews: The Relationship of Ethnic Identity to Behavior and Group Affiliation." *Social Science Journal*, Vol. 30: 1–12.

Knoke, William. (1992). *Bold New World: The Essential Road Map of the Twenty-first Century*. New York: Charles Scribner's Sons.

Kolko, Beth, Lisa Nakamura, and Gilbert B. Rodman. (eds. 2000). *Race in Cyberspace*. New York: Routledge.

Krutwig, Federico. (1984). *Computer Shock: Vasconia, Año 2001*. Estella: Gráficas Lizarra.

Kurlansky, Mark. (1999). *The Basque History of the World*. New York: Walker and Company.

Laguerre, Michel S. (1998). (2003). *Urban Multiculturalism and Globalization in New York City: An Analysis of Diasporic Temporalities*. Basingstoke: Palgrave Macmillan.

——. (2004). "Virtual Diasporas: A New Frontier of National Security." *Virtual Diasporas*. The Nautilus Institute. (June 8, 2004). www.nautilus.org/virtual-diasporas/paper/laguerre.html

Lal, Vinay. (1999). "The Politics of History on the Internet: Cyber-Diasporic Hinduism and the North America Hindu Diaspora." *Diaspora*, Vol. 8, No. 2 (Fall): 137–72.

Larronde, Jean-Claude. (1977). *El Nacionalismo Vasco: Su Origen y su Ideología en la Obra de Arana Arana-Goiri*. San Sebastián: Ediciones Vascas.

Legarreta, Dorothy. (1984). *The Guernica Generation: Basque Refugee Children of the Spanish Civil War*. Reno, Nevada: University of Nevada Press.

Legarreta, Josu. (2001). "Basque Centers: From Associationism to Paradiplomacy," in *Kanpoko etxe Berria. Emigración vasca a America S. XIX–XX. Home Away from Home*. Vol. 1. Bilbao: Museo Arqueológico, Etnográfico e Histórico del País Vasco.

Leonard, Karen. (2003). "American Muslim Politics." *Ethnicities*, Vol. 3, No. 2: 147–82.

Licklider, Joseph C. R. and Robert Taylor. (1968). "The Computer as a Communication Device." *Science and Technology: For the Men in Management*, No. 76 (April): 21–31

Luque Alcaide, Elisa. (1996). "Relaciones Inter-personales e Institucionales en la Cofradía de Aranzazu," in Ronald, Escobedo Mansilla, Ana de Zaballa Beascoechea, and Óscar Álvarez Gila (eds.) *Emigración y Redes Sociales de los Vascos de América*. Vitoria-Gasteiz: Servicio Editorial de la Universidad del País Vasco.

Mackay, Hugh and Tony. Powell. (1997). "Connecting Wales: The Internet and National Identity," in Brian Loader (ed.) *Cyberspace Divide: Equality, Agency and Policy in the Information Society*. London: Routledge.

Mallapragada, Madhavi. (2000). "The Indian Diaspora in the USA and Around the Web," in David Gauntlet (ed.) *Web studies*. London: Arnold.

Matiossian, Vartan. (2003). "The Future is Not Coming, the Past is Gone": Some Notes about the Armenian Reality in Argentina." *Journal of the Society for Armenian Studies*, Vol. 12: 11–29.

McCaughey, Martha and Michael D. Ayers. (eds. 2003). *Cyberactivism: Online Activism in Theory and Practice*. New York: Routledge.

McMillan, Sally J. (2000). "The Microscope and the Moving Target: The Challenge of Applying Content Analysis to the World Wide Web." *Journalism and Mass Communication Quarterly*, Vol. 77, No. 1: 80–98.

Menem, Julio. (2003). *La Pelota Vasca: La Piel Contra la Piedra*. Edición de Gorka
Bilbao. Madrid: Aguilar.

Milikowski, Marisca. (2000). "Exploring a Model of De-ethnicisation: The Case of Turkish Television in the Netherlands." *European Journal of Communication*, Vol. 15, No. 4: 443–68.

Miller, Daniel and Don Slater. (2001). *The Internet: An Ethnographic Approach*. Oxford: Berg Publishers.

Mills, Kurt. (2002). "Cybernations: Identity, Self-determination, Democracy and the 'Internet Effect' in the Emerging Information Order." *Global Society*, Vol. 16, No. 1: 69–87.

Mitra, Ananda. (1997). "Diasporic Web Sites: Ingroup and Outgroup Discourse." *Critical Studies in Mass Communication*, Vol. 14: 158–81.

——. (1999). "Characteristics of the WWW Text: Tracing Discursive Strategies." *Journal of Computer Mediated Communication*, Vol. 5, No. 1 (online). http://jcmc.indiana.edu/vol5/issue1/mitra.html

——. (2001). "Diasporic Voices in Cyberspace." *New Media and Society*, Vol. 3, No. 1: 29–48.

——. (2002). *"Creating Immigrant Identities in Cyberspace."* Paper presented at the Conference 'Media Performance and Practice across Cultures.' University of Wisconsin, Madison. March 14–17, 2002. www.nriol.com/mediakit/awards/anandmitra/

Mitra, Ananda and Elisia Cohen. (1999). "Analyzing the Web: Directions and Challenges," in S. Jones (ed.) *Doing Internet Research*. Thousand Oaks, CA: Sage Publications.

Mitra, Ananda and Schwartz Raelynn. (2001). "From Cyber Space to Cybernetic Space: Rethinking the Relationship between Real and Virtual Space." *Journal of Computer-Mediated Communication*, Vol. 7, No. 1 (October, online). http://jcmc.indiana.edu/vol7/issue1/mitra.html

Molina Aparicio, Fernando and Pedro J. Oiarzabal. (2009). "Basque-Atlantic Shores: Ethnicity, the Nation-state, and the Diaspora in Europe and America (1808–1898)." *Ethnic and Racial Studies*, Vol. 32, No. 4: 698–715.

Moradiellos, Enrique. (2005). *Franco Frente a Churchill*. Madrid: Península.

Moreno, Luis. (1999). "Local and Global: Mesogovernments and Territorial Identities." *Nationalism and Ethnic Politics*, Vol. 5, Nos. 3–4 (1999): 61–75.

——. (2001). "Ethnoterritorial Concurrence in Plural Societies: The Spanish Comunidades Autónomas," in Alain G. Cagnon and James Tully (eds.) *Justice and Stability in Multinational Societies*. Cambridge: Cambridge University Press.

——. (2002). "Global y Local: Identidades Territoriales y Mesogobiernos," in William Safran and Ramón Máiz (Coords.) *Identidades y Autogobierno en Sociedades Multiculturales*. Barcelona: Ariel.

Morley, David and Kevin Robins. (1995). *Spaces of identity: Global media, Electronic Landscapes and Cultural Boundaries*. London: Routledge.

Noivo, Edite. (2002). "Towards a Cartography of Portuguesness: Challenging the Hegemonic Center." *Diaspora*, Vol. 11, No. 2 (Fall): 255–75.

Núñez Seixas, Xosé Manoel. (1998). "Retornados e Inadaptados" el "Americano" Gallego, entre Mito y Realidad (1880–1930)." *Revista de Indias*, No. 214 (September–December): 555–93.

——. (2002). *O inmigrante Imaginario: Estereotipos, Representacións e Identidades dos Galegos na Arxentina (1880–1940)*. Santiago de Compostela: Universidade de Santiago de Compostela.

Oiarzabal, Pedro J. (2007a). "We Love You: The Basque Government's Post–Franco Discourses on the Basque Diaspora." *Revista Sancho el Sabio*, No. 26: 95–132.

——. (2007b). "A Review of Theoretical Approaches to Identity: The Basque Case." *Journal of the Society of Basque Studies in America*, Vol. 27: 24–35.

——. (2009a). *Gardeners of Identity: Basques in the San Francisco Bay Area*. Urazandi Series. Vol. 23. 1st ed. Vitoria-Gasteiz: Servicio Central de Publicaciones del Gobierno Vasco.

——. (2009b). *Gardeners of Identity: Basques in the San Francisco Bay Area*. Basque Diaspora and Migration Studies Series. Vol. 4. 2nd ed. Reno: Center for Basque Studies.

——. (2009c). "Basque Diaspora Digital Nationalism: Designing "Banal" Identity," in Andoni Alonso and Pedro J. Oiarzabal (eds.) *Diasporas in the New Media Age: Identity, Politics and Community.* Reno, Nevada: University Nevada Press.

——. (2010). "The Online Social Networks of the Basque Diaspora. Fast Forwarded, 2005–2009," in Javier Echeverría, Andoni Alonso and Pedro J. Oiarzabal (eds.) *Knowledge Communities.* Conference Series. Vol. 4. Reno: Center for Basque Studies, University of Nevada, Reno.

——. (2012a). "Diaspora Basques and Online Social Networks: An Analysis of Users of Basque Institutional Diaspora Groups on Facebook." *Journal of Ethnicity and Migration Studies*, Vol. 38, No. 9 (2012): 1469–85.

——. (2012b). "Una Verdadera Imagen de Paz: Los Congresos Mundiales de la Diáspora Vasca," in Mercedes Acillona (ed.) *Marcos Interpretativos de la Realidad Social Contemporánea / Egungo Gizarte Errealitatea Interpretatzeko Bideak.* Bilbao: Universidad de Deusto

Oiarzabal, Agustín M. and Pedro J. Oiarzabal. (2005). *La Identidad Vasca en el Mundo: Narrativas sobre Identidad más allá de Fronteras.* Bilbao: Erroteta.

Oiarzabal, Pedro J., Koldo San Sebastián, and Anna M. Aguirre. *Sailing in New York: The Social Origins of the Basque Club of New York, 1905-1955.* Forthcoming.

Oiarzabal, Pedro J. and Ulf-Dietrich Reips. (Eds.). (2012a). "Migration and the Internet: Social networking and diasporas" [special issue]. *Journal of Ethnic and Migration Studies,* Vol. 38, No. 9: 1333–1490.

Oiarzabal, Pedro J. and Ulf-Dietrich Reips. (2012b). "Migration and Diaspora in the Age of Information and Communication Technologies." *Journal of Ethnicity and Migration Studies*, Vol. 38, No. 9 (2012): 1333–38.

O'Neill, Edward T., Brian F. Lavoie, and Rick Bennett. (2003). "Trends in the Evolution of the Public Web 1998–2002." *D-Lib Magazine*, Vol. 9, No. 4 (April, online). www.dlib.org/dlib/april03/lavoie/04lavoie.html

Oregi, Benan and Andoni Martín. (2008). "Evaluation of the Four Year Plan del Plan 2004–2007," in Gobierno Vasco (ed.) *Zubigintzan, 4th World Congress of Basque Communities 2007. Bilbao, July 2007.* Vitoria-Gasteiz: Servicio Editorial de Publicaciones del Gobierno Vasco.

Parham, Angel A. (2004). "Diaspora, Community and Communication: Internet Use in Transnational Haiti." *Global Networks*, Vol. 4, No. 2: 199–217.

Parissi, Julio César. (2006). *Qué fue de Ellos...El Enigma de los Etarras en el Uruguay.* Montevideo: Editorial Planeta.

Park, Han Woo. (2003). "Hyperlink Network Analysis: A New Method for the Study of Social Structure on the Web." *Connections*, Vol. 25, No. 1: 49–61.

Park, Han Woo and Mike Thelwall. (2003). "Hyperlinks Analyses of the World Wide Web: A Review." *Journal of Computer-Mediated Communication*, Vol. 8, No. 4 (July, online). http://jcmc.indiana.edu/vol8/issue4/park.html

Parlamento Vasco. (2003). Official Transcript 031024, October 23, 2003.

Parrish, Rick. (2002). "The Changing Nature of Community." *Strategies*, Vol. 15, No. 2: 259–284.

Perlmutter, Howard V. (1991). "On the Rocky Road to the First Global Civilization." *Human Relations*, Vol. 44, No. 9: 897–1010.

Pescador, Juan Javier. (2004). *The New World inside a Basque Village: The Oiartzun Valley and Its Atlantic Emigrants 1550–1800*. Reno, Nevada: University of Nevada Press.

Plaza, Dwaine. (2010). "Maintaining Transnational Identity: A Content Analysis of Web Pages constructed by Second-Generation Caribbeans," in Andoni Alonso and Pedro J. Oiarzabal (eds.) *Diasporas in the New Media Age: Identity, Politics and Community*. Reno, Nevada: University Nevada Press.

Poster, Mark. (1998). "Virtual Ethnicity: Tribal Identity in the Age of Global Communications," in Steven G. Jones (ed.) *Cybersociety 2.0: Revisiting Computer-mediated communication and Community*. Thousand Oaks, California: Sage.

Presidencia. (2012). "Primer Consejo de Gobierno. Intervención del Lehendakari." October 21, 2012. Vitoria-Gasteiz: Presidencia. Secretaría General de Comunicación.

Raento, Pauliina and Cameron J. Watson. (2000). "Guernika, Guernica, Guernica? Contested Meanings of a Basque Place." *Political Geography*, Vol. 19: 707–736.

Ragnedda, Massimo and Glenn W. Muschert. (eds. 2013). *The Digital Divide. The Internet and Social Inequality in International Perspective*. London: Routledge.

Rai, Amit S. (1995). "India on-line: Electronic Bulletin Boards and the Construction of a Diasporic Hindu Identity." *Diaspora*, Vol. 4, No. 1 (Spring): 31–58.

Rheingold, Howard. (1993). *The Virtual Community: Homesteading on the Electronic Frontier*. Reading, Massachusetts: Addison-Wesley Pub. Co.

——. (1999). "Virtual Community: Another Metaphor." *Whole Earth*, Issue 98 (Fall): 18.

Robertson, Roland. (1990). "Mapping the Global Condition: Globalization as the Central Concept." *Theory, Culture & Society*, Vol. 7: 15–30.

——. (1992). *Glocalization: Social Theory and Global Culture*. London: Sage.

Rodríguez de las Heras, Antonio. (1999). "El Libro Digital." Facultat d'Humanitats de la Universitat Pompeu Favra I els Estudis d'Humanitats; Filología de la UOC. Barcelona, October 21, 1999. www.uoc.edu/humfil/digithum/digithum2/catala/Art_Heras/heras_6.htm

Rudolph, Joseph Jr. and Robert J. Thompson. (eds. 1989). *Ethnoterritorial Politics, Policy and the Western World*. Boulder, Colorado: Lynne Rienner Publishers.

Rubio Pobes, Coro. (2004). "La Primera Bandera de Euskal-Erria." *Revista Sancho el Sabio*, No. 20: 171–82.

Ruíz de Gauna, Adolfo. (1991). *Catálogo de Publicaciones Periódicas Vascas en los Siglos XIX y XX*. Vitoria-Gasteiz: Eusko Ikaskuntza y Servicio Central de Publicaciones del Gobierno Vasco.

Safran, William. (1991). "Diaspora in Modern Societies: Myths of Homeland and Return." *Diaspora*, Vol. 1, No. 1 (Spring): 83–99.

——. (1999). "Comparing Diasporas: A Review Essay." *Diaspora*, Vol. 8, No. 3 (Winter): 255–89.

Santiso González, María Concepción. (1991). "La Segunda Guerra Carlista y su Repercusión en la Emigración Guipuzcoana a América," in Antonio Eiras Roel (ed.) *La Emigración Española a Ultramar, 1492–1914*. Madrid: Tabapress.

San Sebastián, Koldo. (1991). *The Basque Archives: Vascos en Estados Unidos (1938–1943)*. Donostia-San Sebastián: Txertoa.

San Sebastián, Koldo and Peru Ajuria. (1992). *El Exilio Vasco en Venezuela*. Vitoria-Gasteiz: Servicio Central de Publicaciones del Gobierno Vasco.

Savater, Fernando. (2004). *El Gran Fraude*. Madrid: Aguilar.

Sayad, Abdelmalek. (1999). *La Double Absence. Des Illusions de L'émigré aux Souffrances de L'immigré*. Paris: Seuil.

Schiller, Nina Glick, and Georges Eugene Fouron. (2001). *Georges Woke up Laughing: Long-distance Nationalism and the Search for Home*. Durham, NC: Duke University Press.

Schmidt, Garbi. (2002). "Dialectics of Authenticity: Examples of Ethnification of Islam among Young Muslims in Sweden and the United States." *Muslim World*, Vol. 92, No. 1/2 (Spring): 1–17.

Schnapper, Dominique. (1999). "From the Nation-state to the Transnational World: On the Meaning and Usefulness of Diaspora as a Concept." *Diaspora*, Vol. 8, No. 3 (Winter: 225–55.

Shain, Yossi. (1989). *The Frontiers of Loyalty: Political Exiles in the Age of the Nation-state*. Middleton, Connecticut: Wesleyan University Press.

——. (1991). *Governments-in-exile in the Contemporary World of Politics*. London: Routledge.

——. (2002). "Jewish Kinship at a Crossroads: Lessons from Homelands and Diasporas." *Political Science Quarterly*, Vol. 117, No. 2 (Summer): 279–309.

Shani, Giorgio. (2002). "The Territorialization of Identity: Sikh Nationalism in the Diaspora." *Studies in Ethnicity and Nationalism*, Vol. 2, No. 1 (2002): 11–19.

Sheffer, Gabriel. (1999). "The Emergence of New Ethno-National Diasporas," in Steven Vertovec and Robin Cohen (eds.) *Migration, Diasporas, and Transnationalism*. Cheltenham, United Kingdom: Edward Elgar Publishing Ltd.

Shichor, Yitzhak. (2003). "Virtual Transnationalism: Uygur Communities in Europe and the Quest for Eastern Turkistan independence," in Stefano Allievi and Jørgen Nielsen (eds.) *Muslim networks and Transnational Communities in and across Europe*. Leiden, Boston: Brill.

Siu, Paul. (1952). "The Sojourner." *American Journal of Sociology*, Vol. 58, No. 1: 34–44.

Skrbiš, Zlatko. (1991). *Long-distance Nationalism: Diaspora, Homelands and Identities*. Research in Migration and Ethnic Relation Series. Brookfield, VT: Ashgate.

Smith, Anthony D. (1981). *The Ethnic Revival in the Modern World*. Cambridge, United Kingdom: Cambridge University Press.

——. (1992). *National Identity*. Reno, Nevada: University of Nevada Press.

——. (1996). "The Resurgence of Nationalism? Myth and Memory in the Renewal of Nations." *British Journal of Sociology*, Vol. 47, No. 4 (December): 575–98.

Snyder, Joel. (1996). "Get Real." *Internet World*, Vol. 7, No. 2: 92–94.

Sökefeld, Martin. (2002). "Alevism Online: Re-imagining a Community in Virtual Space." *Diaspora*, Vol. 11, No. 1 (Spring): 85–123.

Soraluze, Andoni. (1986). "Prensa Vasca en América." *Euzkadi*, No. 226: 20–23.

Spivak, Gayatri. (1989). "Who Claims Alterity?" in Barbara Kruger and Phil Mariani (eds.) *Remaking History*. Seattle: Bay Press.

Stubbs, Paul. (1999). "Virtual Diaspora? Imaging Croatia On-line." *Sociological Research On-line*, Vol. 4, No. 2. www.socresonline.org.uk/socresonline/4/2/stubbs.html

Tajfel, Henri. (1978). *The Social Psychology of Minorities*. Minority Right Groups.

——. (1981). *Human Groups and Social Categories: Studies in Social Psychology*. Cambridge, United Kingdom: Cambridge University Press.

——. (ed. 1982). *Social Identity and Intergroup Relations*. Cambridge, United Kingdom: Cambridge University Press.

——. (ed. 1984). *The Social Dimension: European Development in Social Psychology*. Vol. 2. Cambridge, United Kingdom: Cambridge University Press.

Tápiz Fernández, José María. (2000). "La Actividad Política de los Emigrantes: El Caso Vasco (1903–1936)," in Óscar Álvarez Gila and Alberto Angulo Morales (eds.) *Las Migraciones Vascas en Perspectiva Histórica (Siglos XVI–XX)*. Bilbao: Servicio Editorial de la Universidad del País Vasco.

Terhune, Kenneth W. (1964). "Nationalism among Foreign and American Students: An Exploratory Study." *Journal of Conflict Resolution*, Vol. 8: 256–70.

Tölölyan, Khachig. (1996). "Rethinking Diaspora(s): Stateless Power in the Transnational Moment." *Diaspora*, Vol. 5, No. 1 (Spring): 3–36.

Totoricagüena, Gloria. (2004). *Identity, Culture, and Politics in the Basque Diaspora*. Reno, Nevada: University of Nevada Press.

———. (2005). "Diasporas as Non-Central Government Actors in Foreign Policy: The Trajectory of Basque Paradiplomacy." *Nationalism and Ethnic Politics*, Vol. 11, No. 2: 265–87.

Turner, Victor. (1969). *The Ritual Process. Structure and Anti-Structure*. New York: Aldine de Gruyter.

Uberuaga, Blas Pedro. (2000). "Basques in the Digital Age." *The Journal of Society of Basque Studies in America*, Vol. XX: 1–16.

Ugalde Zubiri, Alexander. (1996). *La Acción Exterior del Nacionalismo Vasco (1890–1939): Historia, Pensamiento y Relaciones Internacionales*. Bilbao: IVAP.

———. (2008). "World Congresses on Basque Communities: Center proposals, Basque Government Plans and Evaluation of the Results," in Gobierno Vasco (2008) *Zubigintzan, 4th World Congress of Basque Communities 2007. Bilbao, July 2007*. Vitoria-Gasteiz: Servicio Editorial de Publicaciones del Gobierno Vasco.

Van den Bos, Matthijs. (2006). "Hyperlinked Dutch-Iranian Cyberspace." *International Sociology*, Vol. 21, No. 1: 83–99.

Van Hear, Nicholas. (1998). *New Diasporas: The Mass Exodus, Dispersal and Regrouping of Migrant Communities*. London: UCL Press.

Vertovec, Steven. (1997). "Three Meanings of "Diaspora," Exemplified among South Asian Religions." *Diaspora*, Vol. 6, No. 3 (Winter): 277–300.

Virnoche, Mary E. and Gary T. Marx. (1997). "Only Connect—E. M. Foster in an Age of Electronic Communication: Computer-mediated association and Community Networks." *Sociology Inquiry*, Vol. 67, No. 1: 85–100.

Volkan, Vamik. (1981). *Linking Objects and Linking Phenomena: A Study of the Forms, Symptoms, Metapsychology, and Therapy of Complicated Mourning*. New York: International Universities Press.

Ward, Katie J. (1999). "Cyber-ethnography and the emergence of the virtually new community." *Journal of Information Technology*, Vol. 14: 95-105.

Wasserman, Stanley and Katherine Faust. (1994). *Social Network Analysis: Methods and Applications*. Cambridge, United Kingdom: Cambridge University Press.

Watson, Nessim. (1997). "Why we argue about Virtual Community: A Case Study of the Phish.net Fan Community," in Steven G. Jones (ed.) *Virtual Culture: Identity and Communication in Cybersociety*. London: Sage.

Wellman, Barry. (2001). "Physical Place and Cyberplace: The rise of Personalized Networking." *International Journal of Urban and Regional Research*, Vol. 22, No. 2: 227–52.

Wellman, Barry and Milena Gulia. (1999). "Virtual Communities as Communities: Net Surfers Don't Ride Alone," in Marc A. Smith and Peter Kollock. (eds. 1999). *Communities in Cyberspace*. New York: Routledge.

Wellman, Barry and Caroline Haythornthwaite. (eds. 2003). *The Internet in Everyday Life.* Cambridge, Massachusetts: Blackwell.

Wilbur, Shawn P. (1997). "An Archaeology of Cyberspace: Virtuality, Community, Identity," in David Porter (ed.) *Internet culture.* New York: Routledge.

Wong, Loong. (2003). "Belonging and Diaspora: The Chinese and the Internet." *First Monday*, Vol. 8, No. 4 (April). http://firstmonday.org/issues/issue8_4/wong/index.html

Woodworth, Paddy (2009). "Many Flowers in the Basque Garden," in Pedro J. Oiarzabal *Gardeners of Identity: Basques in the San Francisco Bay Area.* Basque Diaspora and Migration Studies Series. Vol. 4. 2nd ed. Reno: Center for Basque Studies.

Zulaika, Joseba. (1998). "Tropics of Terror: From Guernica's 'Natives' to Global 'Terrorists." *Social identities*, Vol. 4, No. 1 (February): 93–108.

Zulaika, Joseba and William A. Douglass. (1996). *Terror and taboo: The Follies, Fables, and Faces of Terrorism.* New York and London: Routledge.

Unpublished works

Álvarez Gila, Óscar. (2013). "'Los vascos vinimos en busca de la libertad'. Reflexiones sobre la emigración desde el exilio (1936-1975)." Paper presented at the Congreso Ciencias, Tecnologías y Culturas. Simposio 4: Migraciones y exilios en América Latina (siglos XIX y XX). Santiago de Chile.

Bilbao, Daniel C. (2006). "Exhorto Antidemocrático del PNV en Argentina." Santa Rosa, Argentina (December 5, 2006).

Casal Lodeiro, Manuel. (2003). "O papel de Internet na Conservación da Cultura e Identidade Galegas entre os Descendentes dos Emigrants."

Corcostegui, Lisa M. (2005). "To the Beat of a Different Drum: Basque Dance and Identity in the Homeland and the Diaspora." Unpublished PhD Dissertation. Center for Basque Studies, University of Nevada, Reno.

Dentice-Clark, Lucia. (2004). "Ethnic Identities in Cyberspace: Italy, Ethnicity, the European Union and the Internet. The URL as *Villaggio Virtuale*." Unpublished MA Thesis. Harvard University (June 2004).

Duany, Jorge. (2004). "Following Migrant Citizens" Puerto Rico's Public Policies toward its Diasporic Communities in the US, 1947–1993." Paper presented at the XXV International Congress LASA. Las Vegas, Nevada (October 7–9, 2004).

FEVA. (2007). "Declaración de la Federación de Entidades Vasco Argentinas." Rosario, Argentina (October 6, 2007).

JO TA KE. (2007). "Comunicado de Prensa." Rosario, Argentina (November 7, 2007).

Junta Extraterritorial de Argentina del PNV. (2006). "A la Colectividad Vasco Argentina." Mar del Plata, Argentina (December 2006).

Lecours, André and Luis Moreno. (2001). "Paradiplomacy and Stateless Nations: A Reference to the Basque Country." Madrid: Unidad de Políticas Comparadas (CSIC). Working Paper 01-06. Paper presented at the Conference "The Institutional Accommodation of Diversity." Saint-Marc-sur-le-Richelieu. Quebec (September 20–22, 2001).

Oiarzabal, Pedro J. (2006). "The Basque Diaspora Webscape: Online Discourses of Basque Diaspora Identity, Nationhood, and Homeland." PhD dissertation, University of Nevada, Reno.

Vazquez, Roland. (1998). "The PNV: The Social and Cultural Life of a Basque Nationalist Party." 2 Vols. Unpublished PhD Dissertation. Department of Anthropology. New Brunswick, New Jersey, Rutgers University (May 1998).

Newsletters and newspapers

ABC. Madrid, Spain.

——. *"El PNV Recurre a sus 'Socios' de Idaho para Implicar a la Embajada de EEUU en un Foro."* C. de la Hoz. September 5, 2002.

——. *"La Embajada de Estados Unidos Desmonta el Carácter Institucional del Foro del PNV."* September 6, 2002.

Aberri. Bilbao, Basque Country, Spain.

——. "El Nacionalismo Vasco en la Argentina." Juan de Artazu. June 12, 1923a.

——. "El Nacionalismo Vasco en la Argentina." Juan de Artazu. July 31, 1923b.

Aberri. Brooklyn, New York, U.S.

——. *"To the Basques in the US."* Issue 1, Year 1. September 1925.

Basque Studies Program Newsletter/ Center for Basque Studies. 1981–2013. Reno, Nevada: Basque Studies Program Newsletter/Center for Basque Studies, University of Nevada, Reno.

——. No. 24, September 1981.

——. No. 26, November 1982.

Berria. English Edition. Basque Country, Spain.

——. *"A Distant Mirror."* Mark Bieter. August 10, 2005.

——. *"Why Jaialdi in Boise is that Important?"* Miren Artiach. August 18, 2005.

Berriak–Asociación Diáspora Vasca, Santa Rosa, Argentina.

——. August 2, 2005.

——. August 10, 2005.

Boletín—Federación de Entidades Vasco Argentinas (FEVA). No. 12, December 1971.

Cinco Días. Madrid, Spain.

——. *"MCC ya tiene más de 1000 Empleados en China y Otros 700 en India."* January 14, 2007.

CNN. United States.

——. *"Washington Tells Idaho it's in charge on Basques."* March 11, 2002.

Deia. Basque Country, Spain.

——. *"S.O.S Batasuna."* César Arrondo. March 4, 2002.

——. *"Idaho aprueba la Moción con Ligeras Variaciones."* March 12, 2002.

——. *"Idaho consigue la Implicación de Washington en la Propuesta de Paz."* Andoni Iturbe. March 13, 2002.

——. *"David Bieter: El Acuerdo con los Nacionalistas no debe llegar desde la Revancha."* Andoni Iturbe. March 20, 2002a.

——. *"El PP enviara un Ejemplar del Estatuto a Cenarrusa: Creen que el PNV 'ha utilizado para sus fines' a un Político 'Ultraderechista."* March 20, 2002b.

——. *"La Ayuda a la Diáspora llegará a Vascos de Iparralde y Navarra."* July 16, 2003.

——. *"Euskadi visto por la Diáspora."* Editorial. July 19, 2003a.

——. *"La Colectividades Vascas piden Diálogo para alcanzar la Paz."* July 19, 2003b.

——. *"Azkarraga: Que sean Agentes Activos de la Justicia y la Libertad."* July 19, 2003c.

——. *"SA acusa a Gasteiz de manipular a los Centros Vascos."* July 20, 2003.

——. *"Publicidad a Bombazos."* Xabier Lapitz. July 24, 2003.

——. *"Iztueta pide Colaboración a los Vascos de Argentina para el Plan Ibarretxe."* Nekane Lauzirika. October 10, 2003.

——. *"El Alcalde de Boise expresa su apoyo al Plan Ibarretxe."* December 13, 2003.

——. *"David Bieter: Yo viví en Euskadi en los Tiempos de Franco y la Situación Actual es parecida."* Arantxa Rodríguez. February 12, 2004.

——. *"Ana Palacio dice en EEUU que la Mitad de los Vascos 'aterroriza a la Otra Mitad."* Javier Velilla. February 13, 2004.

——. *"Azkarraga censura las Palabras de Ana Palacio: Califico de 'Error Político de Gran Magnitud' llamar Terroristas a la Mitad de los Vascos."* Arantxa Rodríguez. February 15, 2004.

——. *"Las Euskal Etxeak tendrán cerca de 900,000 Euros."* June 27, 2004.

———. *Senadores y Diputados de Buenos Aires dan su Apoyo al Plan Ibarretxe."* Elena Ferreira. October 27, 2004.

———. *"Ibarretxe se despide de la Diáspora Americana tras el Exito de Jaialdi 2005 celebrado en Boise."* August 2, 2005.

———. *"La América de Corazón Euskaldun."* Elena Ferreira. July 31, 2005.

———. *"El Gobierno Español no apoya el Dominio '.ct' porque Cataluña "no es un Estado."* October 5, 2005.

———. *"Entidades Vasco Argentinas piden el Archivo de la Causa contra Ibarretxe ya que es 'un Obstáculo a la Paz."* October 29, 2006.

———. *"Ibarretxe afirma que la Diáspora es "la Octava Provincia" Vasca y que debe Ayudar a situar a Euskal Herria en el Mundo."* July 10, 2008.

———. *"La Diáspora Vasca en América considera "Indefendible" que se impida la Consulta."* October 23, 2008.

———. *"Mondragón vendió más pero gano un 90% menos en 2008."* May 29, 2009.

———. "*El octavo territorio vasco*" J. Fernández. June 22, 2013.

Diario Vasco. Basque Country, Spain.

———. *"Ibarretxe pide Ayuda a los Vascos de EE.UU. para alcanzar la Paz."* July 30, 2005.

———. *"La Diáspora constata la Total Identificación que se hace en América entre Vascos y ETA"* Belén Elguea. July 15, 2003.

El Adelanto de Salamanca. Salamanca, Spain.

———. *"Un Político Argentino apoya en el País Vasco la Independencia."* Ana Garbati. July 29, 2004.

El Correo. Basque Country, Spain.

———. *"Idaho por la Autodeterminación."* José María Portillo. March 9, 2002.

———. *"El Gobierno Vasco reclama al Candidato Kerry que rectifique."* February 11, 2004.

———. *"El Gobierno vasco mantendrá las 'embajadas' en el extranjero, pero eliminara su perfil político."* Olatz Barriuso. May 28, 2009.

El País. Madrid, Spain. 1976–2013.

———. *"Benevolencia Uruguaya: Los Etarras Refugiados en Uruguay aprovechan la Ignorancia de la Influyente Colonia Vasca sobre la Evolución de España."* J. J. Aznáriz. April 4, 2004.

———. *"La Irresistible Atracción de Idaho: Una Iniciativa por la Autodeterminación Vasca en el Estado Norteamericano crea Polémica a Miles de Millas de Distancia."* Aitor Guenaga. March 10, 2002.

——. *"La Policía Uruguaya detiene al Presunto Miembro de ETA Jesús María Lariz Iriondo."* July 31, 2002.

——. *"Batasuna desmiente que las Colectividades Vascas aprobaran una Condena de ETA."* July 20, 2003.

——. *"Agotes en Eusketxe."* Iñaki Egaña. July 23, 2004.

——. *"ICANN aprueba un Dominio propio para la Cultura Catalana."* September 15, 2005.

El Periódico de Álava-Arabako Egunkaria. Basque Country, Spain.

——. *"La Vasca es una de las Colectividades que mejor se ha integrado en el Pueblo Argentino."* July 15, 2003.

El Semana Digital. Madrid, Spain.

——. *"Lobby Nacionalista: Bieter y Cenarrusa; los 'Cossiga' de Idaho, Amigos del PNV."* M. Ortega. September 1, 2004.

Euskal Etxeak. 1989–2013. Vitoria-Gasteiz: Servicio Editorial de Publicaciones del Gobierno Vasco.

——. Issue 21, Year 1992.

——. Issue 43, Year 1999.

——. Issue 47. Year 2000.

——. Issue 53, Year 2002.

——. Issue 56, Year 2002.

——. Issue 57, Year 2003.

——. Issue 67, Year 2005.

——. Issue 69, Year 2005.

——. Issue 70, Year 2005.

——. Issue 76, Year 2006.

EuskalKultura.com–Boletín de Cultura y Diáspora Vasca. Basque Country, Spain. 2001–2013.

——. *"Se constituye en Bogotá la Cámara de Comercio Colombo-Vasca en Presencia de Autoridades, Representantes Vascos Locales y una Delegación de Jaurlaritza."* August 9, 2004.

——. *"250 Bat Pertsonek Bi Orduko Ibilaldia Egin Montreal-en (Québec) bertako Bi Euskal Herriturren egoera salatzeko."* March 10, 2005.

——. *"Vascos y Euskal Etxeas de todo el Mundo celebrarán Aberri Eguna con diversidad de Encuentros y Programas."* March 26, 2005.

——. *"Centros Vascos de todo el Mundo se sumaron al Aberri Eguna, en una Jornada Alegre y Emotiva."* March 30, 2005.

———. *"Un Emotivo Acto con Participación Ciudadana realzo la Plantación del Retoño del Árbol de Gernika en Uruguay"*. August 17, 2005.

———. *"Asociación Diaspora Vasca y Udalbiltza firman un Acuerdo para conocer la Situación Vasca Internacionalmente."* October 1, 2005.

———. *"Cuauhtémoc Cárdenas visita a los 6 Vascos Presos en México y declara que su Proceso estuvo 'LLeno de Irregularidades."* April 20, 2006.

———. *"Repaso mediante un Reportaje Fotográfico (I) de la recién concluida Semana Nacional Vasco Argentina de Rosario."* October 9, 2007.

Euskal Paperak. César Arrondo, Laprida, Argentina.

———. *"Tomás Otaegui, un Argentino Vasco y su Predica constante por los Derechos, el Pensamiento Nacional y las Leyes Viejas de Euskalherria."* Issue No. 1. April 2007.

Eusko Etxea of New York. 2004–2007. www.eeny.org

———. *"El Obispo ofreció la Misa 'para que el Pueblo Vasco sea Libre de toda Violencia."* María Mariezkurrena. March 28, 2005.

Euskosare.org. Eusko Ikaskuntza–The Society of Basque Studies. Basque Country, Spain. 2005–2008.

———. *"El Día Internacional del Euskara se celebró en todo el Mundo Vasco."* December 12, 2005.

———. *"Centros Vascos de Europa se reúnen Mañana en Eskual Etxea de París para impulsar Proyectos Conjuntos."* November 30, 2007.

———. *"Opinión de la Lista "FEVA para Todos" en relación a las Elecciones en FEVA y la Existencia de Dos Listas."* March 4, 2008.

———. *"Los Centros Vascos de Europa se reunirán por Segundo Año, en Vísperas del Mundial de Mus de Barcelona."* July 17, 2008.

Euzko Deya. Buenos Aires, Argentina.

———. *"¡Grandiosas Jornadas Vascas en Villa María!"* Year 34, No. 663 (October 1972): 4–5.

Euzko Deya. Paris, France.

———. *"Texto de la Elocución del Presidente Aguirre."* Year 13, No. 285 (April 30, 1948).

———. *"Ante el Congreso Mundial Vasco."* Year 21, No. 399 (September 1, 1956).

———. *"Le Congrés Mundial Basque."* Year 21, No. 400 (October 1956).

Euskonews & Media. Eusko Ikaskuntza–The Society of Basque Studies. Basque Country, Spain.

———. Interview: William A. Douglass. "Creo que la Identidad Vasca tendrá que suponer algo o no persistirá." María Agirre. No. 28 (1999).

——. Interview: Josu Legarreta. *"En el Mundo y Especialmente en América se nos conoce, en parte, Gracias al Fenómeno de las Euskal Etxeak."* María Agirre. No, 72 (2000).

Fitxak–Asociación Diáspora Vasca. Santa Rosa, Argentina.

——. Issue 1, Year 1; May 15, 2005.

——. Issue 2, Year 2; May 22, 2005.

——. Issue 5, Year 1; June 12, 2005.

Gara. Basque Country, Spain.

——. *"Bieter considera que las Presiones Españolas refuerzan la Decisión de Idaho."* March 8, 2002.

——. *"Idaho apoya la Libre Determinación de los Vascos."* March 6, 2002.

——. *"Debate en las Cámaras Legislativas de Idaho: La Diáspora Vasca aplaude la Defensa de la Libre Determinación de Euskal Herria."* March 12, 2002.

——. *"Ajuria Enea hace público un texto contra ETA no aprobado"* and *"Manipulación del Congreso de Colectividades Vascas."* Editorial. July 19, 2003.

——. *"Álvarez: El PNV instrumentaliza la Diáspora y las Colectividades Vascas."* July 20, 2003.

——. *"La Historia de un Manifiesto que no se aprobó tras un Largo Viaje."* July 27, 2003.

——. *"Euskaldun eta Amerikanuak."* Ainara Lertxundi. August 1, 2005.

——. *"Un Camino a seguir en la Red."* September 17, 2005.

——. *"El Camino hacia la Libertad."* Guillermo Canut. January 21, 2005.

——. *"El Senado Chileno respalda la 'Voluntad del Pueblo Vasco."* October 20, 2006.

——. *"Denuncian la Censura de Lakua a un Acto en Argentina."* October 8, 2007.

——. *"Niegan que Lakua censurara la Charla de Ibazeta en la Euskal Etxea de Rosario."* October 23, 2007.

——. *"¡Aguante Euskal Herria!"* Josetxo Ibazeta. October 24, 2007.

——. *"Nota Dantzaris."* November 5, 2007.

Hemen. London Basque Society–Euskal Elkartea's Newsletter, U.K.

——. Special Issue November 2003.

Hizketa. NABO's Newsletter. 1992–2008. U.S.

——. Vol. 9, No. 1. Fall 1998.

——. Vol. 11, No. 1. Winter 2001.

——. Spring 2002.

La Arena. La Pampa, Argentina.

——. *"Represión en el País Vasco."* Federico Borrás. September 20, 2002.

Lokarria. Basque-American Catholic Newsletter, San Francisco, U.S.

——. December 2005.

National Review. New York, United States.

——. *"Impromptus."* Jay Nordlinger. January 28, 2004.

Semanario–Asociación Diáspora Vasca. Santa Rosa, Argentina.

——. Issue 1, Year 1; June 2005.

The Idaho Statesman. Boise, United States.

——. *"Javier Rupérez: A Paper's Ties to Terrorism."* Javier Rupérez. March 19, 2003.

——. *"Basque President visits Boise for Jaialdi."* July 30, 2005.

The Guardian. London, United Kingdom.

——. *"A Bridge Across the Great Divide."* Michael Eaude. October 20, 2001. http://www.guardian.co.uk/books/2001/oct/20/fiction.reviews3

The New York Times. New York, United States.

——. *"10 bombs shatter trains in Madrid, killing 192: 1,400 are hurt—top suspects are Basques and Al-Qaeda,"* and *"Rush-hour blasts kill 192 on Madrid trains: Basques first blamed, but Al-Qaeda role claimed."* March 12, 2004.

——. *"Bombings in Madrid: Spanish officials divided of whom to blame for train attacks: Basques or Islamists."* March 13, 2004.

Voice of the Basques. Boise, United States.

——. *"NABO Emblem Contest."* Vol. 3, No. 5 (March 1977): 8.

Vieiros. Galician Portal. *"Nace a 'Asociación PuntoGal' a prol do Dominio Galego en Internet."* April 6, 2006. www.vieiros.com/especiais/puntog/nova.php?Ed=48&id=49081

In-person interviews by country

Argentina

Arozarena, Miren. October 29, 2009. Bahía Blanca.

Arrondo, César. October 30, 2009. Bahía Blanca.

Auza, Gonzalo. November 3, 2005, and November 2, 2009. Buenos Aires.

Barzola, Verónica. November 3, 2005, and November 2, 2009. Buenos Aires.

Basterra, Ricardo. October 29 and 30, 2009. Bahía Blanca.

Berardi, Pablo. November 3, 2005. Buenos Aires.

Bereciartua, Santiago. October 31, Bahía Blanca.

Borrás, Federico. November 1, 2009. Bahía Blanca.

Carricart, Mariano. November 3, 2005, and November 2, 2009. Buenos Aires.

de Aguirre, Pedro María. October 29, 2009. Bahía Blanca.

de Zavaleta, Teresa. November 8, 2005. Buenos Aires.

Eiheragibel, Felipe. October 29 and 30, 2009. Bahía Blanca.

Esnaola, Julio. October 31, 2009. Bahía Blanca.

Etcharren, Valerie. October 31, 2009. Bahía Blanca.

Etcheverry de Irujo, María Elena. November 8, 2005. Buenos Aires, and October 31, 2009. Bahía Blanca.

Ezkerro, Mikel. October 28, 2009. Buenos Aires.

García Ramos, José Ignacio. November 7, 2005. Buenos Aires.

Irastorza, Coti. October 30, 2009. Bahía Blanca.

Irazusta, Mikel. October 30, 2009. Bahía Blanca.

López de Vicuña, Irene. November 2, 2009. Buenos Aires.

Martin, Alejo. October 31, 2009. Bahía Blanca.

Mignaburu, Magdalena. November 3, 2005. Buenos Aires.

Noblecillas, Raúl. October 29, 2009. Bahía Blanca.

Pointevin, Enrique. October 30, 2009. Bahía Blanca.

Ríos, Norma Beatriz. November 4, 2005, and November 3, 2009. Buenos Aires.

Satostegui, Mariana. November 1, 2009. Bahía Blanca.

Torry, Eduardo. October 30, 2009. Bahía Blanca.

Urruty, Idoya. November 8, 2005. Buenos Aires.

Velasco, Maite. November 2 and 5, 2005. Buenos Aires.

Zubillaga, Xabier. November 8, 2005. Buenos Aires, and October 31, 2009. Bahía Blanca.

Basque Country

Aristorena, Pablo José. July 18, 2003. Vitoria-Gasteiz.

Ayesa, Mariano. July 16, 2003. Vitoria-Gasteiz.

Basañez, Pedro María. July 17, 2003. Vitoria-Gasteiz.

Camus, Argitxu. July 17, 2003. Vitoria-Gasteiz.

Celaya, Julián. November 16, 2009. Vitoria-Gasteiz.

Etxarri, Joseba. July 18, 2005. Vitoria-Gasteiz.

Etxearte, Izaskun. July 16, 2003. Vitoria-Gasteiz.

Foncillas, Luis. July 17, 2003. Vitoria-Gasteiz.

Galfarsoro, Imanol. July 16, 2003. Vitoria-Gasteiz.

Katarain, José Vicente. July 16, 2003. Vitoria-Gasteiz.

Martín, Andoni. November 1, 2009. Bahía Blanca. Argentina, and November 16, 2009. Vitoria-Gasteiz.

Mirandona, Iñaki. July 17, 2003. Vitoria-Gasteiz.

Olave, Carlos. July 16, 2003. Vitoria-Gasteiz.

Oregi, Benan. November 16, 2009. Vitoria-Gasteiz.

O'Sullivan, Patrick. July 17, 2003. Vitoria-Gasteiz.

Panossian, Razmik. July 17, 2003. Vitoria-Gasteiz.

Sommer, Elena. July 17, 2003. Vitoria-Gasteiz.

Sosa, Carlos. July 16, 2003. Vitoria-Gasteiz, and October 30 and 31, 2009. Bahía Blanca (Argentina).

Spectorowski, Alberto. July 17, 2003. Vitoria-Gasteiz.

Urritikoetxea, Irene. July 17, 2003. Vitoria-Gasteiz.

United States

Acheritogaray, Philippe. July 28, Boise, Idaho.

Arrieta, Jaione. July 29, Boise, Idaho.

Corcostegui, Lisa. July 28, 2005. Boise, Idaho.

Foncillas, Luis. July 28, 2005. Boise, Idaho.

Totoricagüena, Gloria. September 3, 2003. Reno, Nevada.

Uberuaga, Blas. July 31, 2005. Boise, Idaho.

Ugalde, Marcelino. March 28, 2005. Reno, Nevada.

Index

B

C

D

E

F

G

H

I

J

S

T

Y

Z

www.ingramcontent.com/pod-product-compliance
Lightning Source LLC
LaVergne TN
LVHW080309110826
845155LV00023B/101

* 9 7 8 1 9 3 5 7 0 9 4 1 1 *